MULTINATIONALS BEYOND THE MARKET

Intra-Firm Trade and the Control of Transfer Pricing

EDITED BY

ROBIN MURRAY

Fellow of the Institute of Development Studies,
University of Sussex

A HALSTED PRESS BOOK

JOHN WILEY & SONS
New York

Published in the U.S.A.
by Halsted Press, a Division of
John Wiley & Sons, Inc., New York

© The Institute of Development Studies, 1981

ISBN 0-470-27240-6

Phototypeset by C. Leggett & Son Ltd., Mitcham, Surrey
on Linotype-Paul VIP in 11pt Times
Printed in Great Britain by
St Edmundsbury Press, Bury St Edmunds, Suffolk

CONTENTS

PREFACE

This book is the outcome of two conferences held at the Institute of Development Studies, and organised by the IDS in conjunction with UNCTAD and the United Nations Centre for Transnational Corporations respectively. These meetings gathered together academic researchers, consultants and public officials, many of whom had been practically involved in the monitoring and control of transfer pricing. The current volume contains a selection of the main papers presented there, re-written and supplemented with two further articles. Together they comprise a principal part of the survey of the field which these meetings initiated. Other papers to the conference have appeared elsewhere (Carlson and Hufbauer 1976, Collins 1977, Hopkins 1978, Lall 1979, UNCTAD 1977, UNCTAD 1978, Ward 1978) as has the work of Constantine Vaitsos which has had such influence on the research and the control of transfer pricing, the most recent parts of which he presented to the conference (see Vaitsos 1974, 1978, 1980). These additional articles and monographs should be read in the context of the debate to which the present volume contributes, and which is summarised in the introduction. A final interpretative text by the present editor will appear shortly, also to be published by Harvester Press.

The current volume is a collective one, not merely by virtue of its origins in common discussions, but also through the extensive support which contributors have given to each other and to myself as editor in the period of re-drafting. I would, however, particularly like to thank Elizabeth Hopkins, who within IDS first raised this project off the ground, following an initiative by Judith Hart, when the latter was Minister of Overseas Development in the British Labour Government. I am also very grateful to Karen Brewer for her help in preparing the text, to Beth Humphries and John Spiers of Harvester Press whose many forms of assistance have enabled this volume to appear so promptly, and to Frances, Marika and Beth without whose support it might never have appeared at all.

Robin Murray,
Institute of Development Studies,
University of Sussex,
May 1980.

CONTRIBUTORS

Sarah Bartlett, who grew up in the Bahamas, has recently completed the M.Phil in Development Studies at the Institute of Development Studies, University of Sussex. She is currently assisting in the production of a television series on Transnational Companies, and editing a book on the IMF for the Latin American Bureau in London.

Daniel Chudnovsky is an Argentine economist who received his doctorate from Oxford in 1973. He was Lecturer in Economics at the University of Buenos Aires, and in the Latin American faculty of Social Sciences, and was chief of the Economic Department of the Registry of Transfer of Technology Contracts in Argentina. He is currently a staff member of the Technology Division of UNCTAD. He is the author of *Empresas multinacionales y ganancias monopolicas*, Siglo XXI Editores, Buenos Aires 1974, and *Dependencia tecnologica y estructura industrial: el caso argentino*, FLACSO, Buenos Aires, 1976, as well as many articles on problems of technology transfer.

Walter Chudson has for many years been an economist at the United Nations, most recently at the Centre for Transnational Corporations in New York. He has written many articles on problems of foreign investment and the developing countries.

Charles Cooper is an economist, and Professorial Fellow at IDS and the Science Policy Research Unit, University of Sussex, where he is responsible for work on the economics of technology. Previously, he worked for seven years at the OECD Science Directorate on problems of technology policy in Southern Europe.

Frank Ellis is currently a Senior Research Fellow at the University of Dar es Salaam, Tanzania, and a home-based fellow of the IDS, University of Sussex. The research underlying his contribution to the present volume was undertaken while he was a consultant to the Union of Banana Exporting Countries between 1975 and 1977.

Peter Fitzpatrick teaches Law and Interdisciplinary studies at the University of Kent at Canterbury. Previously he worked in the Prime Minister's Office in Papua, New Guinea. He has published several case studies and theoretical papers on law in the third world and his *Law and State in Papua New Guinea* is to be published shortly.

Tom Ganiatsos studied Economics at Princeton, where he received a Ph.D for a thesis on foreign investment in Greece. Since 1972 he has been a staff member of the technology division of UNCTAD.

Reginald Herbold Green is a Fellow at IDS, University of Sussex. From 1966-74 he was Economic Advisor to the Tanzania Treasury and since 1976 has been a consultant to the UN Institute for Namibia and has been involved in seeking operational ways to identify, control and avert transfer pricing.

Colin Greenhill, who formerly worked for the Australian Government in Canberra, has for the past fourteen years been with UNCTAD, Geneva, where he is currently chief of the Restrictive Business Practices Section. He has been responsible for many publications in this field, notably the recent report: 'Dominant positions of market power of transnational corporations: use of the transfer pricing mechanism.'

Gerry Helleiner is a Professor of Economics at the University of Toronto. He has been Director of the Economic Research Bureau, University of Dar es Salaam, Visiting Research Fellow at the Nigerian Institute of Social and Economic Research, Institute of Development Studies, Sussex, and Queen Elizabeth House, Oxford. He is the author of *International Economic Disorder* (Macmillan, 1980); *International Trade and Economic Development* (Penguin, 1972); *Peasant Agriculture, Government and Economic Growth in Nigeria* (Irwin, 1966) and editor of *A World Divided* (Cambridge, 1976).

Contributors

Emil Herbolzheimer has taught Economics at Universities in Venezuela, the United States and Spain. He has been Economic Affairs Officer in the Restrictive Business Practices Section of UNCTAD, Geneva, since 1975, and has specialised in research on restrictive business practices in international trade, including those of transnational corporations and their role in exports and imports, especially of developing countries.

Oscar Hernandes Sierra is a staff member of INCOMEX, the transfer pricing monitoring unit in Colombia.

K.M. Lamaswala is a Zambian who studied Economics at Makerere College in East Africa, and Development Studies at the University of Toronto. From 1967 to 1977 he worked in various capacities associated with the Zambia mining industry, ending up as Deputy Managing Director of the Metal Marketing Corporation of Zambia (MEMACO). He has represented Zambia at many international meetings and conferences dealing with copper, and is currently Zambia's Representative at the Paris-based Intergovernmental Council of Copper Exporting Countries (CIPEC).

Robin Murray has been a Fellow at IDS, University of Sussex, since 1970, having previously been a Lecturer in Economics at the London Business School. He has specialised in the political economy of multinational corporations and has both written and lectured widely on the subject. He has worked with a number of departments in the Ethiopian government on questions of the control of multinationals and the transfer of technology.

José Ripoll is a Fellow of the Swiss Actuaries Association. He worked in a reinsurance company in Geneva before he joined, in 1966, the UNCTAD secretariat where he now holds the position of Deputy Chief of the Special Programme on Insurance. He is also 'chargé de cours' at the University of Geneva.

Panayotis Roumeliotis studied Economics at the University of Geneva and the Sorbonne. He worked as a researcher in international economics at CNRS Paris (1970-72) and KEPE, Athens (1972-76). As adviser and director at the Ministry of Coordination, he took an active part in the negotiations of Greece's entry into the Common Market. At the same time he directed the Control Service of Transfer Pricing. In 1978 he became an economic adviser to the Greek Parliament and was appointed to the Office of Professor A. Papandreou, leader of the Greek Socialist Party. From 1979 he has been a Lecturer at the University of Industrial Studies of Piraeus. He has written books about multinational corporations, international business, and the Common Market.

Frances Stewart is a Fellow of Somerville and Senior Research Officer at the Institute of Commonwealth Studies, Oxford, and author of *Technology and Underdevelopment* (Macmillan, 1977) and many articles on development, technology and employment. She has been a consultant to a number of international organisations including UNCTAD, ILO and the World Bank.

INTRODUCTION
ROBIN MURRAY

The term 'transfer pricing' has about it an air of inconsequence. It is a technical term used primarily by accountants, managers and certain officials in Inland Revenue and Customs Departments in the course of their everyday business. It refers to the setting of prices on transactions (or transfers) between different parts of the same firm, as distinct from the setting of market prices on transactions between independent producers. It is a distinction which hardly appears to merit the attention of those with more general economic and political concerns. Indeed, until now, it has been accorded just such a lack of attention by mainstream economic and political theory. The literature on the subject (and it has posed enough practical problems to firms and governments for there to be a literature) is largely confined to finance and business publications, and to the circulated proceedings of specialist international conferences. Only rarely has it reached the pages of the leading journals of the major disciplines. For, in economics at least, it is still the market and inter-firm relations which hold the field. Non-market relations (whether within firms or within the state) are left largely to the practitioners.

Kuhn, in discussing physical sciences, remarked that subjects that were peripheral in an old paradigm, commonly become the centrepieces of the new. In the past few years, a number of economists — mostly concerned with underdeveloped countries — have suggested that transfer pricing, or, more generally, the intra-firm economics of multinational corporations, may be just such a subject in the field of international economic theory and commercial policy.

The context of this argument is as follows. The neo-classical tradition sees international economic relations in terms of the *market* transactions of *national* firms and consumers. Trade takes place between independent national units so that both may increase their 'utilities'. Governments have the power to regulate these international exchanges so that, taken together, they

1

maximise a particular nation's 'social welfare', and they will do so
— if they are well advised — not by attempting to block (for
example through quotas) or replace (through state trading) the
private international market, but by altering the relative prices at
which the exchanges take place. Those familiar with 19th century
social theory will note that in this sphere at least, utilitarianism
remains alive and well, and untroubled by the conceptual attacks
that have weakened its position in other branches of social
enquiry.

Over the last five years two main lines of opposition to
conventional trade theory have emerged. The first is an extension
of neo-Ricardian value theory (drawing much of its inspiration
from the work of Pierro Sraffa), which in England is primarily
associated with the so-called 'new Manchester school' of trade
theory, and in France and many parts of the third world is
embodied in the theories of Unequal Exchange originating in the
work of Arghiri Emmanuel.[1] The main source of difference
between these new theories and the neo-classical tradition is the
theory of value. What neo-classical and neo-Ricardian theories
continue to share is the supposition of private national capitals
related internationally through markets and subject to control by
nation states.

The second stream of opposition — and the one with which this
book is concerned — has based its critique on institutional rather
than value grounds. For this new 'transnational economics'
neo-classical theory is based on assumptions which are inconsistent with the evident structures of contemporary international
trade. Firstly, with the post-war expansion of foreign direct
investment (which rose from $25 billion in 1951 to $287 billion in
1976), trade is increasingly dominated not by competitive national
firms but by oligopolistic multinationals. For example, 69% of US
exports are now associated with multinationals, as are 41% of US
imports. For the UK (in 1973) MNC-related exports accounted
for 72% of the total.

Secondly, an increasing proportion of this MNC-related trade
is *intra-firm trade*, that is to say transfers between different parts
of the same firm. For the US, 39% of MNC-related exports were
of this kind in 1970, and 50% of MNC-related imports. For the
UK, Germany and Sweden the figures for manufacturing exports
are similar and, (at least until 1973) rising. Put in another way, a
growing proportion of international trade is not really trade at all
but transfers *within* single multinational corporations.

This has a third consequence. The prices on these intra-firm

transfers are *administered*, and not market prices, which in
principle play a quite different role in economic activity to
traditional market price. For international transfer prices are
primarily concerned with the accounting allocation of value
between different branches of the same firm. They do not
represent new values appropriated by one firm from another (as
was the case with international market exchange).

Government action which seeks to influence a firm's activity
by changing relative prices may have quite different consequences to those intended. Take devaluation, for example.
With national firms, a fall in the exchange rate would be expected
to increase exports (now cheaper to the foreign buyer) and
decrease imports (now dearer to the domestic buyer). But what
happens when the foreign buyer and the foreign supplier, and the
domestic importer and the domestic exporter are all part of one
and the same firm, a multinational which has established an
international division of labour? To take an example: the plant in
the devaluing country will be specialised in the production of
engines for cars, for example, or keyboards for typewriters. Cars
assembled in the domestic market will now have relatively
cheaper engines (after devaluation) but more expensive components manufactured in the firm's specialised plants abroad.
Cars assembled abroad will also have relatively cheaper engines,
but any consequent price reduction will a) be much less than the
amount of the devaluation, and b) stimulate output in all the firm's
specialised plants — in whichever country they are located — and
not preferentially in the plant of the devaluing country. With
oligopolies there is the further question of whether there will be
any price reduction at all.

In the longer term, devaluation might be expected to attract
new specialised plants and new foreign capital. But by this time
relative foreign exchange rates may well have changed. This
aside, devaluation becomes an ever blunter short-term instrument as multinational specialisation increases.

This is only one instance of how the substitution of transfer
prices for market prices may undermine a government's power of
economic management. Monetary policy and exchange controls
can be by-passed by a firm with the capacity to move company
funds internationally by adjusting transfer prices. As far as direct
taxation is concerned (which is generally levied on the basis of
national financial accounts), multi-nationals can use transfer
pricing to adjust *what* profit is declared *where*, according to
comparative international tax rates and other fiscal incentives.

All these instances serve to question one of the basic assumptions of the traditional model, namely that the state has the *power* to control national economic activity, both internally and with respect to the international economy. Transnational economics considers the whole area of state policy not just in terms of what that policy should be, but how any policy can be implemented. It is concerned with the mechanisms of policy — with the material practice of policy — as much as the compass bearings by which a government should set its course.

Fourthly, in addition to the question of what power the state has over its economy, some contributors to the new approach have raised the question of what power the economy has over the state. In place of the traditional assumption that the state represents some abstract 'social utility', it introduces a notion of conflict, and the control of the state in the interest of particular groups or classes. It recognises in short that policy is politics, and that these politics are grounded in the relations of the economy. For this reason we should call it perhaps the new 'transnational political economy'.

I hope it is now clear why transfer pricing — seen from this new perspective — assumes an importance which belies its unassuming technical appearance. It is one of the main points of contact between multinationals and nation states, and highlights the crisis for national economic regulation which arises when the system of national economic prices (on which much state regulation is based) is rendered ambiguous by the growth of international transfer prices. Traditional theory (and much national economic practice) has not been able to address the problem adequately since transfer pricing strikes at the basis of its main assumptions: the prevalence of arm's-length market relations, and the power of the state to regulate these relations by adjusting relative prices. The new theory — by starting from firms rather than states, and from intra-firm economics rather than the market — has raised these questions in a way which alternative theories and practices can no longer ignore.[2]

The papers in this book should be read as a contribution to this debate. With the stakes so high it is not surprising to find conceptual and empirical disputes in most of the issues under discussion: on the definition of transfer pricing; on the extent of intra-firm trade; on its significance; on the incentives for international firms to manipulate transfer prices, and the degree to which they have done so; on the most appropriate measures (if any) to be taken by states to control such manipulation, and the limits to government action in this field. Nor is it surprising to find that two basic camps in the disputes are the new transnational political economy, on the one hand, and the traditional 'liberal' economy on the other. Though both may be subject to immanent theoretical critique, any new theoretical developments including those of the neo-Ricardians must necessarily relate to the theses which are debated here.

Let me summarise the main points of contention:

1. THE DEFINITION OF TRANSFER PRICING

The extent of transfer pricing clearly depends on its definition. The narrowest definition would be the manipulated prices on trade flows between units which have a common centre of control (usually via a majority shareholding). This definition may be expanded by: i) extending the definition of control to include (in Gerry Helleiner's paper) those trading partners in whom a parent has 5% or more of the shares, or indeed those which are subject to other forms of control such as license agreements or management contracts; (ii) including services as well as trade flows, and financial practices (such as transfer accounting or transfer parking in the case of international banks) which have similar effects to transfer pricing; (iii) including intra-firm pricing which may not be intentionally 'manipulated' but whose very existence (as in the case of royalty payments) involves an ambiguous allocation of international value and flow of funds. The broadest definition abstracts altogether from questions of control, and relates transfer pricing rather to the outflow of foreign exchange. It exists, argues Reginald Green, 'whenever for reasons related to inadequate national knowledge or bargaining skill a country or nationally controlled enterprise pays too much or receives too little for goods and services bought or sold.' Thus transfer pricing can, under this definition, take place between independent parties. The criterion for such a broad definition is public control. Forms of government control relevant for transfer pricing narrowly defined are equally applicable (and for the same end) in cases of non arm's-length prices between independent firms, when these deviations are caused by imperfect information and lack of bargaining skill. Interestingly the Greek monitoring unit — based as it is on the review of product prices rather than firms — has adopted in practice the wide definition suggested by Green. If, however, we shift back from the practicalities of government control to the argument on the new structures of the international economy, then some element of company control (and therefore intra-firm flows) must necessarily be maintained in the definition of transfer pricing — however broadly these forms of control are defined.

2. THE INCENTIVE TO TRANSFER PRICE

The minimisers have argued that the net incentive for multinationals to transfer price is small. Legislation in many of the advanced industrial countries has limited the tax benefits that multinationals enjoy through transfer pricing. Income remitted to the home country is liable to the full rate of taxation. The use of tax havens (certainly by US companies) has been strictly circumscribed. Transfer pricing can be used to evade exchange controls, but this too involves costs. Overinvoicing imports will often attract higher duties. Underinvoicing exports may incur loss of export subsidy. There are costs to the multinationals in manipulating transfer prices, particularly where such manipulation runs counter to the 'economic' transfer prices required by management accounting and profit centre decentralisation. There is, too, the cost of being found out.

The transnational approach argues that the tax incentive is subtler. To begin with, transfer pricing allows a firm to consolidate its profits and losses internationally. For example, the home operations of a multinational — burdened as they are with overheads, research and development, and so on — may well be loss makers in an accounting sense, but these losses are funded by hidden profit remittances from foreign operations which are taxed nowhere. (Vaitsos calls this the relative expenditure requirement, and has suggested an order of magnitude for it in the case of the US; see Vaitsos 1974). Further, where the main expansion of multinationals is taking place outside their home country, the deferral rule (which allows multinationals to defer tax due in the home country on foreign income until it is repatriated) means that profit realised in low-tax countries can be used to fund overseas expansion.

They also suggest that the costs to multinationals of operating transfer pricing systems is declining. Where profit centre systems still operate, dual sets of books can be kept with increasing ease in the age of computerised finance, while some firms have dispensed with profit centres altogether, and 'economic' transfer prices come then to play a less important role in systems of managerial control. In most countries transfer pricing transgressions are kept confidential and are in any case often difficult to prove unambiguously. The cost of being found out is therefore small.

All in all, the advice of international finance manuals, tax consultants, and the practice of large multinationals, suggest that the benefits of transfer pricing outweigh the costs.

3. THE EXTENT AND NATURE OF INTRA-FIRM TRADE

Gerry Helleiner's paper in this volume provides a comprehensive summary of the US data on intra-firm trade and its growth which has been the main statistical basis (together with some UK data) for the transnational case. Walter Chudson's paper presents an interesting counter argument. 60% of US intra-firm exports, he points out, are finished goods for resale or lease abroad, and their monitoring against arm's-length prices should thus be a relatively straightforward task. Of the remainder, there is a strong concentration by sector and firm. Thus, 60% of the exports for further processing were in the transport, non-electrical machinery, and chemical sectors. More than half were shipped to only 25 overseas affiliates. On the import side, the bulk of US intra-firm trade was in primary commodities, but here again Chudson notes that the problem appears to be decreasing. Nationalisations, co-production agreements and state marketing boards have reduced intra-firm transactions. Where intra-firm trade still exists, negotiated transfer contracts are now ruling out manipulation (in bauxite, for example), while the existence of arm's-length markets allow for prices to be checked against international market prices. In sum then, the main transfer pricing problem is confined to a relatively small proportion of intermediates and companies, and it is to these restricted, high technology sectors that government control policy should be addressed.[3]

Between Helleiner's growth in intra-firm and related party trade, and Chudson's decline of intra-firm (non petroleum) primary imports and restricted intra-firm intermediate trade lies a shadow: one best illuminated by case studies. The pioneering work of Vaitsos in Colombia and the Andean Pact countries concentrates chiefly on imports in the electrical, chemical, pharmaceutical and rubber sectors, all intermediates, and many from the high-technology branches whose openness to transfer price manipulation is not in question.[4] As far as primary goods are concerned the conference case studies suggest that the transfer pricing problem can not be generally regarded as settled in the case of vertically integrated sectors (bananas, bauxite and pineapples were three such cases discussed).

Taxes imposed on the quantities of these exports were ways of trying to control the effect of underinvoicing on government revenue, but these taxes (like any transfer pricing adjustment) had to be set and re-set on the basis of exactly the same kind of evidence as is needed for an adjustment of the transfer price itself, while the freedom of the companies to vary their prices still has balance of payments consequences outside those settled by the government tax take. Moreover, in many sectors where there was no evident vertical integration and/or an apparent arm's-length market, there were problems of discounts and switches (copper), quality specification (diamonds), or purchaser dominance (tea, coffee) which laid exporters open to losses similar to those suffered through more evident forms of multinational control. Even where nationalisation has taken place, many exporting operations are still subject to management contracts operated by multinationals, in which international sales and purchasing are under the control of the foreign contractor (sugar is one example; Zambian copper was until recently another).

On transfer pricing in final goods, there is, as yet, little public evidence. Two things should be borne in mind. First, the margin of earnings on sales is generally small, particularly in the case of trading companies with rapid turnovers. Second, even with relatively standardised products there is often a considerable price range. With product differentiation the range widens. For example, an EEC survey showed that prices between different brands of the same product could vary by as much as 79% for small transistor radios, 56% for tape recorders, 52% for washing machines, and 27% for coffee grinders — all in the absence of tariff barriers and import restrictions. This makes it almost impossible for an external agency to prove that, say, an intentional 2% intra-firm price change constitutes a manipulated transfer price.

The case study on banking in this volume provides evidence on this point for a commodity which could be argued to have the most 'perfect' of international markets: money. Half the monthly profit of Citibank's German subsidiary was transferred to the Bahamas through a single set of exchange operations which took place within exchange rate ranges almost undetectable to the outsider.

4. APPROACHES TO CONTROL

Assuming both the capacity and incentive for multinationals to transfer price, there is then the question of a strategy of control. Once more the arguments fall into two broad camps. On the one hand there are those who want to restore the market system, and/or the unambiguous relation of firms and states, either in fact, or by account. Among the proposals put forward to this end are: a) those arguing for anti-trust action to reduce excess profits and the monopoly abuse of transfer pricing, thus restoring the competitive if not the national private firm; b) those arguing for a standardisation of different national taxes and controls, thus reducing the incentive to avoid one channel by using another, and for an internationalisation of income tax which would reduce the incentive to transfer price for tax reasons; c) those which seek to control transfer prices by an accounting comparison with arm's-length prices. This last is the main approach adopted by Customs and Inland Revenue Departments in both developed and underdeveloped countries, and takes as its criterion an implicit competitive international market economy as elaborated by traditional theory.

The arm's-length approach has provoked substantial debate. For many products, there may be no comparable market price. Where there is one, it may be a monopolistic or a competitive one. Even where competitive market prices exist, it has been pointed out that neo-Ricardian trade theory suggests that such prices can in no way bear the implication of being 'just' prices. Indeed, in Emmanuel's argument, they would be the means by which profit was transferred from low wage to high wage countries.[5]

The approach of the transnational economists is one which emphasises bargaining. Cases should be dealt with one by one. There is no objective 'just' price. World market prices could be used to strengthen a government's bargaining position and indicate the extent of the surplus profit (or rent) hidden in a price. The task of government is not to restore some traditional version of market relations, but strengthen itself *vis-à-vis* the transnational corporations which now dominate the world economy. These arguments are examined in more detail in the section of the volume on General Strategies.

5. MECHANISMS OF CONTROL

The above differences carry over into the discussion of control. One position — put most articulately by developed country officials — sees a government's relationship with multinationals as equivalent to its relationship with individuals. Multinationals, like individuals, must be protected against the arbitrary use of state power. The burden of proof in transfer pricing, as in matters of crime, should be on the state not on the accused. Information, given in confidence to one government department, should not be circulated to others. Indeed, in many countries such confidentiality is protected by law. Control systems must be built up within these constraints. Information could be obtained as and when necessary. In the case of the British Customs, the gathering of information and methods of investigation of large multinationals appear very similar to those methods used to spot check individuals or small firms.

The counter argument is that multinationals can in no way be equated to individuals in their relationships with states and systems of control. A lawyer, Peter Fitzpatrick, suggests that a concept of administrative law is needed to replace what he calls the private law model — a form of law which gives governments scope and discretion in dealing with economic units commonly larger than themselves. Similar arguments have been advanced on methods of information gathering and investigation. Not only should governments have legal powers to acquire any corporate information they need, they should also develop methods of systematic data gathering on a scale equivalent to that used by the multinationals. The economics of such an information system would require a co-ordination of departments concerned with transfer pricing (from tax, customs, and exchange control departments, to industry and planning ministries, and anti-trust and price control bodies) and an end to the principle of confidentiality.

The question of the economics of information became one of the central issues at the second conference, with the introduction into the discussion of a private company which undertakes transfer price monitoring for eight African countries. The question of whether a private firm can satisfactorily undertake a public function in the sphere of information gathering and checking led all concerned to recognise that information for transfer pricing control could not be left to simple artisan methods but was a sphere of production subject to economies of scale, externalities, and so on. Gerry Helleiner's paper in Part Three of this book examines information production and circulation in systems of transfer pricing control from this perspective.

For the transnational approach, the question is one of strengthening the countervailing power of states (the echo of Galbraith is a relevant one), rather than confining states to archaic methods of investigation, law and enforcement. The last section of this book includes case studies of public control systems which have attempted a more rigorous monitoring of transfer pricing, and whose experience should be seen as evidence for the more general debate. What is striking, both from these and other cases, discussed at the conference (see, for example, Hopkins 1978) is the substantial rates of return that follow relatively small outlays in the field of financial control.

The arguments over the methods (and limits) of transfer pricing control illustrate the way in which the broader theoretical controversy between traditional trade theory and transnational economics is carried over into practice. Both indicate quite different ways in which nation states should relate to private capital. Take the sphere of information, for example. Data on trade flows is structured by virtually every government in the world according to product, volume and price, for it is these which traditional trade theory suggests are important. To also classify trade flows by firm would be a trivial task with modern computer technology, but with a few exceptions (Brazil, Mexico and the United States) this is not done. So we have the anomaly of small countries, with limited trade, producing volumes of trade statistics with fine distinctions by product, but none by firms, when the top twenty companies may account for upwards of half their national trade. (In Britain, with a large and differentiated economy, a recent government survey found that half of total exports were accounted for by 87 firms).

We have already noted the implications of the debate in the field of law, government organisation, and the principles of confidentiality. We have referred also to the significance of the transnational thesis for many fields of government economic policy. What is at issue is whether — in an era of international transfer pricing — government control of the private economy based on national price systems is any longer adequate.

There are a number of possible answers. First, there are those who — as we saw — regard the problem as still relatively restricted in importance. Secondly, there are those who say that effective arm's-length prices (and therefore an adequate system of national prices) can be restored 'by account'. The transnational approach rejects both these positions and argues for a case by case bargain with multinationals. This would apply to all government departments whose actions could in any way be influenced by transfer prices. But what this leaves us with is not a price *system*, let alone *general* government policies aimed at the macro-economy, but a multitude of serial relations with specific firms, whose unity is established not in the sphere of the private economy, but through some form of co-ordinating mechanism in the state.

Many contributors to the new transnational perspective — concerned as they have been with specific areas of state control — have not posed this more general question. Their interest has been primarily with how states can reimpose their power over firms in the sphere of circulation (the control of prices). In Western Europe the debate has gone farther than this — or rather, I should say has gone on different lines, since relatively little attention has been given to the detailed subject of transfer pricing control as discussed here. What has been argued is that the state should establish its unified control through planning agreements with individual multinationals, which agreements would be co-ordinated in a single national plan. Since traditional, impersonal, general interventions into the price system are rendered obsolete by the growth of the transnationals (or as the leading theorist in the UK, Stuart Holland, has put it, the meso economy) specific, discriminating bargaining relations are required with the major companies in order to re-establish state control over the economy.[6]

The major question posed to the policy of planning agreements as to those transnationalist policies aiming to control transfer pricing through firm-by-firm bargaining is whether states can enforce such control as long as the power of production remains in the hands of private capital. There are two points at issue. The first is the technical one. Can monitoring systems be developed which will provide a government with adequate information to control transfer pricing (or any other aspect of transnational operations)? A number of the papers in this book suggest ways in which such systems could be (and have been) established. The paper by the former head of the Greek technical monitoring agency outlines a blueprint for a transfer pricing commando unit of the kind proposed by a number of participants to the discussion. The rare and comprehensive detail of the US Internal Revenue Service paper (and their extensive guide for tax officers auditing multinationals for transfer pricing) suggests that another way of posing the question would be to ask what were the minimum requirements (in terms of skilled staff, legal rights to obtain information, and powers to penalise transgressors) for a monitoring system to be at least partially effective. The issue remains an open one.

Secondly, there is a political question. Even if a government develops an effective technical system of control, the political forces representing multinationals may be strong enough to prevent a control system being adequately enforced. In Greece, the under- and overinvoicing discovered by the monitoring unit was never acted upon, and indeed its operations were curtailed for political reasons. Similarly, in the Central American republics discussed in Frank Ellis's paper, the fact that the major multinationals were underpricing bananas was public knowledge. So extreme was the practice that the IMF itself recalculated a higher price for statistical purposes and published it in its official statistics. The issue was not information, but rather the power of those who suffered from this underpricing to do anything about it. Some transnational theorists have attempted to grasp this problem by extending their analysis of multinationals from the economic into the socio-political sphere, and raising the further issue of whether the very presence of multinationals in a country will undermine official attempts at control for political reasons. According to this thesis, the power of those in control of production will always tend to dominate those whose power is limited to the spheres of circulation. To overcome the conflict between nations states and multinationals it would be necessary to restore effective state control over the national economy by replacing private multinational production with public national production. This is the programme of those in Western Europe who argue that the option of planning agreements cannot succeed for the technical and political reasons I have just outlined.

Yet, just as transnational critics have asked of neo-classical theory: 'trade policy for whom?', so the same question can be posed of those who argue for state control of production. In whose interest is the establishment of such control? The answer will vary according to circumstance.

Similarly we can ask of the central theme of this book: for whom is transfer pricing a problem? To answer this will be to understand more fully the debates about policy. For, as is so often the case, what is a solution for one, only deepens the problem for others.

Notes

1 For the new Manchester school see Ian Steedman, *Trade amongst Growing Economies*, Cambridge University Press 1979 and Ian Steedman (ed.) *Fundamental Issues in Trade Theory*, Macmillan 1979. On Unequal Exchange see Arghiri Emmanuel, 'Unequal Exchange Revisited', IDS Discussion Paper no. 77, Institute of Development Studies, Sussex 1975.
   For a survey of this new literature see David Evans, 'International

Commodity Policy: UNCTAD and NIEO in search of a Rationale' in *World Development*, March 1979.

2 For further reading, see the works of Norman Girvan and Constantine Vaitsos cited in the general bibliography.

3 Lall presented a similar argument to the conference, see Lall 1979.

4 The results are summarised in Vaitsos 1974. Similar studies in Greece are summarised in the paper by Ganiatsos in this volume, but are more fully reported in Roumeliotis 1978.

5 See the paper by David Evans in Ellis and Joekes 1978.

6 See Holland 1975.

PART ONE
The Growth of Intra-firm Trade

1.
INTRA-FIRM TRADE AND TRANSFER PRICING
WALTER A. CHUDSON

It has long been recognised that the valuation placed by transnational corporations on transactions in goods, technology and services between the national units comprising the total enterprise — and particularly between the 'parent' enterprise and its overseas affiliates — may affect the value of their imports or exports, and hence the national allocation of profits among the respective units. Such transactions, particularly intra-firm trade in commodities, are inherent in the nature of the transnational corporation. What creates a problem of potential importance is the fact that control over the valuation of such transactions may permit a transnational corporation (TNC) to allocate foreign exchange transactions and profits internationally in a different way from 'arm's length' transactions between independent enterprises.

Broadly speaking, the main objectives of such manipulation are twofold: (1) to maximise the *realised* (that is, transferred) profits after taxes of the TNC as a whole; and (2) to reduce reported profits (before taxes) in certain jurisdictions, by recording increased costs for various operational purposes (for example, to justify requests for increased protection against imports, to show a 'low profile' of profitability for collective bargaining purposes, or to justify exceptions from national price controls). The importance of these motives may differ from sector to sector, firm to firm, and from developing to developed countries as a whole.

Independently of such manipulation by TNCs, the international allocation of profits after taxes may also be affected by whether national tax authorities in 'home' countries assert jurisdiction over foreign source income (as in the application of 'worldwide' or 'territorial' definition of taxable income), and in particular by a determination that a certain portion of central costs (for example, for research and development) are attributable to overseas operations and may not be deducted in determining income subject to tax in the 'home' country's

jurisdiction. This may lead to a clash between national ta:
authorities independently of any manipulation of transfer price
by a TNC, and is, of course, the *raison d'être* for international ta:
treaties.

Since the bulk of international production by TNCs is i:
industrialised countries, a corresponding amount of inter-affiliat:
transactions takes place among such countries. While som:
motives for manipulation of such transactions are common t:
TNCs wherever they operate — notably to take advantage o:
differences in effective tax and tariff rates — attention here i
directed to the developing countries.

An assessment of intra-firm transactions involves thre:
considerations:

  1. The nature and extent of such transactions;
  2. The motives for manipulation of such transactions;
  3. The policies that may be employed by governments in hos:
     and home countries to determine an 'appropriate' taxabl:
     profit.

1. NATURE AND EXTENT OF INTRA-FIRM TRANSACTIONS

Although comprehensive data are lacking, by far the larges:
amount of intra-affiliate transactions consists of commodit:
trade, primarily exports and imports of the parent corporation t:
and from its affiliates, but also, to some extent, between affiliate:
within the corporate network. Other significant items includ:
royalties for both patented and unpatented technology, man:
agement and service fees, allocations for central research an:
development costs and other central office expenditures, an:
interest on intra-firm loans.[1]

Largely on the basis of data obtained by the US Governmen:
from TNCs for the late 1960s and early 1970s it is clear tha:
intra-firm commodity trade is substantial. It seems reasonable t:
assume that such trade would grow more or less in step with th:
volume of international production by TNCs; whether it is :
growing proportion of international trade for other reasons is no:
possible to demonstrate conclusively from available evidence.

The statistics revisited

Estimates of intra-firm trade have perforce to be based almos:
entirely on official US data (Department of Commerce).[2] Th:
most complete data ('census') refer to 1966, with supplementar:
data for a large sample in 1970 (and 1966); there is also a sample b:

Business International, a private US consulting firm, which gives some interesting data on the character of intra-firm transactions through 1975.

Most writers have focused attention on total exports from the United States by US-owned parents (TNCs) to their majority-owned affiliates overseas (MOFAs). In 1966 these were 36% of the TNCs' total exports and 29% of all US non-agricultural exports. However, there has been a general neglect of the fact that almost 60% of total intra-firm exports consisted of finished goods for resale or lease without further processing by the affiliate, which was typically an offshore sales subsidiary.[3]

In 1966 only $2.7 billion of a total of intra-firm exports of $6.4 billion consisted of intermediate goods for further processing; this represented 12% of total US exports of manufactures, compared with the estimate of 29% for total intra-firm trade.

The US Department of Commerce samples for 1966 and 1970 also provide a classification of exports to MOFAs according to 'developed' and 'other' (presumably developing) areas.[4]

The data for 1970 are as follows. Of a total of $8,623 million shipped to a large sample of MOFAs, $7,118 million went to developed areas and $1,505 million to 'other' areas. Of the $1,505 million, some $606 million were for resale without further manufacture or lease abroad, $223 million were for capital equipment for use for foreign affiliates, and $699 million were for further processing or assembly (less than 10% of TNC shipments to LDCs but about half of intra-firm trade). In this sample, total US exports to developing countries were $12,159 million, total exports by TNCs to developing areas were $5,977 million and, as indicated above, exports to MOFAs for further processing were $699 million, or about 5% of total US exports to developing countries.

An important question is whether there is reason to expect that manipulation of transfer pricing in the case of finished goods for resale would be significantly different from the treatment of intermediate goods for further processing. Without mentioning the magnitudes involved, Lall, in his well-known article, states that 'it is possible that intra-firm trade in finished goods is easier to check, and thus less subject to misuse, than trade in intermediate and capital goods.'[5] Granted that there is no evidence either way on this matter, a stronger note of caution would seem warranted. Manipulation of transfer prices of finished goods for resale is not only much easier to detect but such goods generally bear much higher import duties. It seems quite reasonable to assume that such trade would be less likely to be subject to the extreme overinvoicing that occurred in several dramatic cases (e.g., Colombian pharmaceuticals). Further, the internal management routine of TNCs in the case of finished products would seem to lead to the same conclusion.

Assuming that it is worthwhile to distinguish between these two categories of intra-firm trade, it is interesting to note certain more recent data. A survey by Business International of 147 firms representing over half the total value of all US-owned manufacturing affiliates overseas disclosed a trend toward a larger share of intra-firm trade in the form of finished goods, requiring no further processing (or assembly). Finished goods as a percentage of total exports to foreign affiliates by the TNCs rose from 53% in 1970 to 59% in 1974 and again in 1975.[6]

The significance of the distinction is also indicated in comparisons relating to broader aggregates. Thus, US intra-firm receipts (from merchandise exports, fees and royalties, and income on direct investment) represented 35% of total US private exports in 1976, but only 19% if finished goods for resale are excluded.[7]

Other interesting aspects of transfer pricing in commodity trade are suggested by further disaggregation of the data.

In 1966, sales of capital equipment by US parent TNCs to MOFAs represented only $0.6 billion of $6.4 billion total sales to affiliates. Further, of the $2.7 billion of intermediate goods sold for further assembly or fabrication, $0.9 or fully one-third went to the transportation industry (mainly automotive) and another $0.7 billion to non-electrical machinery and chemicals combined. This left only $1.1 billion of intermediates shipped to all other industries combined throughout the developed and developing world, representing 16% of intra-firm exports and 6% of the firms total exports.

The concentration within the TNCs of sales of intermediate goods to foreign affiliates is also interesting, particularly in relation to the issue of monitoring. A 1965 sample survey of 350 firms by the US Department of Commerce (*Survey of Current Business*, article by Marie Bradshaw, May 1969) reveals that relatively few firms and affiliates account for a very large part of intra-firm trade. Well over half of the total intra-firm exports for further processing in this sample were shipped to only 25 individual affiliates. Five of these were automobile manufacturers in Canada, who purchased almost one-third of the total intermediate shipments. On the other hand, more than 90% of the

3,579 affiliates in the sample made no purchases from their parent firm in the US for further processing or assembly abroad.

These data do not indicate the importance or unimportance of intra-affiliated trade in particular industries or particular countries. For example, it may be noted that in the US 1966 survey, the proportion of finished goods for resale shipped to MOFAs in Europe was 60% of total intra-firm shipments, whereas in Latin America it was only 30%.

No doubt a significant part of the difference is explained by difference in industrial composition. As pointed out by Lall (*op. cit.*) traditional industries like food, paper, metal products have a relatively small incidence of intra-firm exports from parent to affiliate, compared with technologically more dynamic sectors such as pharmaceuticals, rubber, transport equipment, non-electrical machinery and office equipment.

Some data compiled by Reddaway suggest a similar pattern of industrial incidence of transfer pricing, as shown below:[8]

Table 1.1

Percentage of Intermediate Imports from UK in Total Production
by UK Affiliates Overseas, 1955-64

Sector	%	Country	%
Vehicles	12.8	South Africa	13.0
Non-electrical		Jamaica	12.1
engineering	10.2	Australia	8.0
Electrical engineering	4.1	Malaysia	6.0
Textiles	4.3	Ghana	6.0
Metals and metal		India	4.5
products	2.5	Federal Republic of	
Chemicals	2.9	Germany	4.1
Food, drink, tobacco	0.9	Nigeria	4.0
Paper	0.2	Argentina	3.2
		Denmark	2.6
		Canada	1.8
		Italy	1.4
		Brazil	1.1
		France	0.6
		United States of	
		America	0.5

With the exceptions shown in the table, these are, however, global exports to affiliates in developed and developing countries. Presumably the role of intra-firm imports would be greater in a number of assembly and packaging industries in developing countries, such as the pharmaceuticals, electrical equipment, consumer durables and transportation equipment industries. Unfortunately, data are almost completely lacking on a country or industry basis for the developing countries. This is a statistical gap which can and should be filled.

The sketchy statistical review presented above certainly does not settle the importance of intra-affiliate trade as a basis for assessing the extent and nature of the problem of manipulated transfer prices. But it does signal caution against hasty conclusions drawn from aggregate data. More important, perhaps, it suggests some practical guidelines for directing the regulatory activities of host governments in developing countries.

A very large part of the imports of US-based transnational corporations (and presumably of transnational corporations based in other countries) consists of primary commodities, predominantly petroleum.[9] The rate of growth of imports of manufactures from the developing countries has increased, but their share in intra-firm trade remains small.

Transfer pricing in primary commodities thus becomes an issue of some importance. To begin with, the case of petroleum requires isolation, given the pricing practices in that industry and the recent radical changes in the industry's organisation and control, particularly at the level of crude petroleum production.

As long ago as the early 1950s, so-called 'posted prices' for petroleum, set by the international petroleum companies, began to be used for the determination of income subject to host country taxation in Saudi Arabia and elsewhere, following the introduction of the '50/50' regime for division of profits. This effectively removed the issue of manipulation of *transfer* prices for crude petroleum. This position was formalized by an OPEC resolution of 1966 which affirmed that the 'posted' price would be the relevant price for determining the net income of the affiliate subject to taxation.[10]

Since 1973, of course, the issue of a posted price in petroleum has become academic. This trend has been reinforced by the progressive nationalisation of the oil production in the Middle East and elsewhere, and by such new contractual formulae as production-sharing agreements (which also apply in other mineral projects).

The development of new forms of foreign participation in the petroleum and mining industries has also reduced the significance of transfer pricing. So-called production-sharing arrangements (for example, in Indonesia) simply eliminate the issue of a transfer price, since the host government takes its share of the profits through acquiring the commodity itself.

In the case of bauxite, where for a long time the issue of the transfer price was a sore point, there has emerged a formula by which the royalty on bauxite exports is determined in relation to the price of ingot aluminium on the world market.[11] This comes close to a contractual agreement on the transfer price of bauxite.

Similar changes have subsequently occurred in a considerable number of other bauxite- or alumina-producing developing countries, for example, the Dominican Republic and Surinam. In the Dominican Republic, negotiations on an increase of royalty have occurred, and the royalty rate increased (though it is not clear that it is based on ingot price); and it was reported that ALCOA was negotiating with the government concerning the transfer price paid by ALCOA to the Dominican subsidiary, which forms the basis of the subsidiary's profit and income tax.[12]

Increasingly, host countries are inserting, in their contracts with multinational corporations, standard clauses linking the transfer price of the product concerned with the world price of the final, processed product, whether it be for purposes of export tax, income tax or other levies. Since the world market prices of these commodities are increasingly well known (even in the case of iron ore) through published sources and producers' councils, the policing of these agreements does not appear to present major problems for the host country.

The establishment of an independent sales corporation in the host country *ipso facto* breaks the link with downstream activity of a transnational corporation. This is the case in much copper production (where the state is not already the sole owner or part owner of the production facilities) and in certain other non-ferrous metals, and also in some cases of iron ore production. Transfer pricing issues have been reported in a manganese project and some problems may exist in certain other non-ferrous metals projects.

In certain primary commodities, where the final product is sold in a less perfect international market, problems of transfer pricing may remain. One of the more important cases is probably timber, affecting sales particularly from Asian countries to Japan and the United States. However, even here instances of negotiated transfer pricing formulas have been reported (e.g., sawn timber linked with the price of finished timber in the home country).[13] A rather special situation arises in the case of fishing operations by transnational enterprises (mainly Japanese) based in certain developing host countries.

In certain other cases where the host government has not been able, for various reasons, to negotiate or enforce a transfer price for an exported raw material in a vertically organized operation, the objective of gaining an increased share of the profits has been achieved by imposing or increasing an export tax. A significant example of this seems to be the case of bananas, particularly from Central America. In what is essentially a bargaining situation, the host government (in some cases the government is no longer a host government, since the issue is only the export price of bananas by what was *formerly* an integrated part of a TNC e.g., United Fruit in Honduras) has levied an increase in export taxes. In principle, bargaining could also take place over the charges for downstream services, particularly shipping, but in this respect the host country's position is relatively weak because it is completely dependent on shipping and distribution channels controlled by transnational corporations. The extraction of rents through export taxation of course depends in considerable measure on a degree of concerted action by competing producer countries.

The conclusion of this impressionistic review seems to be the following. Owing to the dramatic developments in the petroleum industry there has been a major decline in intra-firm transactions in primary commodities in recent years within the developing world. Excluding petroleum, a similar trend has occurred, through nationalisation, co-production agreements, establishment of state marketing boards in host countries and similar action.

Measures have also been taken by host countries which substantially reduce the problem of manipulated transfer prices (underinvoicing) of primary commodity exports. In the case of commodities (like copper) in which world market prices exist, there is a built-in regulatory mechanism based on availability of information, supported in many cases by contractual clauses. In the case of unprocessed or semi-processed products (like bauxite or alumina), the control mechanism has been reinforced by standard clauses linking the price of the intermediate commodity to that of the finished product (e.g., ingot aluminium). Cases of manipulated transfer pricing no doubt remain (particularly where there is no established open market price in the 'final' product), but the broad conclusion seems warranted that the problem of transfer pricing of exported primary commodities has been substantially reduced and is of decreasing importance.

Thus, the problem of transfer pricing for most developing countries, with certain exceptions, lies mainly in the manufacturing sector (primarily imports of intermediate goods by developing countries) rather than in the export of primary products. As the volume of manufactures exported from the developing countries hopefully increases, the industrialised importing countries will be vigilant against underinvoicing of such products, if only for narrowly protectionist reasons. The disaggregation of the data by sectors in the manufacturing category should guide the authorities in deciding where to focus their monitoring efforts. This view is reinforced by the large volume of intra-firm trade concentrated in a relatively small number of corporations. All of this does not imply that developing countries may not have problems of transfer pricing in particular sectors, especially when other channels of earnings, particularly dividends or royalties, are blocked.

2. MANIPULATION OF TRANSFER PRICING

A large part of the literature concerning manipulation deals with the reaction of TNCs to international tax differentials. However, in general, it appears that in developing countries differential tax and tariff factors are much less important than others. Effective corporate income tax rates in home countries that tax world-wide income are generally higher than in developing host countries; there is thus no incentive from relative corporate tax rates to overinvoice exports to affiliates in developing countries or underinvoice imports from such affiliates.[14] However, where international shifting of income remains possible by transferring transactions through sales subsidiaries located in 'tax havens', this is an important potential source of tax avoidance at the expense of both the home and host countries concerned. At present the US, Germany, Japan and France generally tax profits accumulated in so-called tax havens.

Further, in any situation where an affiliate is piling up 'excessive' taxes — that is, taxes exceeding the amount that can be used as tax credits to offset tax liabilities in the home country — there is an obvious incentive to overinvoice intra-firm imports shipped to the affiliate concerned. Another important exception may arise in the taxation of royalties by developing countries, when such charges are between related parties or are disallowed altogether. As shown below, stricter taxation of royalties encourages TNCs to shift profits through commodity transactions.

Import duties have the opposite effect from taxes as a factor in the manipulation of transfer pricing. High import duties tend to discourage overinvoicing of imports. But since tariffs on intermediate products are normally kept low in developing countries as a matter of industrial policy (except where a realistic possibility of import substitution exists), there is little likelihood of a significant offsetting pressure from this quarter. High taxes on exports would, other things being equal, tend to encourage underinvoicing of exports, even though this might well be offset by their possible contribution to capturing a larger share of economic rents from TNCs for the host country.

It appears that a stronger motivation for manipulating transfer pricing, particularly of commodities, in developing countries arises from host country limitations on the transfer of profits or restrictions on the amount of payments for various services. One effect of such restrictions is to encourage the capitalisation of intangibles or overinvoicing of imported capital goods, especially when a remittance limit is expressed as a fraction of equity investment. Probably foremost among these are exchange restrictions (on profits but also, to some extent, on imports), or the fear of intensified restrictions; quantitative limits on profit remittances (by law or *de facto*); high withholding taxes on royalties; obligation to remit profits at less favourable exchange rates; restriction of foreign equity to a minority position in joint ventures, leading TNCs to wish to capture a large share of monopoly rents through overinvoicing and other procedures; and desire to show lower profits in order to justify application for increased protection against imports in production for the local market. An additional group of reasons concerns the avoidance of risk and uncertainty; anticipated devaluation or tightened exchange control, and the aim of recording lower profits in order to resist trade union pressures or the risk of attracting competition from other firms (national or transnational). In the case of host countries pursuing a policy of enforced divestment (as under the Andean Pact), another motive may be the desire to record low profits in order to discourage potential local private purchasers of shares in the enterprise.

We have already noted the motive to shift profits away from high tax jurisdictions to tax havens or low tax countries. Some cases have been cited of deliberate underinvoicing of imports to developing host countries to assist local affiliates in the early build-up phase of operations; this is, in effect, like a short-term loan, though not so designated.[15] Still another case, frequently cited, is the tendency in past years of transnational petroleum companies to overinvoice exports of crude petroleum in order to obtain tax credits against home country tax liability and to discourage competition from independent firms in downstream refining and marketing operations.

Various studies have been made by business analysts of transfer pricing practices by individual firms. These indicate some responses to motivations like those described above, but also constraints from internal managerial considerations. The practices reflect in part the degree of decentralisation in management (which, in turn, may depend on the nature of the product) and on the managerial policy of establishing 'profit centers' which are subjected to a more or less arm's-length pricing regime in order to promote managerial efficiency. There is also some indication that the extent of centralised control of transfer pricing, among other operations, may vary with the size of the corporation.[16]

3. MONITORING AND REGULATION

This discussion has anticipated numerous issues of monitoring and regulation that confront host countries, particularly developing countries. An active policy on transfer pricing, however it is formulated, must rest on a supportable finding that the unregulated profits in question are unjustifiably low. Such a finding should take into account shifting of profits, through alternative channels, to commodity trade including all accounting profits and quasi-rents.

This approach is well known and has been articulated at length. Despite the difficulty of applying the arm's length standard, it remains the only benchmark available for administering direct control, unless it is used as a platform for extending regulation to the realm of indeterminacy and bargaining. Extension of control to royalties and central services pushes administration further from an 'objective' foundation of facts and figures.

On the basis of information about a few developing countries, some patterns seem to be emerging. The relatively rudimentary regulation of the terms of technology transfer seems to imply that this form of *ex ante* control will be taken as the surrogate for control of this type of intra-firm transaction. With some important exceptions, on the export side, little thought has been given to a process of negotiation, through which 'equitable' prices or shares of profit are determined. Disallowing the expensing of royalties or subjecting royalty payments to high withholding taxes has been tried. There is very little information on the effect.

Differential tax rates between industrial and developing countries are not an important motive for manipulation of transfer pricing. Non-tax factors must be predominant. But there are certain exceptions, the most important of which is the elimination or sharp reduction of tax havens. In recent years important action has been taken by the US, Federal Republic of Germany, Japan and France, to assert jurisdiction over income accumulated in tax havens. A broader assertion of jurisdiction over world-wide profits as earned (abolition of the 'deferral' policy) would encourage the cessation of competitive tax holidays and similar subsidies. Bilateral tax-treaties are concerned with transfer pricing to a limited extent. Nevertheless, their provision for exchange of information and other forms of cooperation between the governments concerned could be helpful.

As indicated, several possibilities can limit the scope for manipulation of transfer pricing. One is simply a large and relatively free international market in the commodity, though this may require a higher degree of processing. Posted prices seem to offer a solution in some instances. Another possibility, thus far tried only in petroleum, is a formula for production-sharing.

There remains, however, a strong indication that a substantial amount of intra-firm trade will continue to consist of intermediate materials, subject to considerable monopoly power. Despite the availability of 'representative' prices and other data, it seems that any regulatory mechanisms will result in negotiation and bargaining, as in the case of screening royalties and services. To undertake such a policy a host country would need both information and bargaining power. An important corollary might be the advance clearance of intra-firm transactions. This, however, is contrary to the legal procedures of enforcement agencies in the industrial countries, who employ an audit system linked to their income tax administration. The obvious objection to advance clearance is the clogging of administrative channels, with undesirable deterrent effect. Thus, a reasonably effective policy would require the selecting of sectors and firms, and the identification of quantitatively important trade and other transactions. Since such firms would be subject to taxation in two jurisdictions, a procedure for 'correlative adjustment' would be important.

Indirect measures could bring this about. One such measure is a requirement by host countries for greater degree of disclosure. Another is a change in corporate law relating to branches which would tend to reduce unwarranted allocation of headquarters expenses to affiliates.

NOTES

1 For convenience in the following discussion we use the phrase transfer pricing to refer to intra-firm transactions generally except where specific reference is to commodity trade (imports and exports) or services of the factors of production (fees for technology, research and development, management, central office expenses, interest on intra-firm loans, etc.).

2 The primary sources are: (1) US Department of Commerce, Bureau of Economic Analysis (BEA), *U.S. Direct Investments Abroad*, 1966, Part II, containing data on 1,750 US 'parent' firms with 13,400 majority-owned overseas affiliates (previously published in instalments in the *Survey of Current Business* ending April 1972), and (2) a sample of 298 US parent firms and their 5,237 majority-owned foreign affiliates (MOFAs), for 1970 in *Special Survey of U.S. Multinational Companies*, 1970, US Department of Commerce, 1972. The latter contains comparable data on 1966. The 1966 data relevant to intra-firm trade are summarised in D. Wallace, (ed.), *International Control of Investment* (New York; Praeger, 1974), chapter by Anthony M. Solomon, 'International Control of Investments in the Trade Sector', pp.15-30. The Business International Study, New York, May 1977, is entitled *The Effects of US Corporate Foreign Investment, 1974-75*, one of a series. Questions of definition of TNCs arise which are not of central importance here. These become increasingly important as investment in joint ventures, particularly with minority TNC participation, increases. The United States 'census' data refer to 'majority-owned-foreign-affiliates' (MOFAs) which exclude firms' transactions with affiliates having less than 50% equity.

3 This point was noted by W. A. Chudson and L. T. Wells, Jr., in a report written in 1973 and published by the United Nations in 1974 (*The Acquisition of Technology from Multinational Corporations by Developing Countries*, Sales No. E.74.II.A.7), and also by Anthony Solomon, *op. cit.*

4 *Survey of Current Business*, December 1972, p.26.

5 S. Lall, 'Transfer Pricing by Multinational Manufacturing Firms', *Oxford Bulletin of Economics and Statistics*, August 1973, p.182.

6 *Op. cit.*, pp.4-5.

7 Based on data from US Department of Commerce, *Survey of Current Business*, March 1977, cited in a private note by Gerald Helleiner. I have reduced total intra-firm trade by 60%, using the fraction shown in the Business International Study.

8 W. B. Reddaway, *Effects of United Kingdom Direct Investment Overseas: Final Report*, Cambridge, Cambridge University Press, 1968, p.365. The data represent 62 firms constituting an estimated 71% of UK overseas investment in mining and manufacturing, excluding petroleum, in 1964.

9 In 1975 petroleum constituted 84% of US intra-firm import trade with developing countries compared with 68% in 1973.

10 Lall and Streeten (*Foreign Investment, Transnationals and Developing*

Countries, Macmillan, 1977.) refer to 'OPEC's brilliant device of levying income tax on a notional [the "posted"] price' (p.205). In fact the OPEC decision merely ratified an arrangement of more than ten years' standing and was primarily aimed at discouraging Libya from offering market discounts from the posted price in competition with the major oil producing countries at a time when the market price of crude petroleum was declining.

11   The Jamaican government now taxes bauxite exports at 50 cents per ton royalty plus 7.5% of whatever aluminium ingot is sold for by the parent company. This basic rate will remain in force for eight years, before redetermination. Prior to May 1974 the aluminium companies in Jamaica had been paying a royalty of approximately $2.50 per ton of bauxite. The shift to 7.5% of the ingot *price* (not physical quantity) is estimated to yield in 1974 ingot prices a revenue of $11.00 per ton, an increase of 700%.

12   According to information supplied by the Dominican Republic to ECLA, an agreement reached in December 1974 resulted in an approximate doubling of royalties and of income tax. See I. A. Litvak and C. J. Maule, 'Transnational Corporations in the Bauxite-Aluminium Industry, with Special Reference to the Caribbean', ECLA, Division of Economic Development ECLA/CTC Joint Unit, Working Paper No.2, July 1977. See also Economist Intelligence Unit, *Quarterly Review of Cuba, Dominican Republic, Haiti and Puerto Rico*, London, No.3, 1974.

13   Contract between Western Samoa and Potlatch Timber, Inc. (USA), reported by W. A. Chudson from field observation, 1974.

14   This is, of course, a simplified statement of a complex situation, the description of which is outside the scope of this paper. There remains the question of the impact of tax havens. In the US tax code, under so-called Sub-part F, introduced in 1962, the scope for shifting profits to tax havens was reduced, and under new regulations introduced in 1975 the scope for use of tax havens by industrial enterprises has been greatly reduced.

Also, there are significant differences among industrial home countries in the taxation of foreign source income; among the 'tightest' (most comprehensive) policies in this regard are those of the US, Federal Republic of Germany, Japan, the UK and, to a smaller extent, France. It is interesting to note that a current proposal by the US administration to abolish the so-called deferral of US tax on foreign source income until the income is actually transferred to the United States would *reduce* the incentive to shift profits overseas for tax reasons either to tax havens or other foreign jurisdictions. This is, of course, the opposite of the situation envisaged in the concern expressed in developing countries over overinvoicing of imports by affiliates or the underinvoicing of exports. An incidental effect of such legislation would be to reduce further the scope for effective granting of tax holidays unless an exception was made for developing countries in the application of this proposed new policy. See President Carter's message to Congress on taxes (extracts), *New York Times*, 22 January 1978. In an unofficial summary, it was stated, however, that 'deferral could be continued under tax treaties [between the USA and] individual countries', *Wall Street Journal*, 23 January 1978, p.21.

15   Donald T. Brash, *American Investment in Australian Industry*, Cambridge, Mass., Harvard University Press, 1966, pp.217-20.

16   Sidney Robbins and Robert Stobaugh, *Money in the Multinational Enterprise*, New York, Basic Books, 1973, pp.143-61.

2.
INTRA-FIRM TRADE AND THE DEVELOPING COUNTRIES: AN ASSESSMENT OF THE DATA
G. K. HELLEINER

INTRODUCTION

Intra-firm international trade is not a new phenomenon in the developing countries. The problems of the export enclave of traditional development literature are, in large part, those associated with intra-firm trade; and many of the ills of import-substituting manufacturing are also associated with it. With the new interest in transnational enterprises, intra-firm trade is emerging as an object of concern in its own right. A remarkably high proportion of international trade in goods and services now takes place *within firms*. Transactions of this type can be expected to take place as a result of central commands, rather than in response to price signals, and the prices at which they are recorded need have nothing to do with 'market' prices. The fact of intra-firm trade therefore poses problems for both theory and policy which, on the face of it, are more serious than those created by 'intra-industry trade' which, perhaps because of the availability of data, has received greater attention (Grubel and Lloyd 1975).

Developing countries, conscious of their relatively weak administrative capacities, are particularly concerned with intra-firm trade. This is primarily because of the enormous potential it provides to transnational enterprises, through the manipulation of transfer prices, for the evasion of domestic taxes, exchange controls, and other laws; the reduction of host country owners' legitimate shares of profits; and the undesirable redirection of earnings towards investments in other countries. The literature on transfer pricing is by now a substantial one, e.g. Horst 1971; Robbins and Stobaugh 1973; Lall 1973; Vaitsos 1974; Kopits 1976; Booth and Jensen 1977). It has long been recognised that illegal practices such as smuggling and faked invoicing 'are important in scope in the less developed countries, in particular, where frequently the methods of enforcement are lax, the frontiers many and large, and the rewards from illegal activity high relative to the returns from legal activity.' (Bhagwati 1974,

31

p.1). It is *not* that transnational enterprises are more motivated toward tax evasion than others, but rather that they have a much greater *capacity* to do so without breaking the law or, if breaking it, being caught.

Intra-firm trade is also of concern to developing countries because it permits not only prices of traded goods and services but also their volume and direction to be controlled by transnational enterprises in their own interests, rather than by host country residents in theirs. This may be of particular concern to countries seeking to build economic links with one another when foreign-owned firms insist on trading with extra-regional affiliates. 'Unintrusiveness' of external relationships is an important and legitimate aspiration of developing country governments. (Diaz-Alejandro 1975, pp.223-4).

At the more global level, there should also be interest in the phenomenon of intra-firm trade for other reasons:

1. The meaning of statistics on the prices of goods and services moving in international trade is called into some question if intra-firm trade accounts for a large share of any one market. Prices for items moving internationally within firms may be set on the basis of the firms' own tax or other requirements rather than by the market, while those on the thin residual markets which *are* truly open and competitive are more volatile than they ought to be. The signals registered by either type of price series may therefore be quite misleading. (This implies problems for benefit-cost analysis based upon border prices, among other things.)

2. In a period when there is great interest in the potential for international commodity price stabilisation through the maintenance of buffer stocks, the use of long-term contracts, etc., the experience of transnational enterprises in stabilising their intra-firm commodity prices (which, on the face of it, has been quite successful) deserves greater attention.

3. There are some indications that the transnational enterprises and the governments of the countries in which they are based are disproportionately promoting the growth of intra-firm trade, relative to arm's-length trade; if so, it is important to understand the extent and nature of this trade if one is to analyse the implications.

4. If decisions to buy (sell) are made by the same firms that are doing the selling (buying), there is an unusual degree of risk that there may be abuse of dominant positions or 'conspiracies in restraint of trade' (UNCTAD, 1977); intra-firm

trade, and the rights and obligations it should entail, are thus important elements in the discussion of international antitrust policies.

5. There has always been interest in the relative merits of decentralised markets, and planning or command systems in the organisation of economic activities. Intra-firm trade data may shed rather more light on this debate than has frequently been possible from the relatively data-scarce assessments of centrally planned economies.

This paper surveys the state of general empirical knowledge of the extent of, and trends in, intra-firm international trade. It has not been possible to produce a total survey of the field with the time and resources available to me. Disproportionate attention is therefore devoted to US and Canadian data sources, which are those best known to me; most of these relate to these countries' imports of merchandise.

CONCEPTUAL AND DEFINITIONAL DISTINCTIONS

Discussion of intra-firm trade and the role of transnational enterprises therein frequently concerns itself with a variety of different issues simultaneously. Clarity, however, requires the drawing of certain distinctions between different sets of issues and problem areas.

First, while intra-firm trade is frequently found in industries or sectors in which there is a high degree of market concentration (oligopoly, oligopsony), it is not *necessarily* associated with it. It is quite possible for intra-firm trade to be dominant in the international trade of an industry characterised by a high degree of competition. The question of market power is therefore *not* the same question as that of the extent of intra-firm trade or the degree of openness of markets. The empirical discovery that a particular developing country pays more for a particular import sold in intra-firm trade than is paid by other countries may indicate *either* price discrimination by selling firms possessing market power *or* the manipulation of transfer prices *or* both.

Second, intra-firm trade may or may not be associated with vertical integration in the productive process of a particular industry. While it *is* trade within vertically integrated firms which is usually meant when the term 'intra-firm trade' is employed, there are other instances of the phenomenon. In particular, there may be international trade between branches or subsidiaries of the same producing firm, each of which is in a totally different and basically unrelated industry; that is, horizontal integration, as found in the modern conglomerate firm, can give rise to intra-firm trade. There is also the possibility that intra-firm trade takes place within what are essentially trading or brokerage firms which do not themselves engage in production at all. These possibilities highlight some of the difficulties associated with the term's definition and interpretation.

Third, whether one is dealing exclusively with intra-firm trade within vertically integrated industries or one employs a broader interpretation of the term, it is necessary to arrive at a uniform definition of 'intra-firm'. How close a relationship between buyer and seller must there be if the two are to be deemed 'the same firm'? The problem is similar to that of defining the circumstances in which 'foreign ownership' or 'foreign control' is said to exist for the purpose of measuring direct foreign investment. Trade between parents and wholly-owned subsidiaries is clearly 'intra-firm'. Trade between parents and majority-owned foreign affiliates (MOFAs) is also fairly clearly 'intra-firm'. With further degrees of arm's-lengthness — minority ownership (in a joint venture with the state, or with a variety of local private investors); management, technology or marketing contracts; longstanding 'customer relationships' involving a high degree of mutual trust, etc. — things become a little more uncertain. Some arbitrariness is bound to be necessary in the writing of a definition suitable for all occasions.

US TRADE WITH US MAJORITY-OWNED FOREIGN AFFILIATES

The US Department of Commerce's published statistics on export sales by majority-owned foreign affiliates (MOFAs) of US companies to the US constitute the most complete, and certainly the most quoted, series available on the nature and trends in international intra-firm trade in goods and services. The data are based on an annual sample survey of 282 US firms and their 5,900 foreign affiliates, the results of which are bench marked to a 1966 census of US foreign direct investment. These data nevertheless are not without their problems. Some of the most important *caveats* which must be issued concerning their use for the assessment of the importance and nature of intra-firm trade flows are the following:

1. Only the export sales of foreign affiliates of *US* firms are included; there may well be significant intra-firm trade flows in US imports which are 'managed' by foreign-owned

(non-US) firms, as, for example, in the case of some of the petroleum 'majors'.

2. The data presented are for foreign affiliates' *total export sales* to the US; some of these sales (18% of those from developing countries in 1975) are at arm's-length to 'unaffiliated' US buyers. (United Nations Economic and Social Council, 1978, p.221).

3. Only *majority-owned* foreign affiliates of US firms are included, i.e. firms 'in which US equity interest — both directly and indirectly held — is at least 50%' (Chung 1975, p.25). (Indirect ownership occurs when equity is held by another foreign affiliate of the US parent firm rather than by the parent itself.) There are substantially larger flows, which are frequently of just as great economic significance, from firms which are related by ownership but which do not meet the 'majority ownership' test.

4. The trade between foreign affiliates and the US parents is measured at the recorded *transfer prices* rather than at market prices. 'No adjustments have been made to reflect possible differences in valuation between sales to affiliated and unaffiliated customers' (Chung 1975, p.25). Transfer prices may, of course, be higher or lower than market prices; and the relationship may differ between different periods of time, different countries, different industries, etc. (Actually, the data are based on the affiliates' books, and these raw data must be converted into US dollars. This generates a further complication in inter-temporal or inter-country comparisons but it is one which equally affects non-affiliate trade.)

5. There are certain respects in which the data for affiliates' trade cannot be compared directly with US import statistics. In particular, this is the case with pre-1974 data, for until 1974, US import trade was valued at 'customs value' which could have been a matter of foreign market value, American selling price, or other criteria. A further difficulty arises in the classification of country of origin: US import statistics report imports according to the country in which the goods truly originate, whereas the affiliate trade data relate to the country in which the affiliate making the sale is located. Neither these nor some other minor statistical problems are likely to alter significantly the conclusions one might draw from the aggregated trade series or those for broadly defined categories. 'Generally, the more detailed the area classification, the larger the differences between the two series'

(Chung 1977, pp.37-8).

6. The recent data relate only to US *imports*. There have been no data reported on the extent of intra-firm merchandise exports from the US since 1970. (The post-1970 balance of payments accounts distinguish, however, US earnings of fees and royalties from affiliated foreigners and others; the former has slowly been rising as a proportion of the total and in 1976 stood at 82% of these earnings.) In 1970, higher proportions of total US export trade took place between US firms and their affiliates, or were associated with US-based transnational enterprises (21% and 66%, respectively) than was the case in US import trade, where the corresponding percentages were 16% and 46% (Barker 1972).

7. The degree of aggregation in the published data is much too great to permit one to investigate transfer pricing practices. Whenever, indeed, there is risk that data relating to individual firms might be revealed the tables contain a 'D' in the relevant box, for which the footnote reads: 'Suppressed to avoid disclosure of data of individual reporters.' (Valuable raw data relating to transfer pricing certainly are collected in this annual survey. It would be worth exploring whether disclosure regulations might permit research upon them to be somehow undertaken without their breach, perhaps under the auspices of a 'trustworthy' institution such as the National Bureau for Economic Research.)

Despite their limitations, these data deserve close scrutiny. They provide the only available general indication of trends in the intra-firm trade between developing countries and their major industrialised country market and the principal home base for transnational enterprises over nearly a ten-year period.

Table 1 shows the percentage of total US imports over the 1966-75 period which has been accounted for by US majority-owned affiliates, classified by area of origin. Imports from developing countries are imported from such affiliates in considerably greater proportions than those from developed countries (on average over the period, 32% as against 25%). The contrast is even more striking if the special case of Canadian trade is omitted from the developed country total; only 12% of imports from Europe and only 1% of imports from Japan emanate from US affiliates. The proportion of US imports stemming from majority-owned affiliates, moreover, seems to be rising in the case of developing country trade (as well as the trade with Canada and Europe). The limited available data also indicate that between 1971 and 1975 the share of developing country MOFA exports to their parents in their total exports to the US rose from 69% to 82%, while the equivalent share for developed country MOFAs fell from 76% to 65% (United Nations Economic and Social Council 1978, p.221).

These aggregative data are misleading, however, in that they conceal the enormous importance of petroleum in US MOFA imports from developing countries. In 1975, petroleum made up fully 84% of this US trade with developing countries, a proportion which, of course, greatly increased (from 68% in 1972) with the petroleum price increases of recent years. Although the published statistics do not facilitate such analysis, one must consider the non-petroleum data separately in the case of the developing countries. (There is no such necessity in the case of developed country trade data since petroleum's share of the analogous US imports was only 15% in 1975.)

When one looks at the trends in US imports from majority-owned affiliates in developing countries, *exclusive of petroleum*, (Table 2), it becomes necessary to revise sharply the conclusions one might draw from looking only at the aggregative data. Excluding petroleum, US imports from affiliates have made up proportions of total US imports from developing countries which are of the same order of magnitude over the 1966-75 period as their share of total imports from Europe.[1] Even more surprising, while the affiliates' share of total imports from Europe has been slowly rising, their share of non-petroleum imports from the developing countries has dropped markedly. MOFA imports, which had made up 20% of US non-petroleum imports from developing countries in 1967, accounted for only 11% of these imports from developing countries in 1975, whereas they made up 14% of total imports from Europe and 28% of those from all developed countries.

It would seem that, contrary to widely-held views, vertically integrated transnational enterprises may *not* be taking over increasing shares of developing country trade. At least as far as US-based enterprises are concerned, the much-discussed increasing internationalisation and vertical integration of production is confined to Western Europe and Canada. (It does not noticeably apply to Australia, New Zealand, South Africa or Japan either. Indeed, even in the Canadian case, between 1971 and 1975, MOFA exports to their US parents have fallen both as a proportion of their exports to the US and as a proportion of total Canadian exports to the US; see United Nations Economic and

Table 1   MOFA Sales to the United States as Percentage of Total US Merchandise Imports by Area of Origin, 1966-75

	1966	1967	1968	1969	1970	1971	1972	1973	1974	1975	1966-75 Average
All areas	25	27	26	27	25	28	25	28	31	32	28
Developed countries	22	25	24	25	25	27	24	25	24	28	25
Canada	49	54	53	54	55	59	55	55	51	58	55
Europe	10	11	11	11	11	12	11	12	12	14	12
United Kingdom	13	17	14	15	15	16	15	13	14	17	15
European Communities (6)[1]	7	9	9	9	10	11	11	13	13	15	11
Other Europe	11	12	13	10	10	11	9	9	10	12	10
Japan	1	1	1	1	1	—	—	1	1	1	1
Australia, New Zealand and South Africa	10	12	13	14	13	12	9	9	11	8	11
Developing countries	30	29	28	28	23	30	27	32	36	35	32
Latin America	38	38	37	37	30	39	36	39	34	41	37
Other Asia and Africa	18	17	16	17	13	21	18	25	36	32	27

[1]   Consists of Belgium, Luxembourg, France, Federal Republic of Germany, Italy and the Netherlands.

Source: William K. Chung, 'Sales by Majority-Owned Foreign Affiliates of US Companies, 1975', *Survey of Current Business*, vol. 57, no.2, February 1977, p.35.

Table 2

MOFA sales to the United States as a percentage of total and non-petroleum
US merchandise imports from developing countries 1966-75

	Total %	Total excluding petroleum %
1966	30	n.a.
1967	29	20
1968	28	n.a.
1969	28	18
1970	23	14
1971	30	14
1972	27	11
1973	32	13
1974	36	12
1975	35	11

Source: Calculated from data in Chung (1975: 35), and OECD, *Foreign Trade.
Commodity Trade: Imports*, various years.

Table 3

US Exports by MNCs/MOFAs Relative to Total US Exports, by Area of Destination,
1966 and 1970
($ millions)

	1966			1970		
	Developed Countries	Developing Countries	Total	Developed Countries	Developing Countries	Total
Exports from US parents to MOFAs	4,098	940	5,038	7,118	1,505	8,623
Total US exports	19,960	9,327	29,287	29,804	12,159	41,963
MNC/MOFA exports as % of total	21	10	17	24	12	21

Source: Calculated from Betty L. Barker, 'U.S. Foreign Trade Associated with U.S.
Multinational Companies', *Survey of Current Business*, September 1972.

Table 4

US Exports of Manufactured Products: The Role of MNCs and MNC/MOFA Trade, 1970‡
(millions of dollars)

	US Total Exports (1)	Exports of US MNCs (2)	Exports of US MNCs as % of US Total* (3)	Exports of US MNCs to MOFAs		
				Amt. (4)	% of US MNC Exports (5)	% of Total Exports* (6)
All manufacturing	34,969	21,718	62 (65)**	7,707†	35 (32)**	22 (21)**
Food products	2,578	1,062	41	362	34	14
Grain mill products	578	227	39	106	47	18
Beverages	87	58	67	11	19	13
Combinations	—	40	—	9	23	—
Other	1,913	737	41	236	32	12
Paper and allied products	1,109	609	55	150	25	14
Chemicals and allied products	4,012	2,342	58	845	36	21
Drugs	511	361	71	138	38	27
Soaps and cosmetics	154	130	85	70	54	45
Industrial chemicals	1,702	1,198	70	181	15	11
Plastics materials	941	318	34	279	88	30
Combinations	—	114	—	114	100	—
Other	704	221	48	63	29	9
Rubber	344	383	111	148	39	43
Primary and fabricated metals	3,749	2,237	60	278	12	7

Table 4 – *continued*

US Exports of Manufactured Products: The Role of MNCs and MNC/MOFA Trade, 1970‡
(millions of dollars)

	US Total Exports (1)	Exports of US MNCs (2)	Exports of US MNCs as % of US Total* (3)	Exports of US MNCs to MOFAs		
				Amt. (4)	% of US MNC Exports (5)	% of Total Exports* (6)
Primary	1,700	976	58	51	5	3
Fabricated, excluding aluminum, copper and brass	1,356	554	41	131	24	10
Primary and fabricated aluminum	336	627	187	56	9	17
Other	358	80	22	40	50	11
Machinery, except electrical	7,917	3,795	48	1,674	44	21
Farm machinery and equipment	372	392	105	192	49	52
Industrial machinery and equipment	4,181	1,694	41	457	27	11
Office machines	358	576	161	431	75	120
Electronic computing equipment	1,243	399	32	298	75	24
Other	1,763	734	42	296	40	17
Electrical machinery	3,007	2,060	69	575	28	19
Household appliances	172	157	91	39	25	23
Electrical equipment and apparatus	729	978	134	151	15	21
Electronic components, radio, and TV	1,628	734	45	210	29	13
Other	478	191	38	175	92	37
Transportation equipment	6,589	6,750	103	2,748	41	42
Textiles and apparel	724	244	34	97	40	13

Table 4 – continued

US Exports of Manufactured Products: The Role of MNCs and MNC/MOFA Trade, 1970‡
(millions of dollars)

	US Total Exports (1)	Exports of US MNCs (2)	Exports of US MNCs as % of US Total* (3)	Exports of US MNCs to MOFAs		
				Amt. (4)	% of MNC Exports (5)	% of Total Exports* (6)
Lumber, wood and furniture	741	352	48	40	11	5
Printing and publishing	335	144	43	36	25	11
Stone, clay, and glass products	477	267	56	86	32	18
Instruments	1,315	848	65	522	62	40
Other manufacturing	2,121	625	30	146	23	7

Sources: Columns (1) to (5): US Senate, Committee on Finance, *Implications of Multinational Firms for World Trade and Investment and for US Trade and Labor* (Washington, 1973), p.367, 372.

Column (6): Calculated from columns (1) and (4)

*   Customs classifications are not identical to the industry classifications for MNC exports. Hence, this percentage can exceed 100%.
**   Bracketed figure is the percentage in 1966.
†   The total for US MNC exports to MOFAs is stated as slightly different in the presumably more authoritative *Survey of Current Business*. (Leonard A. Lupo, 'Sales by U.S. Multinational Companies', Jan. 1973). The figures are slightly smaller — 7,079 in 1970 — with the result that the estimated percentage which these exports make up of total US manufacturing exports is only 20%, both in 1966 and in 1970. The latter presentation provides no industry breakdowns, which is why the data here presented are from the stated slightly less 'reliable' source.
‡   These data have been 'blown-up' to estimates for totals on the basis of sample data which were summarised in Table 2.

Social Council, 1978, p.221.) The increasing extent to which North Atlantic trade seems to be taking place between MOFAs and their home countries is undoubtedly associated with the falling trade barriers of recent years, and the developed countries' tariff reductions which have been structured so as to favour transnational enterprises (Helleiner 1977).

The declining share of US nonpetroleum imports from developing countries which originate in MOFAs requires further investigation and explanation. It is probably attributable to two main influences:

1. the increasing degree to which the governments of developing countries have been driving wedges into what were formerly 'closed systems' through nationalisation, the creation of marketing boards, etc., particularly in the resource industries;

2. the increasing share of developing country exports which consists of manufactured products, the trade in which is typically less subject to management through majority-owned affiliates than is primary product trade. (Actually, MOFAs account for decreasing proportions of the developing countries' manufactured exports to the US as well; see Nayyar 1978, p.65.) The growth in the role of non-US-based international business may also contribute to this trend.

It is also worth noting that such data as there are indicate that far smaller (although rising) shares of US exports to developing countries move to MOFAs than is the case with US exports to developed countries. In 1970, the respective figures were 12% and 24%, up from 10% and 21% in 1966. The 12% share of exports to developing countries in 1970 can be compared with the 14% shares of US non-petroleum imports from developing countries in the same year, though the latter has since fallen (see Table 3). In Table 4 can be found such information as there is on the industrial composition of exports by US transnational corporations to MOFAs and to others. Lall (1078) has attempted to 'explain', through regression analysis, the decisions on the part of US transnational corporations as to whether to export on an intra-firm basis rather than on an arm's-length basis. He used as his dependent variable the quite highly aggregated industry-level data (given in Table 3) on the share of exports by US transnationals (not of total US exports) which are made on an intra-firm basis. This percentage share was significantly related, positively, to research and development expenditures as a proportion of sales, to foreign assets as a percentage of domestic assets, a dummy for usage of US value added tariff provisions, and (weakly) to value added per employee. The relation between research and development and intra-firm exports by US transnationals has also been noted by Buckley and Casson (1976, p.22).

US RELATED-PARTY IMPORTS

A relatively new and unpublished source of intra-firm trade data, prepared by the Foreign Trade Division of the US Bureau of the Census, provides information based on a much broader definition of 'related-party trade' (to employ their terminology). Since 1974, on a quarterly basis, estimates have been made of the value and volume of US imports within each individual tariff classification and from each country of origin which originates from 'related parties'. (The relevant document, numbered IQ246, is not confidential but only five copies are retained and it is therefore not easily accessible.) A 'related party' is defined, for the purpose of these estimates, as a firm in which 5% or more of the voting stock is owned by the other party to the transaction.[2] The parent firm may be either the buyer or the seller; and neither need have any US ownership. Clearly, such a broad definition of intra-firm international trade will include many transactions not usually the concern of those interested in the subject. For example, trade between buying agents and their employees, or between branches of brokerage or trading firms, will certainly be caught in this definition of 'related party' trade. On the other hand, the 5% cutoff point in ownership share and its application on a reciprocal basis is probably a better basis for defining and measuring 'intra-firm trade' than the 50%, US ownership only, rule employed by the Department of Commerce. (The Canadian Foreign Investment Review Agency, not renowned for the toughness of its regulations, uses 5% ownership of the voting stock by any one foreign source as one of its definitions of 'foreign control' of a Canadian corporation.)

The data are compiled directly from customs declarations filed by US importers. US importers are required to declare whether their imports originate with a related party or not. In the case of imports which are declared as transactions with related parties, the importer is required to state an arm's-length equivalent price as well as the *actual* transaction price which the importer pays. (US c.i.f. data are based on these arm's-length price declarations rather than upon customs declarations.) A complete count is undertaken of the amounts shown on the importers' declarations, and therefore one can obtain comprehensive quarterly data on related and non-related party imports with a fairly high degree of detail.

These data indicate that in 1977 fully 48% of total US imports from all sources consisted of related-party trade. (Recall that in 1975 the proportion of total US imports originating with majority-owned affiliates of US firms was 32%.)

Table 5 shows that the share of trade which takes place between related parties rises as one moves from primary products (excluding petroleum) to semi-manufactured and manufactured products; it is also higher in US imports from other OECD members than it is in those from developing countries. There is strong evidence to suggest, however, that much larger proportions of related party imports from developing countries (and Canada) are associated with international production systems than is the case with similar imports from Europe or Japan, many of which are purely 'distributional' in character. (Helleiner and Lavergne 1979).

Table 6 shows the related-party importing of primary products by the US in 1975. Related-party imports of several major primary commodities originating in less-developed countries accounted for much larger proportions of US total imports of these commodities than the overall 1975 related-party import share of 45%. Bananas, rubber (milk or latex), bauxite, and cotton are well above the US average in this respect. The proportion of Third World commodity exports to the US which takes place between related parties is, in other cases, quite low — zero for copper, phosphates, sugar, kapok, tin and some vegetable oils; under 10% for cocoa and coffee, vegetable oils, hard fibres, and mahogany. In the majority of cases in which developed countries were also suppliers of a particular commodity, the proportion of this developed country trade which took place between related parties was greater than that for developing country trade. (The significant exceptions were bauxite, manganese, and some edible oils.)

In Table 7 may be found the related party share of US imports of manufactured products of various kinds in 1977. There is clearly a very wide range: from the remarkably high shares found in such sectors as machinery, pharmaceuticals and professional and scientific instruments, on the one hand, to the low ones found in leather manufactures and footwear, on the other. Attempts to 'explain' these inter-industry differences have suggested that related party imports are most likely to be a high proportion of

Table 5

US Related-Party Imports as a Percentage of Total Imports, by Product Class and Origin, 1977

| | Petroleum | Primary** | | Semi-Manu-factures** | Manu-factures** | Total | |
| | | Primary excluding petroleum | Total primary | | | | Total excluding petroleum |
	%	%	%	%	%	%	%
OECD*	57.2	35.9	41.3	43.4	61.1	53.7	53.6
Centrally Planned*	0	3.2	2.8	8.9	8.1	7.7	7.8
Third World*	59.6	13.6	49.1	17.0	37.0	43.4	28.1
Total	59.4	23.5	47.3	37.6	53.6	48.4	45.2

*   Country classifications are according to the *United Nations Standard Country Code*, except that Cuba and Yogoslavia have been included among the Centrally Planned Countries.

**   Products classified according to UNCTAD system, reported in 'The Definition of Primary Commodities, Semi-Manufactures and Manufactures,' 1965, TD/B/C.2/3.

Source: Helleiner and Lavergne, 1979.

Table 6

US Imports of Primary Commodities from Related Parties in Less Developed
and Other Countries, 1975

Commodities	Related Party imports as a % of total imports		Total value of US imports ($ million)	
	From ldcs %	*From others* %	*From ldcs* $	*From others* $
a. *UNCTAD 'core' of 10*				
Cocoa beans	1.8	1.9	345	1
Coffee	7.1	54.3	1,771	12
Copper	0	57.7	13	27
Cotton	67.8	0	22	1
Hard Fibres				
Abaca	9.5	88.3	18	1
Kapok	0		5	
Sisal	1.3		5	
Jute	9.6		5	
Rubber				
Milk or latex	79.9		65	
Dry	23.8	71.5	449	1
Sugar	0	0	1,662	290
Tea	27.1	44.7	114	17
Tin	0		45	
b. *Others*				
Bananas	67.5		525	
Bauxite	88.3	77.6	533	3
Iron ore				
Concentrates	17.2	63.1	318	150
Other	24.1	80.8	364	762
Manganese	22.9	0	85	21
Phosphates	0		2	
Tropical timber				
Mahogany	8.2		25	
Balsa/teak	39.3		13	
Vegetables oils and oilseeds				
Coconut oil	2.5	4.2	211	5
Palm kernel oil, inedible	0		2	
Palm kernel oil, edible	0.9	0	33	8
Palm oil, edible	0.4	0	214	1
Sesame seed	0.2	1.0	17	1
Castor oil	0	0	18	1

Source: G.K. Helleiner, 'Freedom and Management in Primary Commodity Markets:
US Imports from Developing Countries,' *World Development*, 1978, 6,1, p.26.

Table 7   US Related-Party Imports as a Percentage of Total Imports, by Category, from Third World and OECD Sources, 1977

	OECD %	Percentage 3W %	Total %	Import Value Total ($ millions)	3W ($ millions)
00 Live animals	16.4	3.9	12.3	254	87
01 Beverages and tobacco	26.0	16.4	19.9	1,287	291
02 Dairy products	13.7	2.6	12.9	229	10
03 Fish and fish preparations	34.5	8.8	23.1	2,047	890
04 Cereals and cereal preparations	13.3	4.5	12.1	151	19
05 Fruit and vegetables	18.9	45.1	39.9	1,523	1,230
06 Sugar, sugar preparations	5.5	2.7	3.3	1,219	966
07 Coffee, tea, cocoa, spices	59.0	6.3	9.0	5,538	5,238
08 Feeding stuff for animals	14.5	22.3	16.3	95	22
09 Miscellaneous food	28.3	11.5	23.6	91	23
11 Beverages	23.8	16.7	23.5	1,218	40
12 Tobacco and manufactures	10.9	8.6	8.1	373	263
21 Hides and skins	1.5	0.3	1.2	219	50
22 Oil seeds, nuts and kernels	33.2	2.7	19.1	48	21
23 Crude rubber (including synthetic)	86.8	27.1	37.9	794	649
24 Wood, lumber, cork	17.9	5.1	17.2	1,996	105
25 Pulp and waste paper	41.2	9.0	41.1	1,194	2
26 Textile fibres	20.6	10.1	16.7	238	67
27 Crude fertilisers and minerals	38.1	36.2	37.6	872	162
28 Metalliferous ores and metal scrap	63.4	40.7	52.3	2,024	943
29 Crude animal and vegetable materials	17.3	12.8	13.6	499	235
32 Coal, coke and briquettes	13.6	70.9	13.5	211	1
33 Petroleum and petroleum products	48.8	57.7	56.8	41,285	37,597
34 Gas, natural and manufactured	59.0	12.1	55.0	2,499	215

Table 7 – continued
US Related-Party Imports as a Percentage of Total Imports, by Category, from Third World and OECD Sources, 1977

	OECD %	Percentage 3W %	Total %	Import Value Total ($ millions)	3W ($ millions)
41 Animal oils and fats	15.5	0.2	15.0	8	—
42 Fixed vegetable oils and fats	9.1	8.7	8.7	505	458
43 Animal and vegetable oils and fats, processed	16.4	1.9	5.2	15	11
51 Chemical elements and compounds	44.0	40.7	43.3	3,178	367
52 Mineral tar and chemicals from coal, petroleum and natural gas	34.3	—	33.7	11	—
53 Dyeing, tanning and colouring materials	73.4	15.7	69.8	209	11
54 Medicinal and pharmaceutical products	46.7	60.3	46.9	318	42
55 Essential oils and perfumes, etc.	41.3	2.1	26.7	239	82
56 Fertilisers, manufactured	20.6	75.1	23.4	353	19
57 Explosives and pyrotechnic products	14.0	4.5	8.9	39	9
58 Plastic materials, etc.	57.6	14.4	54.9	402	25
59 Chemical materials and products n.e.s.	53.2	5.9	48.9	329	22
61 Leather and leather manufactures	7.0	5.0	5.8	256	145
62 Rubber manufactures, n.e.s.	78.0	31.6	73.3	999	96
63 Wood and cork manufactures	22.6	9.4	15.1	1,034	576
64 Paper, paperboard etc.	20.0	39.8	20.6	2,404	81
65 Textile yarn, fabrics, made-up articles	35.1	7.8	22.6	1,776	736
66 Non-metallic mineral manufactures	18.0	10.4	16.4	2,802	479
67 Iron and steel	65.9	20.4	61.8	5,982	483
68 Non-ferrous metals	43.7	16.7	33.7	3,938	1,289
69 Manufactures of metal, n.e.s.	28.0	12.4	24.9	2,499	455

Table 7 — *continued*
US Related-Party Imports as a Percentage of Total Imports, by Category, from Third World and OECD Sources, 1977

	OECD %	Percentage 3W %	Total %	Import Value Total ($ millions)	3W ($ millions)
71 Machinery other than electric	60.3	63.5	60.3	9,777	658
72 Electrical machinery, apparatus, appliances	55.2	75.2	63.4	8,451	3,541
73 Transport equipment	84.7	32.6	83.9	18,229	304
81 Sanitary and other fixtures	17.3	14.2	15.8	109	47
82 Furniture	34.0	13.6	26.3	666	169
83 Travel goods, handbags, etc.	28.4	10.3	13.4	309	254
84 Clothing	12.0	11.5	11.3	4,049	3,221
85 Footwear	11.7	4.4	7.3	1,890	1,013
86 Professional and scientific instruments, etc.	50.9	51.2	50.9	2,316	488
87 Miscellaneous manufactures	33.4	17.1	27.6	5,394	1,825

Source: Helleiner and Lavergne, 1979.

total US imports where the US competing industry pays a high average wage, has a high percentage of its work force in large establishments, and spends a high proportion of its revenues on research and development; in the case of imports from developing countries, only research and development expenditure is significantly related to the related party share (Helleiner and Lavergne 1979).

The degree of detail in this data source permits the calculation of unit values recorded for related-party imports and for unrelated-party imports for most tariff classifications at the country level on a quarterly basis. There are frequently great differences between the declared total unit values of imports and those of imports from unrelated parties. (There are well-known potential pitfalls in the use of unit value data, particularly where there is product differentiation; see Kravis and Lipsey, 1971, p.4.) Here, in principle (and provided that the quality of the data justify the effort), is a goldmine of data on transfer-pricing practices simply waiting to be worked.[3] (In some cases, unfortunately, volume data are not recorded. In others, 100% of the trade with a particular country is either related-party or unrelated-party, so that comparative unit value data at the country level do not exist.) As more time series data accumulate it will become possible to observe not only cross-sectional differences between unit values of related-party imports and those of unrelated party imports, but also their trends and their relationship to *changes* in tax provisions, foreign exchange practices, and political circumstances in particular countries.

INTERNATIONAL SUBCONTRACTING AND VALUE ADDED TARIFFS

As far as manufactured goods trade is concerned, some further evidence on the growth of intra-firm trade is provided by the fact of 'value added tariffs' in many of the industrialised countries. Their exact provisions vary from country to country but all permit, in certain circumstances, manufactured articles to enter national markets partially free of tariff duties when raw materials have originated in the country of importation. The organisation of such trade and manufacturing activities implies a degree of transnational management, although it can be undertaken by brokers and trading houses as well as vertically integrated transnational enterprises. In the case of the US, data on the use of such provisions in the tariff (items 807.00 and 806.30, the former being by far the more important) extend back over a ten-year

Table 8

US Imports under Tariff Items 807.00 and 806.30, 1966-77
($ millions)

	Total Value		*Dutiable Value*		*Value of US Products*	
	Total	*Developing Countries*	*Total*	*Developing Countries*	*Total*	*Developing Countries*
1966	953.0	60.7	805.5	31.4	147.5	29.0
1967	1,035.1	99.0	837.2	42.6	197.9	55.8
1968	1,554.4	221.7	1,263.7	97.7	290.6	124.0
1969	1,838.8	394.8	1,396.7	177.3	442.1	217.6
1970	2,208.2	541.5	1.671.8	245.9	536.3	295.5
1971	2,765.8	652.5	2,105.9	314.1	659.9	338.4
1972	3,408.8	1,066.5	2,540.4	547.3	868.3	519.2
1973	4,247.1	1,557.3	3,238.3	845.4	1,008.8	711.8
1974	5,371.8	2,350.1	4,059.0	1,303.0	1,312.8	1,047.1
1975	5,161.2	2,261.7	3,895.5	1,238.7	1,265.7	1.023.1
1976	5,719.0	2,807.0	4,173.2	1,548.6	1,545.7	1,258.4
1977	7,188.1	3,306.8	5,212.0	1,721.4	1.976.1	1,585.3
1978	9,735.3	4.286.6	7,143.7	2,175.8	2,591.5	2,110.9

Source: United States International Trade Commission.

period and are reported annually by the Data Development Division of the US International Trade Commission. Table 8 presents summary data on the growth in this trade from 1966 to 1977. With the exception of the recession year of 1975, it has grown at extremely rapid rates in recent years — rates considerably in excess of the rates of growth in total US manufactured imports. Table 7 also shows the less developed countries' role in these US imports, of which Mexico has accounted for the largest share (followed by Taiwan, Singapore, Hong Kong and Malaysia). For most of the 1970s, exports under this tariff provision have also been rising more quickly than their total manufactured exports to the US. By 1975 this trade made up 22% of total US manufactured imports from developing countries,[4] though this percentage subsequently fell slightly again; in 1978, it was 19% (Jarrett 1979, 351).

Value added abroad, however, constitutes a significantly smaller, and falling, proportion of the value of this trade in the case of developing countries than in that of developed countries — in 1977, 52% as against 90%. Countries of origin and commodity groups are not cross-classified in the available documentation (although these data can no doubt be obtained from the USITC), so that it is not possible to discover easily the commodity composition of this trade with the developing countries. The bulk of developing country trade of this kind is known, however, to be in electronic components and made-up textiles.[5]

Equivalent data are no doubt available showing recent trends in this type of intra-firm trade in Europe and Japan. (Some are reported in a recent paper by Finger 1975.) Since some international subcontracting is undertaken without benefit of 'value added tariff' provisions, these statistics understate the extent of this type of trade. (On the other hand, these data may slightly overstate its rate of growth, if some of the subcontractors formerly did not take advantage of these tariff concessions and have now begun to do so.)

CONCLUSIONS

This paper has attempted to outline the reasons for the growing concern with the phenomenon of intra-firm trade, and summarise the most readily available data on its nature and growth. It seems that such trade already accounts for substantial proportions of international exchange. From the US data, one can derive a figure for the intra-firm share of total US imports. In 1977, 48% of all US imports originated with a party related by ownership (5% of the voting stock or more) to the buyer (see Table 5); the figure includes firms based outside the US as well as US firms. Of this amount, a little over half is intra-firm importing by US parents from majority-owned foreign affiliates (i.e., 24% of total US imports, 74% of the 32% of total US imports from MOFAs).

To this basic 48% should be added at least some of the US imports which are obtained on a subcontracting basis from overseas firms which use US imports since, while these do not all originate with firms which are related by ownership to the buyers, this trade is fully dependent on them for technology and marketing, and can be regarded as equivalent to intra-firm trade. US imports under items 806.30 and 807.00 of the US tariff (the provisions which exempt the value of US inputs from import duties in certain circumstances) amounted to 5.4% of total US imports in 1975; in 1977, they were 5% of total US imports, 9.7% of US manufactured imports, and fully 18% of manufactured imports from developing countries (Jarrett 1979, 351). How much of this importing is from 'independent' firms is not known. Nor are there data on the extent of such trade which takes place, despite the fact that it does not benefit from the provisions of tariff items 806.30 and 807.00.

There is certainly a case for also including some of the trade which is associated with licensing agreements, management or marketing contracts with ostensibly independent foreign firms. It seems safe to say that US intra-firm transactions must make up as much as half of US imports.

The availability of information on intra-firm trade in merchandise exports from the US is unfortunately more limited. In 1970, 22% of US manufactured exports went from US parents to their own MOFAs. This figure sets a *lower* bound to the importance of intra-firm trade in US exports; it is comparable to the 24% figure for US MOFA-parent import trade cited above.

Among the more important points made in this paper were the following:

1. It is essential to arrive at clear and uniform definitions of what is meant by 'intra-firm trade' and, for that purpose, it is important to know exactly why one is interested in it (is one concerned with concentration of market power? the capacity to manipulate transfer prices? or both?).

2. The share of US non-petroleum imports from developing countries which originates in majority-owned foreign affiliates of US firms is falling (while the equivalent share of US imports from Western Europe and Canada is rising); this runs contrary to most 'conventional wisdom' and deserves further investigation.

3. Very high proportions of some US imports from developing countries originate with 'related parties'; there are frequently large differences between import unit values in related-party trade and those in non-related-party trade.

4. International subcontracting, as indicated by the usage of value added tariff provisions, continues to be a rapidly growing element in manufactured goods trade between the US and the developing countries.

5. Further data should be collected and empirical research conducted through the following:

    (i) resort to the raw data collected in the US Department of Commerce annual survey of majority-owned foreign affiliates' sales, in some way which does not breach confidentiality regulations;

    (ii) more detailed analysis of US data on related-party imports, including more careful econometric testing of unit value differences between related-party and non-related-party trade on both a cross-country basis and a time series basis

at the individual country level;
(iii) more detailed and comprehensive compilation of data on the usage of value added tariff provisions not only by the USA, but also by other countries, so as to discover the commodity as well as country composition of this trade and identify the principal transactors in it.

NOTES

* An original draft of this paper was prepared for the conference on Intra-firm Transactions and their Impact on Trade and Development at the Institute of Development Studies, Sussex, November 7-11, 1977. I am grateful for comments and criticisms to the participants in that conference and particularly to Robin Murray. Versions of the material have appeared in the *Journal of Development Economies*, 1979, and in G.K. Helleiner, *Intra-Firm Trade and the Developing Countries*, Macmillan, 1981. I am grateful for their permission to reprint.
1 These figures for MOFA shares of US non-petroleum imports were obtained by subtracting MOFA petroleum imports from total MOFA imports, and dividing by total US imports, less petroleum imports. (Imports of petroleum from US MOFAs amounted to 61% of these imports from developing countries in 1967, 59% in 1975. Some intra-firm petroleum imports into the US do not originate, however, with US majority-owned affiliates; the intra-firm share of US petroleum imports is actually higher.) In an earlier paper, I reported slightly different numbers based on a cruder estimating procedure detailed there (Helleiner 1979). It is unfortunately not possible similarly to disaggregate the few data showing the share which MOFA exports to parents make up of total MOFA exports to the US.
2 The full definition includes cases in which the importer and exporter are members of the same family, partners, employer and employee, etc., as detailed in section 402 (g) of the Tariff Act of 1930.
3 Some first attempts are reported in Helleiner 1978a.
4 The exact percentage depends upon what one places in the denominator. Nayyar (1978) comes up with a smaller percentage but also finds a sharp rise therein (p.67).
5 Some 1976 data were kindly provided for my use by the US International Trade Commission, but it would be most useful if these were available to the public on a regularised basis. I have reported on some of them in Helleiner 1979.

BIBLIOGRAPHY

Barker, B.L. (1972), 'U.S. Foreign Trade Associated with U.S. Multinational Companies', *Survey of Current Business*, U.S. Department of Commerce, 52, pp.20-8.
Bhagwati, J. (ed.) (1974), *Illegal Transactions in International*

Trade, Theory and Measurement, North-Holland, Amsterdam.

Booth, E.J.R. and Jensen, O.W. (1977), 'Transfer Prices in the Global Corporation under Internal and External Constraints,' *Canadian Journal of Economics*, X, pp.434-46.

Buckley, P.J. and Casson, M. (1976), *The Future of the Multinational Enterprise*, Macmillan, London.

Chung, W.K., (1975), 'Sales by Majority-owned Foreign Affiliates of U.S. Companies, 1973', *Survey of Current Business*, (U.S. Department of Commerce), 55, 9, pp.22-37.

—— (1977), 'Sales by Majority-owned Foreign Affiliates of U.S. Companies, 1975', *Survey of Current Business*, U.S. Department of Commerce, 57, 2, pp.29-39.

Diaz-Alejandro, C.F. (1975), 'North-South Relations: The Economic Component,' *International Organization*, 29, 1, pp.213-41.

Finger, J.M. (1975), 'Tariff Provisions for Offshore Assembly and the Exports of Developing Countries,' *Economic Journal*, 85, pp.365-71.

Grubel, H.G. and Lloyd, R.J. (1975), *Intra-Industry Trade, The Theory and Measurement of International Trade in Differentiated Products*, Macmillan, London.

Helleiner, G.K. (1977), 'Transnational Enterprises and the New Political Economy of U.S. Trade Policy', *Oxford Economic Papers*, 29, pp.102-16.

—— (1978), 'Freedom and Management in Primary Commodity Markets: U.S. Imports from Developing Countries,' *World Development*, 6, 1, pp.23-30.

—— (1979), 'Structural Aspects of Third World Trade: Some Trends and Some Prospects,' in *Development of Societies: The Next Twenty-five Years, Proceedings of the ISS Twenty-fifth Anniversary Conference*, Institute of Social Studies, The Hague, Martinus Nijhoff, The Hague.

—— and Lavergne, R. (1979), 'Intra-Firm Trade and Industrial Exports to the United States,' *Oxford Bulletin of Economics and Statistics*, 41, no.4, November.

Horst, T. (1971), 'The Theory of Multinational Firm: Optimal Behavior under Different Tariff and Tax Rates,' *Journal of Political Economy*, 79, 1059-72.

Jarrett, J.P. (1979), *Offshore Assembly and Production and the Internalization of International Trade Within the Multinational Corporation: Their Causes and Effects on U.S. Manufacturing Industry Wage and Profit Rates*, PhD thesis,

Harvard University.
Kopits, G.F. (1976), 'Taxation and Multinational Firm Behaviour: A Critical Survey', *International Monetary Fund Staff Papers*, 23, 624-73.
Kravis, I.B. and Lipsey, R.E. (1971), *Price Competitiveness in World Trade*, National Bureau of Economic Research, Columbia University Press, New York.
Lall, S. (1973), 'Transfer-Pricing by Multinational Manufacturing Firms,' *Oxford Bulletin of Economics and Statistics*, 35, no.3, August, pp.173-95.
—— (1978), 'The Pattern of Intra-Firm Exports by U.S. Multinationals,' *Oxford Bulletin of Economics and Statistics*, 40, no.3, August, pp.209-23.
Nayyar, D. (1978), 'Transnational Corporations and Manufactured Exports from Poor Countries,' *Economic Journal*, 88, pp.59-84.
Robbins, S. and Stobaugh, R. (1973), *Money in the Multinational Enterprise, A Study in Financial Policy*, Basic Books, New York).
United Nations Conference on Trade and Development (UNCTAD) (1977), *Dominant Positions of Market Power of Transnational Corporations: Use of the Transfer Pricing Mechanism*, ST/MD/6.
United Nations Economic and Social Council, Commission on Transnational Corporations (1978), *Transnational Corporations in World Development: A Re-examination*, E/C, 10/38.
Vaitsos, C.V. (1974), *Intercountry Income Distribution and Transnational Enterprises*, the Clarendon Press, Oxford.

PART TWO

Transfer Pricing in Practice

(A) Exports

3.
EXPORT VALUATION AND INTRA-FIRM TRANSFERS IN THE BANANA EXPORT INDUSTRY IN CENTRAL AMERICA*
FRANK ELLIS

SIGNIFICANCE AND STRUCTURAL PECULIARITIES OF BANANA EXPORTS FROM CENTRAL AMERICA

Since the turn of the century four Central American countries — Costa Rica, Guatemala, Honduras and Panama — have been the principal locus of production for fresh bananas imported into non-preferential, developed country markets. In post-war years each country has experienced periods in which bananas have represented as much as 70% of export earnings; and value added in the banana export sector has constituted up to 30% of GDP in two of them. Although in recent years the traditional predominance of the sector has been eroded by a certain amount of internal diversification, it remains today the largest employer and most important single source of foreign exchange in three out of the four countries.[1] Between 1971 and 1975 the four countries exported, on average, a total of 134 million 40-lb. boxes per year equivalent to 38% of all bananas entering world shipping channels.

The historical evolution of the banana export sector up to 1947 was characterised by the near-monopoly status achieved by one US transnational corporation, the United Fruit Company.[2] In 1930, for example, this company owned 1,409,148 hectares of land in Latin America of which 76,553 hectares, or 5.4%, were in banana production.[3] In that year it was responsible for 80% of the 43.3 million bunches of bananas exported from the four countries. In the post-war period, the company has lost some of its former dominance; but it remains the biggest single producer and exporter in Central America, and it maintains a share in world banana trade of approximately 35%.

Table 1 summarises the company composition of the banana sector in 1947 and 1976. In the immediate post-war period, the United Fruit Company had seven banana divisions: two each in Costa Rica, Guatemala, and Panama and one in Honduras. The only other significant producer of export bananas in the region was the Standard Fruit Company, with one division in Honduras.

These two companies were responsible for 100% of the banana exports of all four countries from 1930 to 1967.

Table 1

Distribution of the banana exports of four Central American countries by transnational company, 1947 and 1976

COMPANY	1947		1976	
	thousand boxes*	%	thousand boxes	%
United Fruit Company	51,409	80.6	61,037	47.2
Standard Fruit Company	12,344	19.4	35,782	27.7
Del Monte	—	—	27,288	21.1
Others	—	—	5,157†	4.0
TOTAL	63,753	100.0	129,264	100.0

*   converted from bunches at 1.60 boxes per bunch.
†   mainly Afrikanische Frucht Compagnie exporting from Costa Rica.

Source: Government statistics and trade sources.

Between 1947 and 1976 there were some alterations in the distribution of banana divisions between transnational corporations, though these did not affect the fundamental character of the organisation of production and exportation in each division. The United Fruit Company, which became United Brands in 1969, closed down two divisions in 1956 and 1964 respectively, and sold one to the Del Monte Corporation in 1972 under compulsory divestiture proceedings begun nearly two decades earlier.[4] The Standard Fruit Company, which was absorbed by Castle and Cooke Corporation in 1968, opened a new division in Costa Rica in 1956. The Del Monte Corporation entered the industry in 1967 through the purchase of an independent trading company in Costa Rica, and subsequently acquired the Guatemala division of United Brands under the compulsory divestiture.[5]

All three banana transnationals are vertically-integrated from production and purchase in the exporting countries to sale at the free-on-rail (f.o.r.) stage inside importing countries. In addition, the process of production and exportation is itself undertaken as an integrated operation within the framework of the banana division. Throughout the post-war period, all corporate banana divisions have contained most, if not all, the following characteristics in common:

(a) a banana plantation, preferably in a single block, divided into districts and farms;

(b) the ownership (or lease) and operation of a railway system linking each farm and district to a main line running to the port of exportation;

(c) the ownership (or lease) and operation of port facilities, including a pier constructed for the stevedoring of bananas;

(d) a complete social infrastructure composed of labour encampments, schools, medical facilities, and playing fields;

(e) a complete service infrastructure consisting of electric plant, telephone and telegraphic system, water purification and distribution system, and sanitary works;

(f) a banana-purchasing operation from national growers located in the vicinity of the plantation, and bound to the division by exclusive contracts of sale;

(g) a divisional headquarters located at the plantation or port, and composed of a departmental system of management functions.

Each division thus integrates every facet of the banana activity from production or purchase through to exportation. It is a self-contained sub-system which is part of a larger system of economic activities described by the global operations of its parent company, rather than part of the national economy in which it is located. In short, the banana division constitutes almost a pure case of the export 'enclave' discussed in the literature on trade and development.

EXPORT VALUATION

For an export such as bananas there evidently exists a considerable potential for flexibility in the declarations which the transnationals make to the government authorities of the respective countries. This applies to the declared value of banana exports, and to declarations on the volume of exports, prices of imported intermediate inputs, costs, and certain components of value added (eg. depreciation).[6] In many cases there is no certainty attached to any dimensions of production and exportation short of painstaking research aimed at examining inconsistencies between alternative figures. In part this situation results from the geographical isolation of banana zones and the degree of autonomy exercised by companies in the areas under their control. It also derives from the nature of original concessions granted to companies, and the generally permissive environment in which banana divisions were established.

Let us look first at the question of export valuation. There is no arm's-length market price for bananas either at f.o.b. ports of exportation or at c.i.f. ports of importation. The first point at which market prices may be obtained is at the free-on-rail stage in importing countries, which refers to the sale of the fruit ex-customs at ports of importation. Even this price is, however, difficult to obtain due to the confidential nature of contracts of sale between the transnationals and ripener distributors. For most importing countries, published price series on bananas are restricted to wholesale and retail transactions, where they are collected in the course of routine monitoring of fruit and vegetable price levels.

Before 1950, the governments of the case-study countries depended entirely on values declared by the companies as the basis for registering the contribution of banana exports to their balance of payments. The extent of under-valuation in these declarations was so large, and represented such a distortion of the true balance of payments position of the four countries, that the International Monetary Fund initiated the practice of supplying governments with alternative figures to enter in their accounts.[7] The IMF revaluations, which began in 1950 and were subsequently modified in 1953, were applied retrospectively to all export value statistics in each country from 1947 onwards.[8] Their significance in the early years from a purely accounting viewpoint is demonstrated in Table 2.

For the five-year period 1947-51 taken as a whole for the four countries, the IMF revaluation adjustment of itself accounted for 35.5% of the total corrected value of merchandise exports of the four countries. The revaluation increased the value of banana exports by 220% above company declarations, and increased the contribution of bananas to total export value from 25% to 51.6% (Table 2).

The IMF banana-adjustment procedure became an accepted and largely unquestioned part of balance of payments accounting practices in the four countries. Until 1965 it remained possible to compare declared and adjusted values because the IMF itself continued to publish the amount of the adjustment in annual issues of its *Balance of Payments Yearbook*. Thereafter it ceased

Table 2

Effect on Total Merchandise Exports of Banana Valuation Adjustments by the IMF 1947-51*

$ million

Description	1947	1948	1949	1950	1951	Total
Banana value declared	29.1	31.0	32.9	30.5	38.6	162.1
Total export value unadjusted	107.7	122.5	120.7	133.5	165.2	649.6
(Bananas %)	(27.0)	(25.3)	(27.3)	(22.8)	(23.4)	(25.0)
Banana adjustment	65.7	74.1	70.9	77.0	69.8	357.5
Banana value adjusted	94.8	105.1	103.8	107.5	108.4	519.6
Total export value adjusted	173.4	196.6	191.6	210.5	235.0	1,007.1
(Bananas %)	(54.7)	(53.5)	(54.2)	(51.1)	(46.1)	(51.6)

* Totals for Costa Rica, Guatemala, Honduras and Panama.

Source: IMF *Balance of Payments Yearbook*, Vol.5, 1947-53, ·Washington DC, 1954.

to do so, and only one country, Panama, continued to publish declared figures separately up to 1970.[9] Subsequently revaluations have been made directly so that Central Bank authorities merely enter adjusted values in their balance of payments accounts. Declared values are still, however, found in the statistics of other government departments; and their implications are explored further below.

In the early years of the banana adjustment the IMF gave some information on the methodology used to derive corrected values. This aspect of the revaluation has been the subject of critical examination elsewhere.[10] Up to 1952 the approach was based on market prices, with unit values at f.o.b. export being obtained from f.o.r. selling prices in importing countries by the subtraction of freight, insurance and unloading costs. From that year onwards, it was shifted to a cost plus basis, and involved confidential declarations by the transnationals to the IMF about the level of their costs in each country. The definitive statement of this methodology was made in 1954. Since subsequent explanations become more vaguely worded and finally non-existent, this remains the best guide to the adjustment procedure followed during the 1950s and 1960s:

> The method used to estimate the international transactions of foreign-owned direct investment companies engaged in agricultural production differs from that used to obtain estimates published in earlier Yearbooks... The value of their exports from each country is calculated at a unit price designed to apportion their profits or losses, for balance of payments purposes, between their local productive operations and their selling operations abroad. The same unit price has been used for all the countries in which the companies have major operations. Since their profits or losses in each country are estimated as the difference between the value of exports and local production costs, the position of total profits allocated to each country varies in accordance with differences in local costs.[11]

This explanation is confusing about the proportion of profits which were assigned to the exporting countries. An alternative source clarifies the procedure, which consisted of summing the production costs of the transnational companies across all countries in which they operate, adding 50% of their total gross profits on foreign sales, and dividing by the total quantity of bananas sold.[12] Thus:

$$\hat{p} = \Sigma \; \frac{C + .5P}{Q}$$

Where $\hat{p}$ is an estimated common unit value for all countries at f.o.b., C is total production cost, P is total profits on sales before tax, and Q is the total quantity sold. The separate profit or loss for individual countries thus depended on the subtraction from the common price of their own production costs. This was the basis upon which the banana exporters obtained export values for balance of payments accounting purposes at least until the mid-1960s.[13]

REAL FOREIGN EXCHANGE CONTRIBUTION, INTRA-FIRM TRANSFERS, AND RELATED ASPECTS OF BANANA COMPANY OPERATIONS

The adjustment made to banana export values by the IMF has not in itself made any difference to underlying real inflows and outflows of funds associated with banana production and exportation. It has merely been an accounting practice which has altered the balance of trade (goods and services) component of balance of payments accounts on the export side, and may thus have improved the standing or credit-worthiness of the countries in international financial circles. In the absence of government action based on the revised figures (for example, more effective collection of profit taxes), it should not have made any difference to the final outcome of the balance of payments. In effect, for every dollar added by the IMF to the banana export value there would exist a compensating dollar entered as an outflow on the capital account, if all other conditions of operation of the transnationals remain the same.

Until quite recently, the transnational banana companies operated in all four countries under highly favourable currency regulations and taxes. These derived in part from the general absence of constraints on foreign exchange flows in three of the countries which have maintained fixed exchange rates against the dollar (Guatemala, Honduras, and Panama). They also derived from the concessionary nature of contracts negotiated in the first three decades of the century, and which were still in force in all countries up to 1974. Certain relevant provisions of the principal banana contracts are given in summary form in Appendix Table 2.

Data obtained from Honduras show that the quantity of foreign exchange converted to domestic currency by the multinational banana companies was little over half the total export value attributed to bananas in the country's balance of payments accounts between 1970 and 1974. In that five-year period,

Honduras exported an average of 44.3 million boxes of bananas per year, with, according to IMF export value statistics, an average value of $81.0 million.[14] The Central Bank of Honduras registered an average annual inflow of dollars converted to the local currency by the banana companies of $43.9 million, equal to 54.1% of the IMF value. These figures are shown in Table 3 below.

Table 3

Honduras: A comparison between total export value and real foreign exchange inflows 1970-74

Year	Volume (thousands of boxes)	IMF Export value		Foreign Exchange Inflow	
		Unit value $ per box	Total Value $ millions	Value $ millions	Share of total %
1970	40,630	1.76	71.3	38.3	53.7
1971	53,402	1.72	92.0	45.9	49.9
1972	46,629	1.76	81.9	43.5	53.1
1973	45,411	1.77	80.2	42.6	53.1
1974	35,347	2.26	79.7	49.0	61.5
Average	44,284	1.83	81.0	43.9	54.1

Source: Banco Central de Honduras, Depto. de Estudios Economicos. IMF, *International Financial Statistics*, May 1976.

Additional information from the same source indicates that the foreign exchange inflow itself is almost wholly composed of wage payments and taxes. Export production of bananas makes relatively little use of domestic inputs other than labour because fertilisers, disease control chemicals, plastics, and the cardboard used for boxes are all imported in either a fully processed or semi-processed state. Table 4 shows wage payments and taxes as a proportion of the foreign exchange inflow data previously quoted. It is clear from this table that, quite apart from the low net foreign exchange contribution of the industry, domestic multiplier effects deriving from the operations of the transnationals are almost wholly confined to the expenditure of wages and the use made of government revenues.

Evidence suggests that the proportion of total export value which is realised as foreign exchange is similar in all four Central

Table 4

Honduras: A comparison between wage and tax payments of transnational banana companies and foreign exchange inflows from them 1970-74

Year	Foreign Exchange Inflow $ millions	Wages $ millions	Taxes $ millions	Wages & Taxes $ millions	Share of Inflow %
1970	38.3	34.6	4.9	39.5	103.1
1971	45.9	37.4	3.6	41.0	89.3
1972	43.5	37.5	4.9	42.4	97.5
1973	42.6	37.1	5.3	42.4	99.5
1974	49.0	38.2	6.3	44.5	90.8
Average	43.9	37.0	5.0	42.0	85.7

Source: Banco Central de Honduras, Dept. de Estudios Economicos.

American countries. Honduras is not a special case in this respect. Moreover, detailed research on long-run tendencies in the composition of total export value shows that this proportion has been falling over the last three decades. As a consequence of the productivity of labour increasing faster than wages, the wage share of export value — which as we have seen is by far the most important determinant of net exchange earnings — has fallen from about 65% in 1950 to 40% in 1975. The share of imported intermediate inputs has correspondingly risen; while profits and other financial repatriations have tended to vary according to costs and market conditions from year to year.

It is clear that the accounting revaluation of banana exports made by the IMF makes no difference to real financial flows, and that this is largely attributable to the absence of internal regulations which would permit the countries to capture a larger share of the total value generated. These factors are further illustrated with reference to costs and profits for the operations of the United Brands Company in Panama for the year 1973. United Brands (previously United Fruit) has traditionally had exclusive control of the banana exports of Panama, with two divisions located one each on the Pacific and Atlantic coasts of the country. In 1973 the company exported 29.5 million boxes of which 23.7 million (80%) were produced on its own plantations and 5.8

million (20%) were purchased from national producers under contract.[15] Data on total values and costs are given in Table 5.

Table 5
Panama: A comparison of IMF export value, declared value, and declared costs 1973

Description	Total values $ millions	Unit values $ per box	% IMF value
IMF Export Value	63.8	2.16	100.0
Company Declared Value	52.1	1.76	81.6
Difference	11.7	0.40	18.4
Company Declared Cost	47.8	1.62	74.9
Declared Profit	4.3	0.14	6.7
Profit Tax	1.3	0.04	2.0

Sources: IMF, *International Financial Statistics*, May 1976 Government Sources.

The company declared a total gross sales value of $52.1 million, equivalent to $1.76 per box. Notwithstanding a substantial difference between this and the IMF balance of payments value of $63.8 million ($2.16 per box), the taxation authorities used the company valuation to calculate gross profits on the basis of further information declared by the company on costs.[16] With total declared costs of $47.8 million, the gross profit of $4.3 million yielded a profit tax at 30% of $1.3 million. Had the government used the IMF valuation, and assuming the same total cost, they would have obtained taxes of $4.8 million, or three times as much. This demonstrates the ineffectiveness of the IMF valuation to alter the leverage of governments, in the absence of a co-ordinating mechanism to link their valuation procedures to company declarations made in host countries. In this case there is an accounting figure of $11.7 million which has no basis in visible transactions.

It is of some interest to examine the composition of the total cost figure given above. Research indicates that the unit cost per box declared in this particular case ($1.62) is an accurate representation of the production cost of bananas in Central America in that year. In the table below certain categories of costs have been grouped according to whether they definitely represent an inflow of financial resources or whether they represent a direct leakage into imported inputs or repatriated earnings.

Table 6

Panama: Structure of Total Costs in the Banana Export Industry, 1973

Category	Total values $ millions	Unit values $ per box	% Total Cost
Total Cost	47.8	1.62	100.0
Boxes	10.4	0.35	21.6
Other Materials/services	10.7	0.36	22.2
Depreciation	3.0	0.10	6.2
Sub-Total	24.1	0.81	50.0
Wages	17.7	0.60	37.0
Taxes	1.6	0.05	3.7
Fruit Purchases	4.4	0.15*	9.3
Sub-Total	23.7	0.81	50.0

* This is not of course the price paid per box to growers, as the purchase value has been divided by all boxes exported; growers received $0.76 per box for their own output.

Source: Government sources.

The table shows that half of declared costs are definitely attributable to national payments. This consists of payments to labour (37%), payments to governments (4%), and payments to national growers for fruit purchased (9%). This may understate the true share of national payments, since a certain proportion of returns to domestic factors are contained in the category described as 'other materials and services'. On the other hand since this category includes imported fertilisers, fuel, chemicals, plastics and implements, the degree of underestimation is unlikely to be very large. It is worth noting that one single item, the cardboard boxes used for packaging, accounts for over 20% of the total cost. This is an imported item not used in production prior to 1962 (when bananas were exported on the bunch). Its significance in the current cost structure is an additional consideration in the long-run tendency for the share of domestic payments in gross export value to decline.

RECENT POLICIES AND CONCLUSIONS

The problem of export valuation and the measurement of the real foreign exchange contribution of banana exports takes place against a background of declining banana prices in real terms. A predominant characteristic of banana prices, whether studied at the retail, wholesale, or free-on-rail stages of the marketing system is that they remained virtually static in money terms from 1950 through to 1974. Real prices to consumers fell by between 45% and 60% in all major importing countries between 1950 and 1972.[17] The same holds true for the unit values of exports after adjustment by the IMF. According to a United Nations report, the terms of trade of banana exporters fell by 61% between 1954 and 1973.[18] The secular decline in their terms of trade was felt particularly acutely by the Central America banana exporters following the oil price increase of early 1974. Since none of the four countries are oil producers, they all simultaneously suffered a severe deterioration in their balance of payments. Their response to this was to establish their own exporters' association, the Union of Banana Exporting Countries (UBEC),[19] and to impose a new and substantially higher export tax per box exported. These actions led to a serious confrontation with the transnationals which lasted from April to October 1974, and in the course of which an initial tax of $1 per box was lowered to between 25 cents and 35 cents per box.[20] This tax at present stands at between 40 cents and 50 cents per box and yields a total government revenue in the four countries of about $52 million.

The imposition of the export tax led to a restructuring of prices at every level of the banana marketing system. Table 7 gives an illustrative comparison of price structures before and after the event and is based on market prices in the United States, which is the principal destiny of fruit from Central America. Preliminary indications suggest that prices have stabilised at the levels found in 1975 and that the long-run tendency for them to remain static in money terms has been reasserted following the once-for-all change. The transnational companies were able to use the export tax as leverage for increasing their selling prices by considerably more than the eventual level of tax applied. Thus the f.o.r. price increased by $1.50 per box whereas the highest level of tax imposed was 45 cents per box in Costa Rica.

From the viewpoint of the governments of the exporting

countries, the export tax represents the most direct and administratively simple method of capturing a larger share of the value generated up to f.o.b. export. Government revenues as a proportion of the IMF gross export value has increased from about 5% to 20%, and this results in an increase of the share of total domestic payments from about 50% to 60% based on figures previously cited. However, the interesting effect to be noted from the table is that the share of the f.o.b. price in the retail price has fallen, and this has the implication that the proportion of the retail price which is actually retained in exporting countries has hardly changed at all.

Table 7
Illustrative Comparison of the Price Structure of Bananas up to the Retail Level in the US Market, 1973 and 1975

	1973		1975	
Unit values	*$ per box*	*%*	*$ per box*	*%*
Retail	6.60	100.0	9.40	100.0
Wholesale	4.50	68.2	6.20	66.0
f.o.r.	3.00	45.5	4.50	47.9
f.o.b.	2.15	32.6	2.60	27.7
Local Payments*	1.10	16.7	1.60	17.0

* Wages plus taxes plus banana purchases from national growers. Approximate average for all countries except Costa Rica where the share of purchases is higher.

Sources: Retail and f.o.r. prices — US Bureau of Labour Statistics, Washington DC; wholesale prices — US Department of Agriculture, Fruit and Vegetable Price Report; f.o.b. prices — IMF, International Financial Statistics (total value ÷ volume data obtained independently); local payments — diverse government and trade sources.

It is also significant that all three transnational companies have made substantially increased profits on banana sales since 1975 as compared to earlier years of the decade. The conclusion is that the imposition of an export tax, while it has resulted in a substantial increase in government revenues from banana exportation, has made little difference to underlying value relationships in the banana production and marketing system. In the absence of major structural changes in the ownership and control of that system, exporting countries will continue to receive only that proportion of the total value generated which is consistent with the long-run strategies of the banana transnationals. The quantitative dimensions of foreign exchange inflows are not affected by accounting adjustments and measures designed to increase them (such as export taxes) cannot alter capital accumulation outside the exporting countries.

NOTES

*   This paper is based on the author's D.Phil. thesis *The Banana Export Activity in Central America 1947-1976* (University of Sussex, 1978).

1   Averaging 26%, 32% and 35% of the export earnings of Costa Rica, Honduras and Panama respectively between 1971 and 1975. See also Appendix Table 1.

2   The United Fruit Company was incorporated under the laws of the State of New Jersey on 30 March 1899. By the end of that year it was responsible for 70% of world banana trade. Stacy May and Galo Plaza, *The United Fruit Company in Latin America: Case Study in U.S. Business Performance Abroad*, Washington D.C., National Planning Association, 1958 pp.6-7.

3   United Fruit Company, *Annual Report 1930*, Boston 1931.

4   *United States of America vs. United Fruit Company: Final Judgement*, United States District Court for the Eastern District of Louisiana, Civil Action No.4560, 4 February 1958.

5   A substantial literature exists on the banana multinationals, particularly the United Fruit Company. Details of their recent history are given in I.A. Litvak and C.J.Maule, *Transnational Corporations in the Banana Industry: With Special Reference to Central America and Panama*, CEPAL/CTC, Working Paper No.7, August 1977, pp.57-113.

6   Several researchers have noted inconsistencies between exports and imports in published volume statistics. See, for example, H.B. Arthur, J.P. Houck, G.L. Beckford, *Tropical Agribusiness Structures and Adjustments – Bananas*, Boston, Harvard University Press, 1968, pp.77-8.

7   Empirical research shows that, prior to IMF intervention, declared export values were sometimes lower than the total annual wage bill of the companies.

8   IMF, *Balance of Payments Yearbook*, vol.5, 1947-53, Washington DC, 1954, p.2 (Costa Rica), p.1 (Honduras), p.3 (Guatemala).

9   Contraloria General de la Republica de Panama, *Estadistica Panamena: Serie 'D' Balanza de Pagos*, Panama, Direccion de Estadistica y Censo, annual.

10   R.A. LaBarge, 'The Imputation of Values to Intra-Company Exports: The Case of Bananas', *Social and Economic Studies*, vol.10, no.2, June 1961, pp.183-91.

11   IMF, *Balance of Payments Yearbook*, vol.5, *op. cit.*, p.2 (Costa Rica), p.1 (Honduras), p.3 (Guatemala).

12   R.A. LaBarge, *op. cit.*, p.188.

13   In the absence of more recent explanations by the IMF. Subsequent

practice is to enter adjusted values directly presumably in consultation with the local IMF representative. The basis for these adjusted values remains somewhat unclear.

14 IMF, *International Financial Statistics*, May 1976, p.202.
15 Data obtained from the Chiriqui Land Company, subsidiary of United Brands in Panama.
16 Government sources.
17 FAO Committee on Commodity Problems: Intergovernmental Group on Bananas, *Retail Prices, Current and Constant Prices, 1950-1972, Selected Countries*, CCP:BA/ST 73/2 Suppl. 1, July 1973.
18 United Nations General Assembly, *Study of the Problems of Raw Materials and Development: Evolution of Banana Prices Since 1954 and the Significance of Bananas in World Trade in 1970*, New York, Document A/9544/Add.3 29 April 1974.
19 Created 17 September 1974, by the governments of Colombia, Costa Rica, Guatemala, Honduras and Panama.
20 This is not the place to enter into the details of the so-called 'banana war'. An excellent account from the viewpoint of Panama is given in 'La Guerra del Banano', *Revista Loteria*, No. 224-225-226, Panama, October-December 1974.

APPENDIX

Table 1

Volume and value of banana exports: Costa Rica, Guatemala, Honduras and Panama
1971-75

Year	Volume Banana Exports 1000 boxes	Participation World Exports Bananas %	Value Banana Exports 1000 US $	Share of Own Total Exports %	Export Value per Box US $
1971	142,619	40.9	240,038	29.3	1.68
1972	143,696	40.2	257,633	27.4	1.79
1973	142,641	39.6	262,142	22.4	1.84
1974	125,675	35.3	257,714	16.9	2.05
1975	114,623	32.7	270,002	15.9	2.36
Average	133,851	37.8	257,509	20.9	1.92

Table 2

A Comparison of the Duration and Tax Provisions of the Principal Contracts Between Governments and Banana Companies

Details	Costa Rica	Guatemala	Honduras	Panama
Company	UFC	UFC	SFC*	UFC
Original date	1930	1924	1910	1927
Duration (years)**	58	70	99	59
Expiry date	July 1988	June 1981	April 2009	March 1986
Export taxes	1 ¢ (1910)	1 ¢ (1924)	1½¢ (1919)	1 ¢ (1927)
per bunch†	2 ¢ (1930)	1½ ¢ (1936)	+¾ ¢‡	2 ¢ (1934)
		2 ¢ (1949)		
Profit taxes†	15% (1949)	30% (1956)	15% (1949)	15% (1950)
	30% (1954)		30% (1955)	30% (1958)
Import duties and	total	total	total	total
other taxes	exemption	exemption	exemption	exemption
Foreign exchange	local	none	none	none
regulations	payments only			

---

* The United Fruit Company concessions differ in having an indefinite duration and a tax of 1 cent per bunch.

** after subsequent extension.

† Dates of first imposition in brackets.

‡ Separate municipal tax.

Source: Concessions and laws regulating the banana industry in each country up to 1975.

4.
THE PRICING OF UNWROUGHT COPPER IN RELATION TO TRANSFER PRICING

K.M. LAMASWALA

The degree of vertical integration in the non-socialist world copper industry falls into two broad categories. In North America the industry is characterised by a very high degree of integration, with mining, processing and fabricating stages being owned and operated by the same corporate interests. This feature of integration extended for a while to South America, particularly Chile, where the leading US copper companies owned and operated the copper mines and also bought the products from these mines. This connection was broken in the early 1970s when Chile nationalised its copper mines.

Outside North America, there has been no comparable degree of vertical integration, the companies which owned and operated the mines have been different from the ones which bought the output of these mines. The slight exception to this rule came with the growth in Japan's appetite for copper. To satisfy it, Japanese firms supplied finance in the forms of loans to many prospective mines in return for long-term contracts.

This disparity in the degree of vertical integration between North America and the rest of the world is reflected in the way copper is priced in North America and elsewhere. In North America, unwrought copper is priced on the basis of producer prices. In the past, these producer prices were only nominally related to market prices. In recent years, particularly at the depth of the 1975-78 copper recession, this pricing practice led to large unsold stocks, in the hands of American producers as copper end-users preferred to buy from cheaper free market sources. This led some American producers to abandon the producer price system completely. Those who still adhere to it have been able to retain the system only by frequent price adjustments to keep them in line with free market prices.

Outside North America, producing companies in Chile, Peru, Zaire, Zambia and other exporting countries have no corporate connection with their customer fabricators in Europe, Japan,

77

Brazil, China, etc. There has, therefore, always been an attempt, by buyers and sellers alike, to seek the best obtainable arm's-length prices, with copper priced on the basis of free market prices, except for brief periods between 1955-57 and 1964-66 when American-style 'producer prices' were attempted.

By far the largest volume of producer copper is sold by reference to direct London Metal Exchange quotations. LME prices are used in three principal ways: 'spot', 'average', and 'price fixing'. In a spot sale, tonnage is sold according to a single-day market quotation. Such tonnages are usually small, as single-day prices, for obvious reasons, can be very unrepresentative.

Average pricing relates to contracts between producers and customers whose consumption is relatively small, or customers who have no ready access to minute by minute market intelligence, and therefore prefer to entrust their fortunes to the law of averages. In this arrangement, prices are averaged over a 'quotational period' — usually a month. This can be either a calendar month, or a month made up of fractions of adjoining months. The percentage of copper priced on the basis of average prices varies from producer to producer. With some, it is as low as 5%; with others, as high as 50%.

The most common pricing arrangement involves what is known in the trade as 'price fixing'. This means that during the quotational period, a customer has the freedom to pick a price prevailing on a particular market day as the quotation for a specified fraction of his monthly quota. To avoid excessive pricing during depressed periods, a limit is placed on what may be priced on a day, and also in a week. The daily and weekly maxima used to be 25% and 50% respectively, but these have now been reduced to 12% and 25%. Initially, quotational periods were of two months' duration, but this is gradually being reduced to a month. Quotational periods are usually fixed in relation to time of shipment, 'month prior to contractual month of shipment', 'contractual month of shipment' and 'month following contractual month of shipment' being the most popular. As explained below, earlier or later quotational periods can be arranged, depending on the particular merits of each case.

Copper is not a homogeneous commodity, and enters the trade in many forms: concentrates, blister copper, fire refined, electrolytically refined cathode and finally copper wirebars. Outside the USA, the basic quotation is for standard wirebars. Special bars, such as scalped or trolley bars, attract premiums over the LME. Similarly, blister metal, cathodes and concentrates entail various discounts.

This article is not concerned with the appropriateness of the London Metal Exchange as a pricing mechanism, nor whether the pricing terms outlined above are fair to the producer. The point is that the terms are fairly standard throughout the industry outside North America. The prices set by the LME, are accepted by the two separate and unconnected groups in the transactions (namely buyers and sellers), to represent the best obtainable arm's-length prices.

In the early 1970s, most of the copper mines in developing countries, particularly Chile, Peru, Zaire and Zambia, came under different degrees of state control. In Chile, it was straightforward nationalisation, with the Government assuming 100% control of the mines. In other countries there was some form of partnership between state and the former owners.

In the case of Zambia, the Government announced, in August 1969, its intention of taking a majority interest in all the copper-mining operations in the country. The negotiations were concluded fairly speedily, and the nationalisation agreement was signed on 24 December 1969. By 1 January 1970, the Government owned 51% of all the operating copper mines in the country. The takeover agreement provided, among other things, for the issue by Zambia Industrial and Mining Corporation (ZIMCO) of bonds carrying interest at 6%, unconditionally guaranteed by the Government to the former owners of the mines, and representing the Government's 51% interest in the mines. ZIMCO (the Government's holding company) undertook to redeem its bonds over a period of eight to twelve years. Meanwhile, the mining complexes were to be regrouped into two operating companies, Nchanga Consolidated Copper Mines (NCCM) and Roan Consolidated Mines (RCM).

As an integral part of the Government's takeover arrangements, the private companies which formerly owned and managed the mines, were awarded exclusive management and marketing contracts. The original intention was for these to remain in force for at least ten years. The management and marketing services for NCCM were to be provided by the Anglo-American Corporation of South Africa Group. Likewise, responsibility for providing these services to RCM was entrusted to the Roan Selection Trust Group (an affiliate of the US based Amax Group). Two marketing companies were established — Anmersales AG (for the Anglo-Group), based in the tax haven of

Zug in Luxembourg to service NCCM, and RSTIM (for the Amax Group) to service RCM.

For the first time in the history of the Zambian copper mining industry, there were now two separate sets of companies involved in the fortunes of the Zambian copper mining industry. There were the two big operating companies — NCCM and RCM — in which the Government, through ZIMCO, owned 51% of the interest, with the former owners, Anglo-American and Amax groups, holding 49%. The second set of companies — the service companies — providing management and marketing services to the operating companies, were 100% owned by the Anglo-American Group on the NCCM side, and by the Amax Group on the RCM side. Furthermore, these service companies were based outside Zambia.

This article does not concern itself with the management of these service contracts. However, it attempts to show how the marketing side of these dual arrangements was used to siphon millions of dollars from the operating companies in Zambia to the foreign-based and privately owned marketing companies. The two marketing companies of Anmersales and RSTIM operated closely with identically owned sister in-house merchanting companies, Anglo Chemical and Ore, and Ametalco Trading which were (and still are) LME-registered trading companies.

CONTRACTING TO SELL THE ENTIRE PLANNED PRODUCTION

A year's production of copper is usually contracted for sale in or before the 'mating season', generally October to November, of the preceding year. However, planned production targets are sometimes not met. Where a mining company is committed in advance, any subsequent production shortfall carries the potential risk of default on some or all of the advance contracts. The marketing companies therefore contracted to 'firm' end use outlets for about 80 to 90% of planned production. The balance of 10-20% would be contracted on a looser basis to the affiliated merchanting companies.

However, by committing the outlet for this precautionary margin in advance, however loosely, the tonnage only realised standard prices. Meanwhile, the merchanting companies when they eventually got the metal, sold it on an *ad hoc* basis, thereby realising prevailing *ad hoc* premiums. These premiums have been known to reach US$ 50 per tonne. If, therefore, in a particular year, the precautionary margin was fixed at 15% on Zambia's annual production of 700,000, the tonnage involved would be about 100,000 tonnes. At an average *ad hoc* premium of US$ 30 per tonne, the marketing companies stood to gain between them US$ 3 million. This type of money did not accrue to the jointly owned operating companies in Zambia, but to the marketing companies, and through them to their owners, the 49% partners of the Government.

GEOGRAPHICAL DISTRIBUTION OF SALES

The second method by which the marketing companies skimmed off profits from the operating companies in Zambia relates to the geographical distribution of the copper. The copper-consuming countries were arbitrarily grouped into two categories:

(a) those with 'sound' financial structures, usually, but not exclusively OECD, where it was claimed there was no risk of default on payments for copper delivered; and

(b) those with supposed credit risk.

Sales contracts for the 'no risk' countries were made directly between the Zambian operating companies and the fabricating company. However, sales to the 'risky' buyers (for example, China, Brazil, India, the Middle East and South-East Asia), were made in the first instance to the same in-house merchanting companies mentioned above. These companies would in turn and in their own right, resale the material to the fabricators in the 'risky' countries. The subtle point here is that prices of copper to the elite OECD countries were LME, c.i.f., main European or Japanese port. On the other hand, prices to the other countries were LME plus cost of insurance and freight. The differential in prices could sometimes be as high as US$ 85 per tonne. Thus, by selling to these other countries via the in-house merchanting connections, which were OECD-based and therefore paid the ordinary prices to the operating companies in Zambia, the extra juicy differential was skimmed off from the revenues of the jointly owned operating companies in Zambia. The amounts involved from this particular trick could conservatively be estimated at US$ 2 million a year. It was argued that this was a return for undertaking the 'credit risk', but in fact there was no such risk, as irrevocable letters of credit were always opened long before any shipment could be effected.

SWITCHES

Since most sales contracts for copper entering international trade in a particular year are concluded long before the start of that year, this means that both buyers and sellers are basing their plans on expectations. If business is slack, a fabricator could find himself having contracted tonnage in excess of requirements. Similarly, if demand is firm, fabricators could be short of material. This disparity between expectation and actual performance is commonplace; meanwhile, due to the high cost of finance, it is expensive to keep excessive stocks of idle copper. There is therefore always frequent and active trade in these marginal tonnages.

For countries with access to terminal market facilities, overbuying could turn out to be beneficial, as material could be sold to the market ahead of arrival, and only rebought when needed, thereby earning the contango. As a rule, fabricators in Western Europe, where there are extensive LME warehouses, tend to contract copper in excess of requirements. For customers in Taiwan, Brazil, or some such distant countries, the penalty of overbuying in a period of slack demand would be expensive, idle inventories. Such countries therefore tend to be very conservative in their purchases. Now, assume that one of the mining companies in Zambia has an annual copper sales contract with a fabricator in Liverpool. Next, assume that a Taiwanee customer has underbought. He would probably contact an LME merchant to meet his shortfall. The price for this would be LME plus the prevailing *ad hoc* premium, plus cost of freight and insurance from LME warehouse to Taipei. If the Taiwanee fabricator agrees to buy, the merchant selling him the copper would approach one of the 'in-house merchants' with Zambian connections to arrange a 'switch'. The mining company in Zambia would be requested to ship material to Taipei to fulfil the first merchant's contract. This merchant would reciprocate by obtaining a Liverpool warrant to take material from the LME warehouse there, and this would fulfil the delivery requirement of the operating company in Zambia to their customer in Liverpool. The first merchant would then pay the second 'in-house merchant' with Zambian connections in the region of US$ 35 per tonne. Zambian operating companies would be paid a nominal US$ 5. The arithmetic involved in these transactions is as follows:

(a) *Without switching*
  1st Merchant: ships LME warehouse (say
                Liverpool) to Taipei   US$ 85 pt
  Zambia: ships African port (Dar es

Salaam) to European main
port   US$ 55 pt
                        Total freight paid   US$ 140

(b) *With Switching*

1. 1st Merchant: obtains LME Liverpool
   option delivery warrant   US$ 10 pt
2. Zambia: ships African port (Dar) to
   Taipei   US$ 55 pt
3. 2nd Merchant: pays operating company in
   Zambia   US$ 5 pt
   Total outlays by all involved   US$ 70
   Net saving to be split between the two
   merchants   US$ 70 pt

i.e. US$ 35 a piece (or some other combination)

However, such switches were always so arranged that the additional premiums generated accrued to the marketing companies, with only a nominal amount paid to the operating companies in Zambia.

There are other common types of switches relating to quality and to time. On a quality or brand switch, a non-critical copper user, such as a brassmill, would be delivered an acceptable alternative brand, thus freeing high-quality copper for a customer such as a finewire drawer willing to pay a suitable premium for the quality. In a time-switch, a customer with long inventories could be persuaded to take late delivery, to permit delivery to another customer requiring immediate delivery and willing to pay a premium.

It is difficult to estimate how much money the marketing and merchanting companies made out of switches, as this depended on the opportunities available each year. All that can be said with certainty is that in 1976 alone, when such techniques were already under Zambian control, about US$ 3 million was earned from switches.

REFINING CHARGE

Zambia refines almost 100% of the copper it produces in Zambia. Copper from the smelter is cast into anodes which are refined into cathodes in a tankhouse by the electrolysis process. In the normal casting of the anodes, a few are defect and not suitable as feed for the tankhouse. Returning the anodes to the smelter for remelting and recasting not only entails additional costs, but takes up casting capacity, thereby reducing overall output. It is much more economical to market the anodes as a defect shape. The tonnage involved is in the region of 10,000 to 15,000 tonnes a year, or about 2% of annual production.

While the marketing arrangements were in the hands of the minority shareholders, these reject anodes were sold to their affiliated merchanting outlets with a discount on the price of refined metal. The merchanting companies in turn resold them to refineries in Europe or elsewhere.

In time, the discounts allowed escalated drastically, moving from about US$ 40 per tonne in 1970 and US$ 70 per tonne in 1974. It all sounded very logical, especially when it was claimed that the rise in the price of oil had made refining in Europe very expensive!

But in an oversupplied market, forward metal is usually sold at prices significantly higher than prompt delivery quotations, reflecting a contango. By granting buyers of the defect anodes an early quotational period, it is possible for them to earn the contango, which in turn would cover their refining charges.

When the market situation is reversed and near metal commands premiums over forward delivery, this 'backwardation' can also serve as a processing allowance, provided a late quotational period is offered. There are very rare occasions when the contango or backwardation prevailing is not large enough to cover this refining charge. The discount of US$ 40-70 per tonne therefore, which was granted to the in-house merchanting outlets, was pure transfer profit from the operating companies in Zambia.

CONCLUSION

This article has attempted to highlight the principal techniques employed by the marketing companies in Zambia in the early 1970s to enrich themselves at the expense of operating companies. The motives for these complex manoeuvres were threefold:

(a) By accruing these profits to companies which they owned 100%, they would not have to share the profits with ZIMCO, the 51% owner of the operating companies.

(b) As the marketing companies were externally based in tax havens, no Zambian taxation would be payable. Mining taxation in Zambia at that time was twofold: a mineral tax at 51% of gross profits, and a 45% corporate tax on the remainder: a combined rate of 73.05%.

(c) Zambia employed fairly extensive exchange control restrictions which included limits on remission of dividends. By accruing these profits to foreign-based companies, they would circumvent the exchange control restrictions. This consideration became very pertinent because at about the same time, Zambian authorities decreed that henceforth all foreign exchange earned by the mining companies would be paid into accounts belonging to the Central Bank overseas, and the mining companies would only be credited in Zambia with the equivalent in local currency. Prior to that, all the foreign exchange earned on metal sales belonged to the mining companies.

It must be remembered that the Anglo and Amax groups also had the management contracts for NCCM and RCM. This helped the perpetuation of these marketing malpractices. There is reason to suspect that similar devices were also at work on the management side of the services contracts.

On 31 August 1973, the President of Zambia announced his Government's intention of cancelling both the sales and managements contracts, following the Government redemption of the ZIMCO bonds. This decision was announced after the contracts had been in effect for less than half of their intended ten-year life. The negotiations for the termination of these lucrative contracts were protracted. Whereas the negotiations for the takeover of a 51% stake in the mines were concluded within 4 months, those for terminating the sales and management contracts dragged on for an unbelievable 20 months, and only ended on Amax's signature in February 1975. In fairness, it should be mentioned that the new arrangements were backdated and were deemed to have come into effect on 1 August 1974.

The two operating companies, NCCM and RCM, henceforth became self-managing. For marketing, the Government set up a wholly owned (through ZIMCO) state company, the Metal Marketing Corporation of Zambia Limited (MEMACO), to handle all the marketing of minerals and metals from Zambia. MEMACO in a few short years following its incorporation proceeded to demolish the elaborate structures of deceit described above.

5.
UNDERINVOICING ALUMINIUM FROM GREECE
PANAYOTIS ROUMELIOTIS

In Greece, aluminium is produced by a single firm, a subsidiary of a powerful multinational company. This Greek subsidiary was formed in 1960 with the aid of foreign capital. Its production reached a profitable level by 1966, and by 1976 this firm's output of 134,000 tons represented 1% of world production. The major part of this production is exported through its overseas parent company. Local aluminium requirements are covered by local production and by imports.

The Price Commission of the Ministry of Co-ordination undertook an examination of aluminium pricing in 1976. A number of factors were behind the decision to undertake such a study:

(a) the importance of foreign exchange imported into Greece in order to help the exports of aluminium. These represented 3% of the total value of Greek exports in 1976.
(b) the fact that aluminium was being produced by a single multinational company.
(c) the homogeneity of the product allowed comparisons with similar products in other countries.
(d) Greek aluminium was exported to a limited number of countries.

PURPOSE, EXTENT AND METHOD OF ANALYSIS
The purpose of the analysis was to examine aluminium export prices in relation to the practices of the international market. The period covered by the study was January-December 1976. (All exports during this period were the subject of detailed examination.)

The types of aluminium exported from Greece are (according to international specifications):
Primary unalloyed

. A5	99.5%	in the form of
. A7	99.7%	ingots or
. A8	99.8%	slabs.

Primary alloyed for extrusion
. AGS 5Q in the form of 'billets'.
The countries importing Greek aluminium were Japan, Italy and France.
The method of analysis consisted of the following stages:

1. Firstly, we established the base prices of aluminium in France, Italy and Japan during the period under study, i.e., the prices quoted by national producers (French, Italian and Japanese) when selling their product to local consumers. The base price did not include fiscal charges or the profit of intermediaries, and was quoted in terms of the price of a given type of aluminium, specifically of A5 (99.5%) in ingots. The prices of other kinds of aluminium were calculated by adding onto the base price the premiums for quality (in other words the purity premiums, 99.7%, 99.8%) for size, quantity, homogeneity, and so on. In this way we calculated a price at which Greek aluminium could be absorbed by the markets in question.

2. Secondly, the aluminium import duties, and the costs of transport and insurance from Agios Nocolaos (the port of embarkation of Greek aluminium) to the ports of destination were deducted from the base price. Thus we arrived at an FOB export price, at which Greece could sell her aluminium to the countries in question.

3. Thirdly, this FOB export price was compared with the one at which Greece exported her aluminium.

4. Lastly, we examined all the conditions of sale attached to the Greek product. For example, we were able to show that this product was sold on credit, without the seller charging interest to the buyers (as happens in the majority of cases involving a parent of a Greek subsidiary).

STATISTICAL DATA AND INFORMATION

The statistical data were obtained from export invoices and the annexed documents deposited by the exporter at the Ministry of Commerce. The documents annexed relate to the delivery order from the parent to the Greek subsidiary, the export invoices and the certificate of quantity and quality of the product exported.

The information on transport and insurance costs was obtained from the maritime bureaux. The relative sales price of aluminium in the different countries studied were obtained with the help of experts working for the Ministry of Co-ordination, who posed as independent intermediaries in the purchase of aluminium. This information was verified by institutions and official organisations in the countries in question: in France: Direction Générale de la Concurrence et des Prix du Ministère de L'Economie et des Finances; in Italy: Associazione Nationale Industrie Metalli non ferrosi; and in Japan: the Ministry for International Trade and Industry.

The premiums, which are added to the base price of aluminium, were obtained from the consumers of aluminium. Greek aluminium is exempted from duties by the EEC, and, following the system of Generalised Preferences, these duties are 4.5% (*ad valorem*) in Japan. The parities used in our calculations are those of the Bank of Greece. We took 7.5% as a rate of interest for the sale on credit of aluminium, which corresponded to international standards.

RESULTS
The results of our research can be summarised as follows:
  (a) All Greek exports were sold through the parent company of the Greek subsidiary.
  (b) All exports prices of Greek aluminium are lower than the estimated base prices in the three countries studied.
  (c) The percentage of underinvoicing fluctuates between 1% and 19% according to the different types of aluminium and the different destinations. The weighted average of underinvoicing is 8.3%.
  (d) The resulting total loss of revenues to Greece, during the period studied, amounted to a minimum of $4,027,000 (an estimate made on the basis of minimum international FOB prices).
  (e) A supplementary loss of $730,237 was incurred, as the Greek exporter did not charge interest on its sales of aluminium on credit.
  (f) A commission of 3% is charged by the parent company to its Greek subsidiary for promoting its exports. This percentage is very high by international standards (1.5% is a maximum).

(B) Services

6.
TRANSFER PRICES IN THE INSURANCE SECTOR
JOSE RIPOLL

This paper considers why and how (but not how much) transfer prices in the insurance sector affect developing countries. It will also discuss the distinctive features that make this sector more vulnerable to such practices than other economic sectors. Offshore and captive insurance companies will not be considered here, but the reader may consult the paper by Ward (1978) for an analysis of their operations in Bermuda.

Incentives to resort to transfer pricing in the insurance sector mainly stem from a historical factor: the emergence, in developing countries of national insurance markets, and the resistance that the developed insurance markets have put up against efforts to service them locally. Previously, when a London-based insurance company operated in British colonies or new countries through agents and branch offices, local business was dealt with as part of the general business transacted in London. However, increasing awareness of the developing countries' capacity to provide insurance services by themselves, and international recognition (through UNCTAD) of the role of the domestic insurance industries in development, encouraged national initiatives. Subsequent entrepreneurial and governmental action initiated new market structures in many developing countries.

Insurance transnational companies (TNCs) accepted the move with some anxiety: 'The developing countries tend to have ambitions to start up their own insurance organizations . . . British insurers abroad have had to accept the inevitability of national aspirations...' There was still much room for manoeuvre, though, and it was suggested, for example, that they could 'act as expert advisers in such situations, devising methods of reconciling insistence on independence with the essential security which only the international market which London leads can supply.'[1]

This, in fact, is the course which has been followed. In many cases, what used to be a branch office in a developing country has become a national company, meeting local legal and market requirements, often in association with other local or non-local financial interests. To a large extent, however, these have only been facelift institutional changes, which may have had some effect on the volume of business flowing to the central organizations, but have had less on the operational patterns which permitted that flow. Premiums and claims continue to be transferred, with the difference, however, that these transfers have had to be covered by reinsurance contracts, which appear to be underwritten by two separate legal entities in two separate countries.[2] It is probably not an exaggeration to term these contracts 'artificial' reinsurance, and as such they called for 'artificial' prices. By the same token, compatibility which was thus achieved between developing countries' aspirations for independence and London security was inevitably to become an 'artificial' concept as well.

The establishment of domestic companies with foreign ownership (total or partial) has thus become a generalised practice, mainly in oil producing countries and those whose growth potential is considered important. A study by the UNCTAD secretariat (TD/B/C.3/141) identified many newly registered companies in the short period 1975-76. Foreign participation can, and often does, lead to glaring abuses.[3] But even more moderate cases lend themselves to price manipulations in the reinsurance cessions of the company concerned. The UNCTAD document cited above points out that when national companies (in developing countries) with foreign (capital) participation are called on to take decisions on such vital matters as planning and negotiation of rates for reinsurance, there are many indications that these decisions do not always escape the influence of the foreign shareholder....' Now, it seems obvious that, when this happens, the shareholders have participated in the new venture for no other reason than that of wielding influence over those decisions. As a big US insurer has put it: 'a voluntary association with local interest constitutes a suitable arrangement, particularly when the participating (foreign insurance) company obtains in this way a preferential position as reinsurer.' This explains the reason why 'the reinsurance activities of such companies (Western European reinsurance TNCs) are complemented by significant shareholding in companies forming part of the national insurance markets in many parts of the world.'[4]

It appears, in fact, that the shareholding is not a complement, but an integral part of the strategy aimed at maintaining the position held when 'the international insurance scene was virtually our [i.e. British] monopoly.'⁵ This strategy involves transfer prices for reinsurance to the extent that reinsurance transactions take place between related firms, and that freedom to resort to the international reinsurance market is severely curtailed for the company concerned.

Manipulation of prices and transfer practices in the international insurance sector must be considered against this background. It may be true that the above propositions provide a somewhat schematic picture of a more complex situation, and do not take account of a whole fabric of interferences and interactions. However, any explanation of major motives for transfer pricing, other than those prevailing in industrial and commercial sectors, should take this into consideration. To the extent that reinsurance transactions between developing and developed countries provide a fictitious means for insurance flows from one group of countries to another, prices for reinsurance are very likely to fall within a special category of transfer prices.

To what extent these practices actually take place, and the volume of transfers involved is anybody's guess. However, even if it were possible to evaluate that volume in net quantitative terms, the exercise would not prove very meaningful. For transfer prices in the insurance sector may go in two divergent directions: (a) A TNC may impose higher prices for reinsurance which it accepts from a subsidiary company than those prevailing in the international market on an arm's-length basis; (b) A TNC may set lower prices than arm's-length in order to improve the competitive conditions of the subsidiary company in the local market by reducing its reinsurance costs. Either system is likely to be detrimental to the developing country concerned. In the first case, reinsurance costs of the local company amount to more than they would under other circumstances, and the difference, in foreign exchange, is borne by policy-holders and by the country as a whole.

In the second case, the genuine domestic market may not be able to put up with the temporary competitive advantages enjoyed by the foreign-owned local subsidiary, and the conditions of the market may be so upset as to result in local bankruptcies.

In general, the supervisory authorities and other regulatory bodies in developing countries are at a loss to overcome these obstacles. A major difficulty arises in the right assessment of the conditions and terms of a reinsurance contract, which tend to be increasingly complex. The price of reinsurance is closely related to the level of risk transferred to the reinsurer, and this risk is often difficult to evaluate. Reinsurance premiums will eventually be matched by a certain amount of reinsurance indemnities, but these will only come about after much time has elapsed, and because of future random events which do not lend themselves to a correct evaluation when the contract is underwritten. A reinsurance contract also involves a number of services, provided by the reinsurer (evaluation and rating of large and unusual risks, information on markets and tariffs, etc.), which are difficult to assess and to correctly measure in economic terms. Reinsurance premiums, in comparison with the potential liabilities transferred to the reinsurer, are rarely significant rates, so that even a very slight variation of the rate (and the interested party might provide many justifications for that variation) brings about a relevant difference in the amounts of premium. To assess whether reinsurance premiums are adequate or not to the claims expectations requires a sophisticated analysis, which many ceding companies and regulatory authorities are unable to perform; those best able to do so are in fact the international reinsurers.

Measures have already been adopted in a number of developing countries which, rather than being aimed at checking the adequacy of reinsurance premiums, tend to curtail the outflow of national insurance business to international reinsurance organisations. In some countries, local state-owned reinsurance institutions have been created, and local companies are required to reinsure part of their business with them, leaving less for outside markets. In other countries, shareholding of domestic companies is restricted to nationals, to prevent, among other side-effects, external interference in reinsurance policy matters. In still other countries, reinsurance premiums paid abroad are subject to taxation, to stimulate the exchange of insurance business within the internal market. Not all the implemented measures are equally effective. For, while most of them do not aim at the core of the problem, many of them increasingly restrict the actions of local companies, thereby placing them at a disadvantage compared with the foreign companies that are not subject to them.

As an example of such measures, the following extract on Venezuela, from the UNCTAD document referred to above, is interesting in more than one respect:

'In *Venezuela*, the new insurance law introduces for the first time very stringent regulations on reinsurance with foreign enterprises. The reinsurance proportion of risks — and hence the proportion retained — is left for the enterprises concerned to decide for themselves; they may therefore reinsure all or part of a given risk, or even not reinsure it at all, subject, however, to the provisions of article 94 of the law which empowers the supervisory authority to order an increase or a reduction in the amounts which enterprises propose to retain. But once the proportion of retention and reinsurance have been fixed, the following provisions are applicable: (a) The enterprises are obliged to cede 40 per cent or more of all their reinsurance premiums to the national market; but this affects only reinsurance premiums arising from proportional reinsurance contracts: (b) The reinsurance enterprises established in Venezuela must accept this business on economic conditions similar to those which the ceding enterprises obtain from their reinsurers abroad; (c) Beyond the amount of risks covered by automatic reinsurance contracts, the enterprise must place the remainder in optional reinsurance with national insurance or reinsurance enterprises; only saturation of the underwriting capacity of these enterprises can justify recourse to foreign reinsurers: (d) The supervisory authority may take decisions on the conditions of reinsurance contracts. If it considers them too onerous it will ask the enterprise to give the technical and economic reasons justifying them, and if the explanations are found to be inadequate, it may order the necessary adjustments to the contracts in question.'

NOTES

1   Quotations extracted from *Policy Holder Insurance Journal*, London, 17 September 1976.
2   'The loss of traditional markets has to some extent been offset both in home foreign business (foreign risks directly insured in London) and *in the exchange of reinsurance*,' Peter Dugdale, managing director of Guardian Royal Exchange, in *Policy Holder Insurance Journal*, London, 15 December 1978.
3   '(In Burundi) the foreign group subscribed only 10% of the registered capital of the national company (CABU). In exchange for technical services relating to the formation and operation of the new company (which will have a *de facto* monopoly in the main sectors of the domestic market), the foreign minority partners have obtained, among other things, the technical management, a commission of 1.5 per cent on gross premiums, *sole rights to the placing of reinsurance*, and 35 per cent of the company's reinsurance commission' (UNCTAD document TD/B/C.3/141).
4   R.K. Bishop, in *Policy Holder Insurance Journal*, London, 17 September 1976.
5   R.K. Bishop, *op. cit.*

7.
TRANSNATIONAL BANKING: A CASE OF TRANSFER PARKING WITH MONEY*
SARAH BARTLETT

INTRODUCTION
The decade of the 1970s registered a major shift in the source of financial flows to less-developed countries (LDCs); in effect, these flows became privatised. In 1970, private international bank lending comprised only 3% of total financial flows to the LDCs. By 1976 the percentage had reached 28%, with the interesting corollary that direct investment fell from 21% to 12%.[1] Academic studies have tended to focus on multinational corporations which are more directly associated with material production. It is clear, however, that transnational banks (TNBs) are in a central position of power *vis-à-vis* developing countries — as such, their dynamics and mechanisms need to be elucidated.

Since the early 1960s, the banking industry has become transnationalised. In 1960, only 8 US banks had branches in other countries; by 1975, some 125 US banks had 732 branches operating in 59 countries. Total assets of US overseas branches jumped from $3.5 billion in 1960 to $181 billion by June 1976.[2] Although figures are less readily available on French, German and Japanese banks, a similar, although more recent trend has also been noted. According to the Bundesbank, the number of overseas branches of 15 German banks has risen by 16% in the past two years, and the volume of business has almost doubled.[3]

Amongst US banks, concentration is particularly marked: according to one study, of nearly 14,000 commercial banks in the US, only 125 are involved internationally and possess one or more direct means of representation abroad.[4] Of these 125, in 1976 the 13 largest represented over two-thirds of all US bank foreign activity.[5] Initial surveys of European banking show similar trends towards concentration, with three or four top banks dominating the field in each country.

The main vehicles through which the TNBs now operate is the eurocurrency market. Eurocurrencies are deposits of a currency which are held outside their country of origin and which, because they collect in pools outside any national regulatory jurisdiction,

96

can be managed with great flexibility. The market is also unique in that it is 'wholesale' — transactions rarely go below $1 million, with the result that the participants in the market are restricted to the largest: TNCs, governments, parastatals, wealthy individuals and international organisations.

The eurocurrency market, about 80% of which consists of eurodollars, has grown rapidly. It is estimated that its net size has risen from approximately $17 billion in 1964, to $62 billion in 1970, and to about $550 billion at the end of 1979.[7]

Although no *one* factor can be singled out as *the* explanatory one for this market's evolution, a combination of the following have each played their part.[8]

1. In the 1950s, the Soviet bloc transferred most of its dollar accounts abroad, in order to protect against the possibility of US appropriation.
2. Specific national legislation on credit expansion and interest levels hampered banking operations, and led to a greater expansion of branches abroad.
3. Large US balance of payments deficits resulted in increasingly large pools of dollars being held in other nations' central banks, which had to be re-lent.
4. With the growth of world trade and the increasing internationalisation of production, TNCs expanded their 'global reach', and TNBs followed their corporate clients abroad — providing a parallel structure of services in finance.
5. The placing of OPEC petrodollar surpluses with the US TNBs, led them to assume a recycling role of mammoth proportions, especially as regards the non-oil LDCs.

While these factors help to identify the main inputs into the eurocurrency market, it is generally agreed that borrowers and lenders continue to use the market in such a big way because of regulations, and what the lack of them enables the banks to gain. Since eurocurrencies collect in 'free zones' they are free of the restrictions which normally apply to national banks in their domestic markets, such as reserve requirements and exchange controls. (Freedom from reserve requirements means that eurobanks don't have to put aside a certain amount 'in reserve', and so have more interest-bearing funds at their disposal. Freedom from exchange controls means that eurobanks can accept and re-lend deposits without any regard for the local Central Bank's exchange control policies.) When these features are combined with the fact that in this wholesale market, overhead costs are lower, *the result is that eurobanks can offer more competitive interest rates than can national banks in their domestic markets.*

The peculiar spatial pattern of the eurocurrency market reflects this central requirement of avoiding national restrictions. In order to get a 'window' on the market, TNBs must have an office of some kind in one of these free zones or offshore centres, which include places such as Luxembourg, Singapore, Panama, etc.. The focal point of this study is the Bahamas, which is the second largest euromarket centre after London: a careful study of that offshore centre reveals some interesting points about the operations of US TNBs.

THE BAHAMAS

On the capital island, in the Bahamas, there are 285 financial institutions — that is, one bank for every 800 residents, or about 20 times the US ratio. There are many criteria for a country to compete as an offshore financial centre, and the large number of banks present in the Bahamas suggests that the country scores high on all counts. Among these are: (a) geographical proximity to a major metropolitan centre of trade and finance; (b) political stability; (c) time-zone location — Nassau is in the same time zone as New York, which is useful for rate quoting; (d) lack of exchange control regulations, or reserve ratio requirements, or withholding taxes; (e) adequate infrastructure — availability of skilled staff (the Bahamas has 200 qualified accountants on hand, good telecommunications system, etc.); (f) wide use of the English language.

In addition to having these minimal requirements for a eurocurrency centre, the Bahamas has other important attributes. Primarily, as the Economist Intelligence Unit summarised, 'the Bahamas is the archetype of tax havens', having no income tax, corporation tax, inheritance tax, estate duty, capital gains tax, or withholding tax. The Bahamas has also assumed another important characteristic: the commitment to banking secrecy is strictly observed.

Since 1973, the Bahamas has established itself as a full-scale offshore centre, with notable prominence in the eurocurrency market, especially for US TNBs. To illustrate this, at the end of 1973, US banks had only $22 billion of their dollar assets in the Caribbean, while their holdings in London were $40 billion. By September 1977, however, the Bahamas had multiplied its total some threefold to $67 billion, a figure which surpassed the $64 billion then held in London. In other words, by 1977 nearly one-third of the assets of all foreign branches of US banks were held in the Bahamas and Cayman.[9] Moreover, by the end of May 1976, more offshore loans by US banks were recorded in the Caribbean than in London; the Bahamas had 31.9% of the total versus 27.5% in London.[10]

There are two main kinds of banking operations in the Bahamas. At the simplest level, a large number of banks in the USA have a branch in the Bahamas to provide them with access to, or a 'window on', the eurocurrency market. These tend to be the smaller, often regionally-based banks whose main business is domestic, but who want to have the ability to participate in the eurocurrency market from time to time, yet can't afford a London branch. Examples would be the US National Bank of Oregon, the Valley National Bank of Arizona, or the Exchange National Bank of Chicago. These banks are generally represented by no more than a plaque on the wall, and a registered office, post office box and receptionist, all of which are probably shared with 8 or 10 other banks of a similar kind. The procedure for these 'shell' operations is quite simple. The parent bank in the USA will participate in the eurocurrency market for its clients by registering such activities on the accounting records of its Bahamian branch. Statistics suggest that the scale of these banks' operations in terms of assets is relatively insignificant. According to the FINE Report, at the end of 1974, of the 125 banks with overseas branches, 80 had only a single shell branch nominally operating in either Nassau or the Cayman Islands. Their aggregate assets were $4.1 billion or 2.7% of total foreign branch assets, and only 13% of total branch assets in the Bahamas and Cayman.[11] Thus, although it is often these banks which are cited with respect to banking operations in the Bahamas, they are relatively unimportant.

As these shell branches tend to be nothing more than a cheap business address for small-scale national banks, and as the volume of their transactions in the Bahamas is quite small, it is fair to assert that it is the location rather than the tax benefits *per se*, which characterise this particular group of banks' activities in the Bahamas. This is not to say that there are no tax benefits for these banks, but it is important to remember that all US banks are required to pay tax on their global earnings, regardless of which branch those earnings derive from. It would be false to assume, as many do, that these shell branches represent tax-free income for their head office. The only slight tax benefits which do accrue to these small-scale banks relate to withholding taxes (a tax on gross interest payable). As a paper written by the Banker Research Unit in conjunction with the Bahamian Central Bank makes clear: 'By directing their transactions to the shell branches, the banks and their depositors avoid paying withholding tax on a substantial part of the business they operate. But taxes have to be paid anyway, when they are repatriated from Nassau to the head office, and the main advantage is to postpone this payment and utilize this money in profitable operations.'[12]

TRANSFER BOOKING

The basic scheme, known as 'booking' entails the following: whereas the small-scale banks place their loans on their Bahamian books in order to comply with US restrictions on participating in the eurodollar market, the TNBs concertedly 'book' their loans and deposits through their Nassau branch in order to minimise their tax liabilities. For, although it is true that US banks are taxed on their global earnings, the scale and geographical spread of the TNBs' euromarket operations makes it worthwhile for them to have a low- or no-tax jurisdiction. This is because the US government allows banks to earn tax credits from areas where they have had to pay a higher level of tax to a foreign government than they would to the US government. These tax credits are wasted unless the banks can levy them against the normal level of US taxes on a low-tax area. In other words, when the British government in 1975 increased its tax on bank earnings to 52% (in comparison to the standard 48% in the US) the TNBs could use the 4% tax credit against their Nassau branches' earnings, thus lowering the rate there to 44%. (Obviously, as this tax credit incentive only applies to those TNBs with a branch in London, it is irrelevant to the smaller-scale banks, whose limited activities in the Bahamas we have already described.) Reducing one location's tax rate by a mere 4% may seem insignificant, however according to one tax expert,

> 'Much international banking business is carried out for very small margins, say ¼ per cent or even less, particularly where a bank borrows on the interbank market and re-lends to another bank. A tax on net profits, ie, the quarter per cent turn less expenses, is not a major deterrent, but it is enough, other things being equal, to encourage the use of the Bahamas.'[13]

In fact, the use of this booking procedure can save TNBs a substantial amount in tax liabilities. A Bahamian branch affords them the possibility of booking loans to suit their tax purposes — the more loans that are booked on the Nassau accounts, the fewer that appear in a high-tax area such as London, and the greater is the amount against which excess tax can be credited. In addition, by using the Bahamas, the US TNBs are not only able to reduce their overall tax burden, but they can also lower their taxable state and city income.

The only indication of the potential scale of this kind of booking operation comes from internal bank documents which were leaked to the *New York Times*, and which show the extent of one bank's operations (Citibank) in the Bahamas. Citibank was using its Nassau branch so heavily that one-quarter of all the eurocurrency loans then booked through the Bahamas were those of Citibank. 'The bank's documents show that toward the end of last year (1976), more than one-third of Citibank's eurocurrency loans made in dollars outside of the US were booked in the Bahamas. About one-fifth of the bank's total offshore loans, and one-eighth of its loans of all sorts, domestic and foreign, were placed in Nassau.'[14] These same documents showed that for Citibank at least, Nassau was the main springboard for loans to the Western hemisphere. More specifically, Brazil and Mexico were the two most heavily indebted to Citibank's Nassau branch — Citibank's identifiable loans included almost $2 billion to Brazil alone, $850 million to Mexico, and approximately $1 billion in loans to other countries in the rest of Latin America.

With so many of the US TNBs headquartered in New York City, the New York tax officials began to get increasingly concerned about the heavy use of booking procedures. In the wake of New York's fiscal crisis, lost revenue takes on even greater importance. Indeed, the *New York Times* estimated that 'at stake for the state are millions, perhaps tens of millions of dollars in tax revenues'.[15]

It is interesting to consider the procedure of 'booking' in relation to literature on TNCs. For example, the influential report on TNBs which was prepared for the Senate Foreign Relations Committee in 1977 asserts:

> 'These bank-haven branches, which are rarely subject to local taxation, can be extremely useful in helping a bank distribute, or 'book' its transactions among various tax jurisdictions so as to minimize its global tax burden. *Such selective 'siting' of loans and deposits serves much the same purpose for multinational banks as transfer pricing does for other multinational corporations.*'[16]

There is some contention amongst regulators about the degree to which money is a commodity: the banks themselves refer to their operations as an 'industry', and money as the main raw material. But two problems arise with the equation of transfer pricing with booking: these concern the notions of pricing, and of production. For the statement in the Senate report reflects a basic assumption, that merely to allocate the accounting or billing of a commodity, that is, to book with respect to tax differentials, is to transfer price. This confuses a standard strategy of spatial allocation of accounting units, with both the manipulation of prices through their internal determination by a firm (a key characteristic associated with transfer pricing), and with the location of production facilities.

However, there is no evidence at all that TNBs, when booking, alter the terms or amounts of their loans. (This would be exceedingly difficult to do, particularly when these loans are for end-users, ie., go outside the bank's system.) Secondly, the evidence on booking demonstrates that no real production takes place in the Bahamas. This was made clear in the first field audit of banks in 20 years, which was launched by the New York tax authorities in 1977. The auditors claimed, on the basis of their examinations, that the vast majority of loans attributed to Nassau were actually being organised and negotiated in New York, and that tax was due in that State. Specifically, the New York State Department of Taxation and Finance claimed that, 'regardless of where loans are booked their proceeds are taxable where the "mind and management" of the loan is situated.'[17]

The reaction of the US TNBs to this audit is also revealing. According to Euromoney magazine, 'In response to this audit, several New York banks increased their Caribbean branch expenditures. This included, in some instances, enlarging their Caribbean offices. Many New York bankers felt that, in order to justify their allocation of income and expenditures for tax purposes, they would have to alter their Caribbean branches from low-cost shell operations to full-service branches.'[18] The banks' immediate willingness to lease larger office space, purchase new office equipment, and increase their staff numbers from 1 or 2 to 15 or 20 in some cases, gives some indication of the Nassau branches' strategic importance, as well as illustrating the extent to which those branches were little more than shop-windows, rather than actual 'production' facilities.

In sum, we would argue that the booking of loans by the TNBs in tax havens such as the Bahamas is not sufficient to deserve the term of transfer *pricing*. At minimum, some element of manipulation of prices must be involved. With respect to the TNBs, the 'price' of their commodity, money, is usually taken to be the rate of interest. If the foreign exchange rate is considered to be the 'international price' of money, then its manipulation by the TNBs could perhaps qualify as transfer pricing as it is understood with regard to TNCs. The following example of 'transfer parking' by Citibank is intended to show exactly that.

TRANSFER PARKING

Transfer parking is the practice whereby TNBs transfer their foreign exchange positions (which they take as a matter of course in a range of different currencies) from one branch to another. The rates at which these positions are exchanged can be adjusted according to the objectives of the TNB, with the result that money can be exchanged at international prices which fall outside the prevailing market range, often for the purpose of lowering tax liabilities.

The basic mechanisms of this procedure came to light in a court case involving a principled Texan named David Edwards, and his former employer, Citibank. Edwards grew disturbed by what he perceived to be a misuse of Citibank's foreign exchange dealing rooms, so he collected evidence on this practice and sent it off to the senior management, believing they would halt it. He was promptly fired, and a long court case ensued on his claim against wrongful dismissal which, fortunately for members of the public, offered a unique opportunity to examine at close hand the internal workings of a TNB.

It is important to add that the evidence of transfer parking does not emanate solely from the Edwards case. Citibank became so worried by the publicity which the case generated that they commissioned their own accounting firm, Peat, Marwick and Mitchell to conduct an 'independent inquiry'. Rather than disproving Edwards' claims, this report (which we shall call the Citibank Report) both verified the *general* content of those allegations, as well as amplifying, in some ways, the specificities of the mechanism. In sum, these sources show that Citibank, in shifting its foreign exchange positions around its global network, also adjusted the exchange rates at which the transactions took place with others of its branches. The result was to make it seem as if the European branches of Citibank had taken losses on the transactions, thus lowering the level of income which was taxable in those jurisdictions, while the profits appeared to arise in its Bahamas branch.

In order to clarify the actual process of transfer parking, it is helpful to give some examples, taken from the Edwards court files.

Example A: The simplest example of transfer parking involved a transaction between the Frankfurt and Nassau Citibank branches. On 6 October 1976 at 3:44am, the Frankfurt branch instructed the Nassau branch through the New York office (using a special telex number) to sell £6 million to Frankfurt at the rate of $1.6660. On that same day, at 8:43am, the Frankfurt branch again telexed the Nassau branch via New York that it was selling £6 million back to Nassau at the rate of $1.6525. As a result of this transaction, the Frankfurt branch appeared to take a loss of DM200,000, thus lowering its level of taxable income in Germany by that amount. At the same time, on the internal books of Citibank, this same amount was credited back to the Frankfurt branch to compensate for the apparent reduction in earnings.

Example B: This example is only more complicated in that it involves more branches, but the same basic pattern is used. On 11 June 1976, Citibank's Paris branch telexed the New York office under a special telex number, instructing the Nassau branch to buy $6 million at Ffr 4.7275. In the same telex, the Paris branch also directed the Nassau branch to sell the $6 million at the higher exchange rate of Ffr 4.7375: $4 million of it to New York and $2 million to the Brussels branch. When this was accomplished, the Paris branch then purchased the $6 million back from New York and Brussels at the same rate which they had bought it, ie., 4.7375.

The net result of these transactions was that New York and Brussels remained exactly the same, and Paris took a loss. Meanwhile, the Nassau branch appeared to make a profit of Ffr 60,000 (having bought $6 million at 4.7275 and sold at 4.7375). The Paris branch, for the purposes of reporting taxable income in France, had seemed to have reduced its earnings by Ffr 60,000, while on the bank's internal accounts, it was credited with the apparent loss in earnings.

Clearly, the controversy of the Edwards case revolves around the charge of manipulation of the exchange rates of money; as such, it is useful to examine other evidence, such as the statement by the Citibank Report on this subject. This states, in a key passage:

> A profit or loss occurs when there is a differential between the rates used in the two transactions. Such a differential can result from several

circumstances: (1) the rates for each transaction are within the prevailing market range and those rates have changed between the transfers; (2) a rate within the prevailing range and a different rate outside the market range is used on the transactions; or (3) two different rates outside the prevailing market range are used. *Citibank branches have entered into transactions with other Citibank branches using each of these possible combination of rates.*[19]

The responses to the uncovering of transfer parking have been revealing in themselves. Citibank's reaction was both confusing and contradictory. The bank's affidavit to the New York Supreme Court claimed not, as might have been expected, that Edwards' allegations were incorrect, but rather, that the information Edwards had made public was damaging to Citibank, and that he had divulged secret, confidential and proprietary data which he was not permitted to do under the terms of his contract.[20]

The Report by Peat, Marwick and Mitchell took a slightly different tack. The Report went out of its way to demonstrate that the origins of transfer parking were not 'pre-meditated', and that there was no proof of any *systematic* tax evasion on the part of Citibank. Nevertheless, it was forced to admit to finding several examples of apparent tax violations. 'While no *institutional* pattern of transferring tax liability from one country to another in violation of local tax laws was present, we have discovered some specific instances where local counsel advise that tax challenges involving particular transactions would appear to have a high probability of success.'[21] The Report identified the branches where it found discrepancies, and these included Frankfurt, Paris and Zurich. For example, it states: 'During Peat Marwick's field program in Frankfurt, several inter-branch transactions were identified which appear to have been conducted outside the then prevailing market range. Because few such transactions were identified, there is no discernible pattern.'[22]

One firm outcome of the Edwards case involves the Swiss tax authorities. After the publication of the Citibank Report, which noted selected cases of tax manipulations in the Zurich branch, Citibank voluntarily contacted the tax authorities and declared its willingness to negotiate over possible back-taxes. In dealing with the authorities directly in this way, it is probable that any eventual settlement with the Swiss will be reached without details, such as the sums involved, being made public.

In Citibank's defence, the accounting firm claimed that 'in the complex world of taxation and other laws, no bank is entirely innocent', however, such a statement merely serves to implicate other TNBs in the same kind of operation. Indeed, as the *Financial Times* reported in September 1979: 'International bankers are⁻ gravely concerned that their foreign currency operations may come under close scrutiny from tax authorities around the world after a recent highly-publicised court case in New York.'[23]

Interestingly enough, interviews with senior bankers and foreign exchange traders in the Bahamas (although far from exhaustive) demonstrated that, without exception, each was certain of the veracity of Edwards' claim, and each one separately volunteered the information that, to their knowledge, every 'good' TNB used the technique of transfer parking to minimise tax liabilities. One banker went so far as to call the Edwards case the 'Citigate' of banking.

SCALE

Although the evidence that transfer parking occurs is fairly substantial, statistics on its *scale* are unavailable. Nevertheless, the Edwards case does provide an approximation as to the magnitudes involved. Firstly, in the material which Edwards sent to Citibank's senior management, he claims that his documents represent, 'four examples of the use of Nassau by Citibank branches for parking profits earned in Europe. These are not isolated cases. Indeed there is evidence in them of their being merely routine transactions in the ongoing parking of funds.'[24] Furthermore, as far as transfer parking in general is concerned, the Citibank Report also verifies this: 'The most prevalent scenario described is the relatively standard practice of transferring a foreign exchange position either to New York or Nassau, and the subsequent return of that position to the initiating branch.'[25]

Another indication of scale derives from the figure of DM200,000 which was given in Example A as the profit the Nassau branch 'earned' and which was later credited to the initiator branch, Frankfurt. Edwards, in his affidavit to the New York Supreme Court, states that the total profit for the Frankfurt branch during that monthly period amounted to DM900,000.[26] In other words, according to Edwards, it was possible for one branch of Citibank to shift to the Nassau branch 22% of one month's total profits in one telex slip, and thus lower its level of taxable income in Germany by that amount. Clearly, if these kinds of sums can be moved worldwide in one telex, the potential for transfer parking would appear to be substantial.

A further piece of evidence comes from a letter dated 29 June 1976 from Mr F. Redi, a Citibank Vice-President and Treasurer of the London branch, to Mr F.H. Huntington, then a Citibank Senior Vice-President at the head office. In commenting on a confidential bank memorandum (the equivalent to a 'manual' on parking), Redi wrote:

> 'My concern is that the booking units consider these parked positions a special favour, and do not intend spending much time on them. There is, therefore, the potential risk of correspondence which would make obvious the nature of the transaction, and expose ourselves to the following possibilities:
> 1. Severely upsetting the local Central Bank.
> 2. Exposing ourselves to blackmail, for example, by some unhappy staff member.
> 3. Violation of the FX (foreign exchange) limits through parking of positions with various other CMDS (commodity dealers).
> One should question at this point whether it is worthwhile wasting the expertise we have been building up in the field over the last 15 years, and *what are the alternatives to avoiding a substantial reduction of FX earnings in the institution*' (emphasis added).[27]

Several bankers in the Bahamas pointed out one serious difficulty in identifying the scale of transfer parking. According to them, the relative performance of parking need not appear in the statement of consolidated income under the (easily identifiable) category of foreign exchange. Instead, through what one senior vice-president termed 'creative accounting', the profits from parking could be manipulated to appear under the 'interest' category — a much larger and more nebulous one. This is possible because even when currencies are exchanged, they are held for a certain period of time. This is measured in terms of either a premium or a discount rate (depending on which direction that currency is expected to move), and a differential on the interest rates between the two currencies to be traded. The results of transfer parking can thus be attributed to 'interest earned' just as easily as to foreign exchange income.

Although these points suggest that the scale of transfer parking may be indeterminable, this shouldn't lead to the assumption that the benefits of transfer parking to the TNBs are limitless. On the contrary, the most obvious limit arises from the nature of the foreign exchange market, which is a fiercely competitive one. TNBs invest large sums in the most advanced telecommunications systems, which enable them to monitor the market so closely as to make a profit by recognising a movement in exchange rates ('price') of as little as $^1/_{16}$ of a point. Consequently, TNBs are unable to use transfer parking in order to raise their end-price of money. In other words, parking cannot *create* profit for the TNBs, for if one branch appears to make a profit on a foreign exchange transaction, it is at the expense of another branch; any profit from buying cheap and selling dear will be balanced by the loss registered at the other branch. Similarly, if, in one of the parking circuits, a branch of another bank is used, the rates at which that money will have been traded, will be those within the market range, otherwise that other TNB would refuse to enter into such a transaction.

The mechanism of transfer parking reveals some further interesting points about TNBs. Firstly the TNBs' activities in the Bahamas are centrally controlled from the head office. For example, when an initiating branch was in the process of transferring all or part of its foreign exchange position to the Nassau branch, instructions for the transaction were usually telexed through the New York office. The same confidential Citibank memorandum states with regard to contact with Nassau that: 'all communication regarding position parking should be with the Eurocurrency Department of the International Money Market Division at Head Office, by telex numbers: 423712, 236355, and 425848 and not with the Nassau branch directly.'[28] In further streamlining the control over transfer parking, the Nassau branch was never given responsibility for the practice. This also emerges clearly from the confidential parking 'manual'.

'The responsibility for parked positions lies solely with the Parking Branch, while Nassau only acts as a booking unit... The Parking Branches will provide Nassau branch with the exchange rates to be used for revaluation purposes: as of each monthly closing, a letter (in duplicate) will be mailed to each of the Parking Branches (attn: Treasurer, or better, Senior Operating Officer) listing the exchange rates used and requesting the copy to be signed and returned. Naturally, no mention of Parked Positions will be made.'[29]

This feature of centralised control is also clearly visible from Citibank's admission of heavy reliance on its own internal accounting system, which it calls the Management Information System (MIS). Using debits and credits against actual accounting figures, the MIS adjusts profits, losses, income and expenses in such a way as to ascertain what the separate business segments of the institution actually contribute or cost it. The culmination of the MIS is the Management Profit Report (MPR) a monthly record which 'was used to portray the contribution of individuals and organizational units in terms of the goals of management, rather than in terms of accounting entities.'[30]

The MIS was an important component of transfer parking. Citibank staff were reluctant to have it appear on accounting records as if their branch or division had an unusually high proportion of losses, unless they could feel certain that their true participation in the creation of profit could be adequately acknowledged by management. The Citibank Report is explicit on this point:

> 'In the context of foreign exchange trading, MIS adjustments are used to recognize the role of a branch in initiating an exchange profit or loss, even if the actual profit or loss is realized and recorded on the books of another branch. *This reporting system provides an incentive for the various segments of Citibank to make their business decisions with an eye towards global or institutional concerns rather than strictly along divisional lines.*'[31]

CONTROL

Having established that transfer parking as a mechanism *does* exist, and is an important component of the TNB's strategy of minimising global tax liabilities, it is important to examine what, if any, forces are likely to mitigate against the widespread use of such a mechanism. For example, is it reasonable to assume that a TNB can and will voluntarily provide its own effective control over such a tempting procedure?

Citibank's actions inspire little confidence in TNB self-discipline. While Citibank attempted to present an image to the public of innocence of any systematic wrong-doing, the report prepared by its auditors and lawyers is full of implicit admissions on the part of the bank that it knew it was 'skating on very thin ice'. For example, the Citibank Report notes that the somewhat haphazard way in which parking is said to have developed led, not to a halting of those activities, but to 'concern of management in New York about the need to establish operational uniformity and more *effective oversight*' (emphasis added).[32] On the question of taxation, the Report acknowledges that 'Nassau's appearing on the transferring branch's books was perceived to have un-desirable tax-haven connotations that might easily be mis-understood.'[33] Similarly, 'Some branches considered it un-desirable to realise large profits or losses as this could potentially raise questions by regulatory agencies and competitors as to the volume of foreign exchange transactions being conducted by the branch. It was therefore important to conduct inter-branch transactions in such a way that any profit or loss would be realized at the transferee branch.'[34]

It seems the bank's resources were used to avoid detection. Not only were special telex numbers used, but transactions were often diverted through other branches — according to the confidential memorandum, 'the transactions routed this way become less visible on the Parking Branch's books, particularly because Nassau is not very active in Foreign Exchange.'[35] These features, when combined with the statement by the Vice-President quoted above which refers to fears of blackmail, suggest that even at the high level of management, Citibank, rather than being concerned with the *arresting* of such a practice, was more interested in hindering its discovery.

If this is so, then the question of control is likely to rest with those in the state apparatus whose function it is to regulate the banking system and collect revenue. However, the Edwards case also provides an indication of some of the obstacles which lie in the way of any successful monitoring of transfer parking.

The first obstacle lies with the nature of the commodity being transferred. Citibank alone had 1,918 offices in 92 countries in 1978. Moreover, the fungibility of money, and the high-level technology which is used to transfer it, combine to make the shifting of money around the world a flexible and instantaneous operation. In a letter to Peat, Marwick and Mitchell, Edwards offered his advice on this problem of monitoring and producing proof.

> 'Using standard auditing procedure, Peat Marwick and Mitchell may be sampling as few as 7 foreign exchange and money market transactions from among 400 to 1000 generated weekly.
>
> Parking transactions are multi-sided. In order to get a full picture of a Citibank inter-branch transaction, it is necessary to examine its individual components at all branches involved. *The chances of random sampling in several Citibank branches producing a single complete parking transaction are almost non-existent.*'[36]

Edwards goes on to suggest which branches should be most closely examined: Nassau, New York, London, Brussels, Milan, Amsterdam, Paris, Frankfurt, Zurich, Hong Kong, Caracas, Rio de Janeiro, Singapore and Mexico City.

Peat, Marwick and Mitchell found the question of establishing proof to be a problem when preparing the Citibank Report. In their concluding remarks, they noted, 'the question of whether particular conduct constitutes a legal avoidance or an illegal evasion of a rule of law... is normally decided on a case-by-case basis.'[37] Yet the constraints on this procedure had already been outlined in the introduction to their brief, where they admitted, 'Much of the trading room paperwork was not required to be retained under Citibank's regular document retention programs, and was no longer available.'[38]

In addition to these technical obstacles to the appropriate monitoring of transfer parking, there are also the problems of establishing what the legal limitations actually are. For example, on the subject of tax revenue, the central question revolves around the notion of a fair, arm's-length price. As the Citibank Report states, 'as the arm's-length quality of the transaction declines, the likelihood of tax liability accruing to the transferor branch is increased.'[39] Yet the Report then goes to great lengths to stress that the arm's-length price for foreign currency is complex, and that the question of a market range should be left open. It seems that to determine even this is very difficult.

> 'Foreign exchange transactions are conducted in a dealer market, with rates quoted directly between pairs of dispersed trading parties. Thus, there are varying buying and selling rates being quoted among dealers at any one moment. *Since there is no central market, there is no universally recognised "market rate"*, although as a result of the speed and efficiency of modern communications, the rates quoted among major participants will not vary widely in an orderly market, and there will be a prevailing market range at most times.'[40]

One of the leading experts on corporate tax planning, John Chown, commented on the legal aspects of the Edwards case at a conference on international banking held in the Bahamas in March 1979. His opinion then was that: (a) if a bank is transferring a position to another branch in order to comply with local exchange controls, that is perfectly reasonable; (b) if a bank takes a position or view on a currency, this can legally be booked to whichever of its branches will pay the least tax (taking into account exchange control constraints and other local regulations, of course). Where Chown felt a bank's conduct would be unacceptable was in the *delayed* booking of transactions.

> 'It is one thing for a bank to say, "this will make us a profit, therefore let us book it to Nassau where we pay the least tax". It is quite another to open a transaction and to wait a few days (or even a few hours, the way foreign exchanges move these days) and then to decide that, if the transaction

shows a profit it is to be booked to Nassau, whereas, if it shows a loss, it is
to be left as a charge against profits in a high tax country.'[41]

In other words, although Chown was not concerned with the
actual transferring of positions, the delaying of booking seemed to
raise tax and other related questions. The Edwards material
includes one example of a transaction in which the date of the
telex slip was altered. In addition, the Citibank Report refers to a
case in Switzerland where the delaying of booking was generally
frowned upon. This aspect adds a further dimension to the
problem of the detection and enforcement of TNB transfer
parking.

There are other problems, in addition to the technical and legal
limits, to successful state monitoring of transfer parking. For
example, it is difficult to imagine what incentives could be offered
to offshore centres such as the Bahamas to curtail the
international operations of the TNBs. These financial centres
(which are often small, island economies) tend to rely heavily on
the business which is generated from their services, and on the
indirect revenue (such as license fees, work permits, etc.). In
other words, the freedoms they offer are their main bargaining
tools in the market — their restriction would entail a significant
cutback in revenue and employment for that country. Moreover,
the competitive pressures between other offshore centres should
not be underestimated, as a statement from the Chairman of the
Nassau office of the Bank of Nova Scotia highlights: 'There is no
reason whatever to suppose that if this country introduced a tax,
Cayman or Bermuda would follow such an example and thereby
forfeit the advantages which would accrue to them from the
elimination of the Bahamas as a competitor.'[42]

CONCLUSION
It is clear from the discussion above that the TNBs' ability to
transfer park represents a challenge to the state's fiscal role. This
practice also enables TNBs to avoid exchange controls and other
regulations which are designed to protect the banking system.
Use of such a mechanism can cause significant damage to the
structure of a system which relies heavily on confidence as a key
input. In sum, by transfer parking, the TNB's are likely to
provide an increasing threat to governments' control of their
national economies and to the stability of the international
banking system itself.

NOTES

* This paper is a revised version of a thesis presented for the M.Phil degree at the Institute of Development Studies. I would like to gratefully acknowledge the useful discussions held with Philip Wellons, Robert Cohen and David Edwards in the United States, and Robin Murray, Constantine Vaitsos, my supervisor Carlos Fortin and Stephanie Griffith-Jones at IDS, and last but not least, Teddy Brett, who provided a constant source of critical but constructive comment, as well as support.

1 United Nations (1978), p.248.
2 US Senate Report, p.9.
3 *Financial Times*, 9 August, 1979.
4 M. Odjagov, p.2.
5 S. Griffith-Jones, p.3.
6 US Senate Report, p.2.
7 S. Griffith-Jones, p.8.
8 Good summaries are contained in Chase's *Eurocurrency Financing*, the articles by Bankers Trust, by S. Griffith-Jones and by M. Odjagov, and the books by I. Giddy and G. Dufey and S. Robinson.
9 *Financial Times*, Special Survey in 30 May, 1978 issue.
10 A. Crittenden, 3 March, 1977.
11 US House of Representatives, FINE Report, p.811 and 822.
12 Banker Research Unit, in conjunction with the Central Bank of the Bahamas, p.21.
13 J. Chown, speech, p.4.
14 A. Crittenden, 4 March, 1977.
15 A. Crittenden, 4 November, 1977.
16 US Senate Report, p.2.
17 A. Crittenden, 4 November, 1977.
18 *Euromoney*, December 1978, p.160.
19 Citibank Report, p.75.
20 Citibank was successful in having two of its motions approved by the court: (a) that Edwards be forbidden to speak to the Press after September 1978, and (b) that so-far undisclosed evidence be sealed and court hearings be held 'in camera' from December 1978. On 22 June, 1979 Justice Martin Evans of the New York Supreme Court brought the case to a sudden close with a ruling that Edwards had no formal contract with Citibank and no fixed term of employment, so that his claim that he had been wrongfully dismissed had no legal grounds. This would appear to stand in direct contradiction first, to Citibank's initial statements concerning the reasons for Edwards' dismissal, second, to the Citibank Report's 'brief', which included statements such as 'the termination of Edwards' employment', and so on, and third, to Citibank's original affidavit which stated that Edwards' contract didn't allow him to publicly divulge the information he had collected. *Financial Times*, 25 June, 1979.
21 Citibank Report, p.128.
22 Citibank Report, p.85.
23 *Financial Times*, 3 September, 1979.
24 Citibank Report, p.10.
25 Citibank Report, p.25.
26 Edwards' affidavit in New York Supreme Court case file.

27 Letter contained in Edwards' court file.
28 Edwards' court file — Confidential Memorandum internal to Citibank.
29 Citibank's Confidential Memorandum — Edwards' court file.
30 Citibank Report, p.61.
31 Citibank Report, p.60-2.
32 Citibank Report, p.66.
33 Citibank Report, p.67.
34 Citibank Report, p.68-9.
35 Citibank's Confidential Memorandum, Edwards' court file.
36 Edwards' letter — court files.
37 Citibank Report, p.127.
38 Citibank Report, p.20.
39 Citibank Report, p.126.
40 Citibank Report, p.31.
41 J. Chown, speech, p.9 and 10.
42 D. Fleming, address to the Bahamas Chamber of Commerce, p.14.

BIBLIOGRAPHY

Banker Research Unit (1977), *Offshore Investment Centres*, (eds. Chown, J.F. and Kelen, T.F.).
——*The Commonwealth of the Bahamas: Profile of an Offshore Centre*, in conjunction with Central Bank of the Bahamas, (P. Thorn, ed.).
Bankers Trust (1964), Pamphlet on the Eurodollar Market, prepared by Roy L. Peterson.
Chase Manhattan (1975), *Eurocurrency Financing*.
Chown, J. (1979), 'Taxation and International Banking', Paper presented at Conference on the Bahamas as an International Financial Centre, 4-6 March, Nassau, Bahamas.
Citibank (1978), Report by Audit Committee, Prepared by law firm of Shearman and Sterling, and accounting firm Peat, Marwick and Mitchell, published in New York, 20 November; Annual Report.
Crittenden, A. (1977), 'Growing US Bank Role in Bahamas Causing Concern', *New York Times*, 3 March.
——'Citibank Found to Lead in Shifting Loan Activity to Offshore Tax Havens', *New York Times*, 4 March.
——'State is Auditing City Banks as They Expand in the Bahamas' in *New York Times*, 4 November.
Edwards, David, Court Case Files, NY Supreme Court Edwards vs. Citibank, Index No. 12692, 1978.
Euromoney, various issues.

Fleming, D (1975), 'The Bahamas — Tax Paradise', pamphlet 23 May.

——(1976) Address to the Bahamian Chamber of Commerce.

——(1978), 'Benefits to the Bahamian Economy from the Banks and Trust Companies', paper 22 February.

Giddy, I. and Dufey, G. (1978), *The International Money Market*, Prentice-Hall.

Griffith-Jones, S. (1978), 'The Growth of Multinational Banking, the Eurocurrency Market, and the Developing Countries,' *Journal of Development Studies*, January 1980.

Odjagov, M. (1977), *Transnational Banking*, Study prepared for the UN Centre on TNCs.

Robinson, S. (1972), *Multinational Banking*, A.W. Sijthoff.

United Nations (1978), *Transnational Corporations in World Development: a Re-examination* E/C 10/38 March.

US House of Representatives, Committee on Banking, Currency and Housing (1976), 'Financial Institutions and the Nation's Economy' (FINE).

US Senate, Committee on Foreign Relations, Staff Report prepared for the Subcommittee on Foreign Economy Policy, (1977), 'International Debt, the Banks, and US Foreign Policy', with foreword by Senator Frank Church.

(C)   Technology

8.
PRICING OF INTRA-FIRM TECHNOLOGICAL TRANSACTIONS
DANIEL CHUDNOVSKY *

INTRODUCTION
The literature on transfer pricing has been mostly concerned with visible international trade. This is understandable given the amount of resources involved in visible trade and the scope offered by intra-firm trade for transfer price manipulation. Yet the share of intra-firm transactions in total transactions is much larger in the case of intangible technology than in visible trade, and the problem of transfer pricing no less acute.

Pricing of intra-firm technological transactions not only refers to the explicit incomes to be obtained out of the sale or lease of various technological items, but also to the implicit prices imposed by the licensor to the licensee in terms of restrictions. These implicit costs are usually referred to as restrictive business practices. Despite being generally stated in contracts between parent and subsidiaries of TNCs, they only really make sense in inter-firm transactions. However, from the point of view of the host country, the way in which subsidiaries are considered in the TNC global technological policy is of great importance, though this consideration cannot be looked at merely as a restrictive business practice.

Home and host countries have made some attempts to regulate intra-firm technological transactions, trying generally to assimilate them to inter-firm arrangements. The same question has been discussed in the context of the preparation of International Codes of Conduct on transfer of technology and on transnational enterprises.

This article is in four parts. Firstly, there is an examination of the features of intra-firm technological transactions and their pricing; secondly, a review of possible reasons for the use of royalties in intra-firm transactions; thirdly, a discussion of the relation between pricing intra-firm technological transactions and R & D financing; and lastly, on the basis of the above considerations and of policy initiatives taken by some Latin American countries, possible policy approaches by host countries will be discussed.

119

SOME EVIDENCE

The US obtained $5.6 billion in 1978 in receipt of royalties, licence fees and management fees: $4.6 billion, or 82% of the net flows were accounted for by intra-firm transactions.[1] Even excluding management fees, the proportion of intra-firm transactions in total technological transactions was very high — 63% in 1972 — and much higher than the comparable proportions for visible international trade. It is also remarkable that the proportion of intra-firm transactions in total transactions has been growing. Intra-firm royalty receipts accounted for 62% of total receipts in 1960.

If, instead of referring to the world as a whole, a geographical breakdown of the US receipts is made (Table 1), an interesting feature emerges. Japan, and Eastern Europe, have a much lower proportion of intra-firm technological transactions as a result of their policy towards foreign investment. However, the proportion for Japan (as for the UK and the EEC) is growing. The other extreme is Canada, the UK, and the developing countries except Latin America where the proportion of intra-firm trade is higher than the world average (94, 90 and 88% respectively).

Royalties received from US subsidiaries operating in Latin America have decreased not only in relative but also in absolute terms since 1975,[2] probably as a consequence of the government policies implemented in that area (see section 4). Even with this recent reduction, the proportion of intra-firm technological transactions in total transactions is very high.

This US figure is higher than those shown in national studies. In the case of Brazil, intra-firm payments amounted to 52% of total payments in the period 1965-70 in the manufacturing sector,[3] while in Argentina they were 42% of the total in 1972.[4] It is worth pointing out that both the Brazilian and Argentinian studies refer to royalty payments to all countries, not only to the US, and they did not cover fully comparable sectors. However, even compared with the proportion of intra-firm transactions as reflected only in royalty payments (net of management fees) — which was 68% for the US in Latin America in 1972 — the national figures are lower, reflecting that transactions coming from other industrial countries are less affected by the trend under consideration. The Federal Republic of Germany, for example, received only 5% of its royalties from affiliate firms in 1975.[5]

In general, however, for recipient developing countries intra-firm transactions are considerable in the technological area, especially for agreements made with US-based enterprises.

Table 1

Proportion of Intra-firm Royalties in Total US Receipts

Year	All	UK	EEC (6)	Other Western Europe	Eastern Europe	Canada	Latin America	Japan	Australia, N.Zealand S.Africa	Other Developing Countries
1960	62	56	— 44 —		—	80	83	13	65	72
1972	76	81	76	76	0	90	85	30	82	80
of which:-										
royalties	63	72	72	67	0	80	68	26	74	63
management fees	13	9	4	9	0	10	17	4	8	17
1976	82	84	82	81	0	94	82	51	84	91
1978	82	90	83	79	0	94	81	58	83	88

Source: Calculated on the basis of data in Survey of Current Business, December 1973, March 1977 and March 1979.

Once the importance of the phenomenon is acknowledged, the obvious question is: are intra-firm transactions charged at prices higher than inter-firm transactions? This is not an easy question to answer, given the peculiarities of technology as a commodity, the bargaining position of both parties in the arrangement, the financial policies of TNCs, and host and home countries' policy restrictions. These factors make all comparisons very hazardous. However, it is worth trying to see if there is any observable trend in the area of technology.

This was attempted with information collected in Argentina. The results are shown in Table 2. If col.1 is compared with col.3 it is possible to see that royalty rates[6] were lower in inter-firm transactions than in payments between subsidiaries and parent companies in 9 out of 16 selected industries. The average, however, is strongly influenced by two sectors — pharmaceuticals and motor cars — which accounted for nearly 30% of all royalties. It is important to note that the average share of sales under licence in total sales was 40% for national firms (col.2) and 93% for foreign subsidiaries (col.4). Subsidiaries tend to produce almost everything under licence from the parent, though some exceptions were found, especially in consumer goods industries.

If, instead of calculating royalty rates, average royalty payments per contract for all sectors are taken into account, we found that average royalties charged on intra-firm transactions were 4.4 times higher than in inter-firm ones. A similar conclusion was reached in a study on Brazil, using the same procedure. Average royalty payment per contract was higher in agreements between parent companies and subsidiaries than in contracts made by foreign firms with third parties, or in contracts made by national firms.[7]

Even though this is specific evidence, the results are not unexpected. Intra-firm transactions would generally lead to prices higher than those quoted by independent firms. But this general statement cannot be applied so easily to a market as imperfect as the technology market, in which most of the transactions are not made at arm's-length prices. It is important to find the reasons for the use of royalty payments in intra-firm transactions.

THE ROLE OF ROYALTIES IN INTRA-FIRM TRANSACTIONS

Royalty payments are one of the means used by TNCs to transfer funds from one country to another, as well as to reduce tax

Table 2

Royalty rates in inter-firm and intra-firm transactions

Argentina 1972

Sector	Inter-firm		Intra-firm	
	Royalty rate (1)	Licensed Sales on Total Sales (2)	Royalty rate (3)	Licensed Sales on Total Sales (4)
All	4.4	40	2.9	93
Food	1.6	53	1.9	35
Textiles	.6	24	5.8	56
Clothing	6.7	89	3.9	96
Paper	1.8	12	6.2	100
Printing	3.4	29	2.8	94
Pharmaceuticals	5.6	36	6.8	69
Cosmetics	16.7	60	4.4	68
Other chemicals	3.0	14	1.8	65
Rubber	1.3	94	2.0	80
Stone, glass	2.7	34	1.7	94
Fabricated metal products	5.3	24	7.9	69
Non-electrical machinery	4.4	32	2.3	90
Electrical machinery	4.2	62	7.1	50
Electrical household equipment	1.7	63	1.9	100
Motor cars	3.5	31	1.9	97
Scientific Professional equipment	9.8	77	18.2	65

Note: Inter-firm transactions are those made by nationally-owned firms while intra-firm transactions are those made between parent companies and majority-owned subsidiaries. Only selected sectors are shown in the table. The average is made with all sectors including others not shown in the table.

Source: Own elaboration on the basis of the information collected in D. Chudnovsky et al, *op. cit.*, Tables 4 and 11.

payments, avoid government restrictions or, in the case of joint ventures, to avoid sharing them with local partners. Moreover, intra-firm transactions provide for greater control of the technology.

Many countries have a differential tax treatment for royalties. Transferring profits as royalties instead of dividends could lead to an important tax saving for a firm depending on how they are treated in the home country.[8] For instance, in Argentina in the year the research was carried out, it was more convenient for TNCs to use royalties than dividends to transfer profits, and this could be one reason accounting for higher prices in intra-firm technological payments. In addition, royalties are stated as cost items in balance sheets, and therefore the amount of taxable profits may be reduced. As they are usually stated as percentages of sales, they can also be transferred even in cases in which the subsidiary in question declared losses.[9] In the case of joint ventures, royalties paid to the foreign partner do not need to be shared with the local partner (as is the case with dividends) and therefore are usually preferred by TNCs.

TNCs' preference for intra-firm technological transactions can also be explained by some additional factors. One obvious but usually forgotten fact is that royalties are estimated on all sales, and run for ever. This is seldom the case in inter-firm transactions. Secondly, it is harder to change inter-firm royalty rates than intra-firm ones. Thirdly, there is the possibility of capitalising technology i.e., the inclusion of patents, trade marks, know-how or other intangible assets as part of the foreign firm's equity. This is implicit in intra-firm transactions and by definition cannot be made in inter-firm arrangements. Finally, intra-firm arrangements offer the possibility of charging implicit prices — in the form of restrictive business practices — even in cases where these prices are not allowed by the host country legislation. This would occur when restrictive practices, stated in technology arrangements, are declared illegal.

Vaitsos has put forward a comprehensive explanation for the use of transfer pricing, including inter-affiliate charges for technology, even in cases in which no tax differentials between countries or joint ventures exist. He showed that if overhead and variable costs exceed TNC revenues from sales in its home market and to non-affiliates abroad, a firm would find it convenient to transfer untaxed income through transfer pricing.[10] His explanation is valid for royalty payments when royalties are taxed at a lower rate in the host country than dividends, but it does not hold when royalties are taxed in the same manner.

However, Vaitsos raises a more fundamental question (p. 102): how are overhead expenditures like R & D financed by the different national operations of transnational enterprises? This leads us to a discussion of the importance of intra-firm technological transactions in the financing of R & D expenditures.

PRICING OF INTRA-FIRM TECHNOLOGICAL TRANSACTIONS AND R & D FINANCING

The data shown in the US Senate study gives us some idea of the importance of royalties. In 1966 royalties earned in manufacturing overseas operations accounted for 7.7% of the total expenditure in R & D made by US-based manufacturing TNCs.[11] However, taking into account that, on average, only half of the R & D expenditures in the US are financed by the corporations themselves, and that, on average, one-third of the world sales are made abroad,[12] the incidence of royalties in R & D financing is much higher. Assuming that the money spent on R & D is distributed proportionally to every dollar of sales made by the whole TNC, royalties from abroad contributed 47% of that portion of global expenditure allocatable to the overseas activities of TNCs. This suggests that royalties do play an important part in the financing of centralised R & D activities.

To allocate the financing of R & D expenditures according to sales would mean that each subsidiary would be taken into equal consideration when R & D is planned. But this can hardly be the case in subsidiaries located in developing countries. On average, 94% of the sales of the TNCs were made in industrialised countries (including the USA) and so R & D expenditures favour the corporation's activities in those markets. Subsidiaries located in developing countries may be receiving less in terms of technological output than they have actually contributed to finance. This is well stated in the US Senate report: 'Theoretically, all the technology available to the parent MNC is available to its affiliates. In practice, this is rarely the case. The foreign affiliates may have less immediate access to US-developed technology than do domestic operating affiliates in the United States, so that, if they share R & D costs equally with the domestic subsidiaries, they may pay for more than they get' (pp.592-3). If this is the case, and the evidence for developing countries seems to indicate that it is, pricing of intra-firm transactions will simply be based on what the market will bear. The basic point is that, as developing countries are not taken into account when planning R & D expenditures, any royalties obtained out of the subsidiaries operating in those countries is pure profit.

This is a conclusion similar, although based on different reasoning, to those based on the argument that since know-how has no marginal cost, any price obtained from it will be purely monopoly rents. However, though know-how may have no marginal costs from a social point of view, the firm who owns it has private opportunity costs.

A different argument applies if R & D expenditures are made with developing countries' needs in mind, or if the technological output requires special adaptation for these countries. In that case, the price to be paid in terms of profits or royalties should be related to the amount of R & D expenditures. The price to be paid should cover the marginal cost of the special R & D effort undertaken by the corporation.

Finally, another approach would be a contribution on a *pro rata* basis to the financing of the R & D effort instead of paying for the *ex ante* R & D made for developing countries. For example, royalties might be paid by each subsidiary as a proportion of sales in any country, developed or developing, and in this way equally contributing to the financing of the centralised R & D.

There are, then, two different arguments. The first is that the pricing of technology transferred to subsidiaries located in a developing country is purely a monopoly rent. This is because (a) developing countries are not taken into account in the *ex ante* R & D expenditure, or (b) know-how has no marginal cost.

The second argument is that the pricing of technology transferred to subsidiaries in developing countries should be related to R & D expenditures. This can be done either by paying the marginal cost of the *ex ante* R & D planned for that developing country, or as an *ex post pro rata* contribution to the financing of the centralised R & D.

POLICY ISSUES IN IMPORTING COUNTRIES
The regulation of technological transactions is a relatively recent trend in developing countries, at least in Latin America. The majority of regulations have been implemented during the 1970s, the most influential of all being the Andean Pact's Decision 24.

When analysing the pricing of technological transactions, it is important first to see how intra-firm arrangements were approached, *vis-à-vis* inter-firm ones, and then whether the approach is the most appropriate one.

Royalty payments between subsidiaries and parent companies, are not allowed under Decision 24 of the Andean Pact. Neither are they allowed for patents and trademarks in Brazilian legislation. In the 1974 Argentine Law considers royalties in intra-firm transactions as profits. In the recent Argentine Law (No.21617) this provision was changed and only royalty payments for the use of trademarks are currently not allowed.

Capitalisation of technology is also not allowed in those countries which are members of the Andean Pact. No such restrictions exist in Mexican and Brazilian legislation, and both the previous and the present Argentine laws have allowed the capitalisation of technology.

Finally, no legislative distinction is made between intra-firm and inter-firm restrictive business practices.

Let us examine how appropriate these approaches have been. In the case of royalty payments, two different questions are involved: first, non-technological considerations that may favour the use of royalties *vis-à-vis* other means of remitting funds in TNCs; second, the amount of payments for the technology received, independently of the form in which they are remitted.

The simplest solution to the first question is that of the Andean Pact, i.e., not to allow any royalty payments between parent companies and subsidiaries. Another approach is to treat royalties in the same way as other remittances in the fiscal and foreign exchange policy of the recipient country, as in Brazil and under the previous Argentine law. Though this is very attractive in principle, some problems may arise in implementation,[13] mainly because royalties are still a cost item for other purposes. At the same time, in the case of joint ventures, royalties cannot be treated in the same way as profits.

The second question is more difficult. It is unrealistic to consider inter-firm arrangements as a standard of comparison for assessing the pricing of intra-firm technological transactions. This is not only because the majority of international transactions in the technology field are made within TNCs, but because of the imperfections that characterise this market.

This does not mean that intra-firm transactions should be left without special regulation. What is needed are realistic measures. These should take into account the peculiarities of R & D allocation and financing in TNCs, and the needs of developing countries to reduce the costs of technological dependence.

In order to assess the price to be charged for technology, the main issue is the *ex ante* importance of that particular market for that particular technology. This would mean knowing: (a) how country specific is the technology or the adaptation made abroad for that technology; (b) how many markets are going to be used; (c) in how many years will it be amortised; (d) whether it is protected by industrial property rights; and (e) how important it is for the importing country. These questions should be discussed when negotiating with TNCs the reward for the technological contribution. If the technology was not designed for the country in question, which is likely, the price fixed will depend on the opportunity costs both for the firm and for the country. In the case of the transnational firm, the opportunity cost will be given by the royalties or profits which can be obtained elsewhere. For the country, it will depend on the cheapest available alternative offer.

What is clearly not advisable, in any case, is the usual practice of royalty payments as a fixed percentage, calculated on the whole output, or estimated as a fixed portion of the flow of future profits.

The situation is obviously different with new agreements and existing ones. In the latter, it was relatively easy to reduce royalty payments without affecting the flow of technology. Prices in both intra- and inter-firm arrangements were clearly very high, and technology was not only already transferred but also mostly conceived for the markets of industrialised countries.

The future reaction of foreign suppliers towards operating in a more regulated technology market is not clear, and will depend on a number of non-technological and non-economic reasons. The elasticity of supply of technology has still to be assessed, though it is clear that important differences may exist by industries, countries and types of transactions.

Restrictive business practices in intra-firm technological transactions are unlike those between independent firms. Contracts between parent companies and subsidiaries might be free of any formal restrictions but subsidiaries still operate with constraints.

Although the elimination of restrictive clauses in contracts is desirable for host governments, little can be achieved by merely eliminating export restrictions. It is much better to arrange specific export commitments when the foreign investment proposal is negotiated. Instead of eliminating grant-back provisions, it is much better to arrange the R & D efforts of the subsidiary in terms of product adaptation and skill formation. And so on. There is a need to move from a restrictions framework to a policy framework in which the subsidiary can meet certain objectives fixed by the host government.

Restrictive practices that subsidiaries carry out in the market of the host country are a different question. So far, legislation on transfer of technology has approached only the market for an input, not the market in which the output resulting from this input is sold. This question has hardly been tackled in developing countries, and is directly linked with other important policy areas such as tariff protection, the legislation on patents and trademarks, the regulation of advertising, etc. These policies usually help subsidiaries to obtain, among other things, a certain amount of market power. This may result in undesirable effects on the economy of the host country and particularly on nationally-owned enterprises.

For this reason it would be more relevant to approach the matter of restrictive business practices not as an issue between parent companies and subsidiaries but as one derived from the activities of subsidiaries in the host countries' markets.

CONCLUDING REMARKS

Intra-firm agreements form a major part of international transactions on technology, particularly for the USA. These transactions, made between parent companies and subsidiaries, lead to explicit prices such as royalty payments or capitalisation of technology, and to restrictive business practices.

As in the case of visible trade, it appears that prices charged in intra-firm transactions are higher than in inter-firm ones, though the evidence is scarce and many intervening factors make the comparison hazardous. Inter-firm technological transactions, in particular, are made in a very imperfect market and cannot be considered as an appropriate standard of comparison.

For this reason, the question of pricing intra-firm technological transactions should be approached in a different manner. It is important to see, first, the non-technological factors — such as taxes and foreign exchange policy — that play a role in using royalties as a particular form of remittance. Second, is the issue of how the R & D expenditures of TNCs are planned and financed by the different subsidiaries. In most of the subsidiaries operating in developing countries, pricing of intra-firm technological transactions has little to do with the actual or planned R & D expenditures, and is purely profit. This can be explained either by the nature of know-how as a commodity, or by the actual importance of LDCs in the planning of global R & D activities.

The most promising policy initiatives taken in this field in Latin America have dealt mostly with the non-technological factors playing a role in these intra-firm transactions, and steps have been taken in the right direction, particularly in the case of the Andean Pact. Little has been done to tackle the question of what price should be paid for the technology received by subsidiaries as a result of global R & D efforts. It is unrealistic to use the situation in inter-firm transactions as a standard of comparison.

It seems that royalty payments in existing transactions are being reduced, though little comprehensive information is available to assess the effects of such new policies in Latin America. Regarding future agreements, the reaction of technology suppliers is still not clear, though the elasticity of supply clearly differs among sectors and countries.

On the question of restrictive business practices in intra-firm transactions, the approach of many host governments has clearly been short-sighted. Instead of merely declaring illegal formal restrictions in contracts, it is better to transform restrictions into commitments to achieve specific policy targets. And there are virtually no policies on restrictive practices that may have a really serious effect, i.e., those carried out by subsidiaries in a host market as a result of the technology received.

It is clear that the subject of pricing of intra-firm technologccal transactions requires much more attention. Some of the basic questions on which research should be concentrated are:

(a) What has been the importance, by sectors and by importing countries, of US and non-US originated intra-firm technological transactions?

(b) What prices have been paid by intra-firm and inter-firm technological transactions in similar industries in developing and developed countries?

(c) How are R & D expenditures planned and financed — among different subsidiaries — in TNCs?

(d) What are the specific non-technological factors influencing the price of intra-firm technological transactions, particularly in developing countries?

(e) How can concrete policy proposals be designed by developing countries to pay for intra-firm technology transactions?

The little we know on these questions suggests that these are not only interesting academic issues, but also matters relevant to the improvement of the policy frameworks in which the transfer of technology to developing countries has been taking place.

NOTES

*   The author is a staff member of UNCTAD. The views expressed are his own and not necessarily those of the organisation.

1   The data under consideration have been estimated on the basis of balance of payments statistics. Only film rentals have been excluded. Otherwise, the

receipts and payments are the result of formal transfer of technological contracts signed by TNCs with subsidiaries, or with independent parties, or between independent business firms. The limitations of the data are well explained in the Survey of Current Business, December 1973, p.15. The figures refer to all sectors. However, in the US Senate Report, it is mentioned that in 1966, 61% of the net receipts belonged to the manufacturing sector. See US Senate, *Implications of Multinational Firms for World Trade and Investment and for US Trade and Labor*, Washington, 1973, p.600.

2   The flow of intra-firm royalties coming from Latin America to the US was (in $ millions):

1970 : 264	1975 : 389
1971 : 281	1976 : 330
1972 : 272	1977 : 333
1973 : 361	1978 : 330
1974 : 415	

Inter-firm royalties have been growing steadily but slowly from $52 million in 1973 to $81 million in 1978. See *Survey of Current Business* (March issues).

3   See F. Almeida Biato, E.A.A. Guimaraes and M.H. Poppe de Figueiredo, *A Transferencia de Tecnologia no Brasil*, IPEA, Brasilia 1973, Table VI.8.

4   See Daniel Chudnovsky *et al, Aspectos economicos de la importación de tecnologia en la Argentina en 1972*, INTI, Buenos Aires, 1974, Table 3. In the case of Mexico, the proportion of technological payments accounted for TNCs was 79.8% in 1971 (F. Fajnzylber y T. Martinez Tarragó, *Las empresas transnacionales*, FCE, México, 1976, p.325). In the case of Peru, foreign firms accounted for 52% of royalty payments in 1974 (see ITINTEC, *Efecto del proceso de importacion de tecnologia en el Peru*, 1971/74). However, it is not mentioned how much of these payments are directed to affiliated companies and how much to independent suppliers. In Brazil, payments by subsidiaries of TNCs to independent suppliers accounted for 21% of total payments, and in Argentina they represented 19% of the total.

5   See United Nations, *Transnational Corporations in World Development: A Re-examination*, E/C.10/38, 1978, p.279.

6   Royalty rates were defined as royalty payments divided by sales under licence minus imports coming from the licensor. They were calculated for all contracts on the basis of the actual payments. The average reflects agreements with a variety of payment clauses (lump sum, percentage of sales, fixed amount), contracts with royalties and no sales under licence (during the period of construction, for example), or arrangements with sales under licence without royalties (in trademark agreements, for example).

7   See S.K. Fung and J.E. Cassiolato, *The International Transfer of Technology to Brazil through Technology Agreements – Characteristics of the Government Control System and the Commercial Transactions*, Center for Policy Alternatives MIT, Cambridge, Mass., May 1976, Table 3.25.

8   See S.M. Robbins and R.B. Stobaugh, *Money in the Multinational Enterprise*, Longman, London, 1974, pp.88-90.

9   Many technological contracts between parent companies and affiliates establish a standard royalty rate, e.g., 5% on the whole output of the

subsidiary. The amount actually remitted may be lower and will vary according to the business cycle, the general policy of the TNC, and so on. It is, however, worth noticing that this rate may easily be half the amount of the declared profits of the subsidiary.

10 See C.V. Vaitsos, *Intercountry Income Distribution and Transnational Enterprises*, The Clarendon Press, Oxford, 1974, ch. VI.

11 *op. cit.*, p.601.

12 *op. cit.*, p.432.

13 See S.K. Fung and J.E. Cassiolato, *op. cit.*, pp.59-61, for the reasons why, even in cases where royalties and profits are treated in the same way for fiscal purposes, foreign companies prefer the use of royalties.

9.
ASPECTS OF TRANSFER PRICING IN MACHINERY MARKETS
CHARLES COOPER

I INTRODUCTION
Two conditions are necessary for transfer pricing between firms in a transaction. First, one of the firms must dominate in some way: for example, it may be a parent company in a transaction with its subsidiary, or a licensor dealing with its licencee. Usually, dominance comes from having some particular monopolistic advantage (see Vaitsos 1974, ch.1).

Secondly, the dominant firm must be able to restrict the market options of its partner, and to use this to set itself up as sole supplier of various inputs, or sole purchaser of outputs. Government policy on transfer pricing across national frontiers is primarily concerned to ensure that such imperfect 'tied' markets are not used as a hidden means of expatriating income which might otherwise have accrued locally, or as a means of pre-empting taxable income by claiming it in forms which are not taxable.

Machinery is frequently an important input sold by parent firms to subsidiaries, and licensors to licencees. Like any other input, machinery can be used for transfer pricing if a dominant firm can 'tie' markets for it. To control this, policy makers need standards to measure prices against, and guidelines to the circumstances in which tied markets are likely to exist.

Section II of this paper examines aspects of price formation in machinery markets, to see how far theoretical considerations can provide norms about what prices 'should be'. Its conclusions are mostly pessimistic, certainly as far as finding norms are concerned. Section III examines how the organisation of machine markets provides motive and opportunity for transfer pricing. It suggests that empirical understanding of market organisation is necessary for policy and gives at least some rough and ready approaches to the control of transfer pricing.

133

II   SOME GENERAL POINTS ON THE VALUE OF MACHINERY

Under conditions of general equilibrium, the value of a machine can be specified without ambiguity. It is given by the stream of future revenues, net of variable costs, which the machine will yield, discounted at the equilibrium rate of interest and summed. When competition is perfect in all markets, this aggregate value will exactly equal the supply price of the machine, and there will be 'no-profit' equilibrium. If, for example, the supply price of machines were less than the discounted sum of future net revenues, machine users would earn profits above the equilibrium rate of interest. There would be new entrants into the market for final output, whose price would fall, whilst the increased demand for machines would drive their prices up until they equalled the (somewhat lower) discounted net revenue stream. The rate of interest also would adjust.

Obviously, the assumptions that have to be met for general equilibrium are strenuous, especially those needed for specifying machine value. They imply that machine users should be certain about the future in ways that are inherently improbable: they must have certain knowledge of all relevant future prices. Amongst other things, these depend on future cost-reducing innovations for their final output, as well as on innovations which might affect the relative prices of other outputs, and so the demand for their own. Such events cannot be foretold with certainty. An implication is that machine life is uncertain: machines are replaced when unit variable costs are higher than total unit costs on new machinery; innovations which bring down total unit costs and prices obviously hasten replacement,[1] but are difficult to foresee.

These uncertainties about the price effects of future innovations are sufficient to disrupt the simple relationship between future net revenues and the supply price of machinery.

In the face of uncertainty, the amount that potential users are willing to pay for a machine depends on the expected value of the net revenues it may generate, if users are risk-neutral, or on the expected utility of net revenue, if users are risk averse. At any given machine price, demand will be less than under equilibrium conditions. Any change in conditions affecting subjective evaluation of uncertainties about the future will change the equilibrium position in machine markets. Even a modest concession to economic realities leads to considerable ambiguity about the valuation of machinery. *Ex post*, the supply price of machines will always differ from the discounted stream of net revenues. Aside from questions of sub-optimality,[2] this poses considerable practical difficulties about the interpretation of any given price.

In this sense, there is always a puzzle about what the price of a machine 'should be'. The general equilibrium ideal value is no good as a practical norm, because it is not observable. The cost of producing machinery is no guide, partly because it usually varies with the level of output and the equilibrium output is unknown, and partly because it includes a private opportunity cost of capital which is non-optimal. Above all, there are second best problems: it is not clear what normative meaning can be given to an equilibrium price when the rest of the economy is non-optimal.

Puzzles about the value of machines are general, but especially acute in two practically important cases: in the case of innovative machines and in the case of second-hand machines.

The problems about the price of innovative machines are related to the nature of private incentives to innovate in a market economy. These depend on the innovator being able to exclude others, particularly competitors, from the technical knowledge he may acquire through his investment in innovation (see Arrow 1962, for a discussion of the implications for optimal investment in, and use of, technical knowledge.) If there is no exclusion, imitation will be immediate and, presuming a competitive industry, a new no-profit equilibrium will be reached which will prevent the innovator from recovering his costs. Exclusion, on the other hand, permits monopolistic pricing and consequently a possibility of meeting innovative costs.

To simplify matters, consider a machine innovation in an initially competitive industry, which consists simply in reducing costs of production of a machine, without altering its operating characteristics.[3] The highest price the appropriating machine innovator can charge for it is either the monopoly price, or the pre-innovation competitive price for the machine, depending on which is lower (see Arrow 1962). The innovator may charge one of these prices, or a lower price. For example, if the probability of imitation increases with the price charged for the machine, an innovator who seeks to maximise expected utility will charge a price below the monopoly price and conceivably below a pre-innovation competitive price. Price war may also be an option for the innovator.

Whatever he chooses, the innovator who appropriates successfully will get some temporary profit. There are two points to note about this. First, there is no economic mechanism to ensure that the discounted sum of the net profit stream he obtains will equal innovation costs. These are independently determined, the first by demand and supply conditions in product markets, and the second by research and development costs or engineering costs. Generally, one might expect that successful innovators obtain a discounted net profit above innovation costs, especially in the conditions of uncertainty that customarily surround innovations.[4] Thus, even if innovation costs are counted in as fixed costs of production of machinery, the prices charged for innovative machinery will be higher than the competitive costs of producing it (supposing these can be determined), and consequently there will be ambiguities about the value of the machinery. Its private value to the innovator is greater than the social opportunity costs of producing it, and there is no obvious way they can be reconciled without undermining the incentive to innovate.

There are also ambiguities about the valuation of second-hand machinery. Before discussing them, however, there is a point to consider about the relationship between amortisation and the value of second-hand machinery.

If there is certainty about future prices and costs, machine life is known in advance, and amortisation can spread over the machine life in some appropriate way. In practice, of course, this is not possible and firms amortise fixed assets over some conventional or roughly estimated life (moreover, the rate of amortisation is used by governments as an instrument of fiscal policy). It is not surprising, therefore, that the economic life of machinery is quite often longer and sometimes a great deal longer, than the period of full amortisation. No real conclusions can be drawn from this. It merely means that the machine was amortised 'too quickly' in some sense, so that lower net revenues were accounted in the earlier part of its life than would have been, had it been possible to foresee machine life and amortise more evenly over the whole of it. It does not follow, as is sometimes suggested, that when a machine is fully amortised, its proper value is its value as scrap. It is true that the machine owner will have recovered his initial outlay on it, but nevertheless, so long as the machine is expected to yield future net revenues above variable costs whose discounted sum is greater than scrap value, it will continue to have value in use to its owner, and he will incur costs if he relinquishes it.

However, even when it is accepted that the private value of old machinery to its owner is the discounted value of the rents it is expected to yield above variable costs, there still remain difficulties about pricing, especially in international transactions. (The following points are discussed *in extenso* in Cooper and Kaplinsky, 1974, pp.23-60, and 129-42.)

Suppose that the value of an old vintage machine in use is P, given a price level for final output set by total unit costs of 'best practice' machinery (Salter 1966). P, which is assumed above scrap-value, is the minimum price at which the present owner of the machine can afford to part with it, and is specified for the particular factor price ratio ruling in the economy.

Next, suppose that an entrepreneur from a lower-wage, higher-interest rate (Third World) economy, thinks of buying the old vintage machine. We can then find a price P*, which is the highest price the entrepreneur can afford to pay for it, given total unit costs of production with best practice machines, at the high interest/low wage factor price combination in the Third World country. It can be shown that P*, the maximum the Third World entrepreneur can pay for the old machine, is always greater than P, the minimum its present owner can expect for it*[5] (Cooper and Kaplinsky 1974, Appendix 2; Netherlands Economic Institute 1958). In short, the private value of used old vintage machines will in general be higher at the factor price ratios of developing countries than the value of the machinery to its advanced-country owner — a straightforward consequence of persistent factor price differences, i.e., of 'imperfection'.

In the comparatively slight analytic literature on second-hand machinery markets, it is typically assumed that demand for old vintage machines by developing-country businessmen is limited and occasional, so that prices for it will not be pushed upwards because its value in use in a high interest economy is greater (see for example, Sen 1962). There is some empirical evidence that markets for second-hand machines are 'thin' in this way. It does not follow, however, that thin markets prevent prices from rising above P. Precisely because of thin markets, many transactions are done by bargaining between one buyer and one seller, and prices are made between the buyers' and sellers' limits.

Once again, then, there is ambiguity about what the price of a machine 'should be'. There are a number of other problems about second-hand machinery markets — especially problems of risk and uncertainty (see Cooper and Kaplinsky 1974) and of 'asymmetric information' (sellers know more about particular machines than buyers; see Akerlof 1976).

Where do these arguments lead? Their main implication is clear: in economic reality, it is difficult to say what the price of a machine should be: in other words, to find a norm for judging prices that are actually charged. Theory has something to say on the matter, but not very much, and hardly anything that is a practical help to policy makers.

Take the simple case of open-market transactions in a non-innovative machine. There is uncertainty about future prices. This means that *ex post* we might find out that the discounted value of returns to a machine buyer is considerably above the supply price of the machines. We cannot conclude very much about the 'fairness' of the transaction from this. It may be that the transaction would not have taken place at any higher machine price than was actually charged, because *ex ante* the buyer may have perceived the machines as a risky investment. Indeed, in the event, some machine buyers may have made losses. We can no more say of the losers that they were cheated by being charged too much for the machine, than we can say of the winners that they cheated the sellers. It is hard to make any judgment at all.

There are similar problems about innovative machines. If an innovative machine maker is found to charge prices well above the competitive costs of producing a machine we cannot say his prices are 'unfair': he may or may not have covered the costs of the innovation. An *irreducible* requirement for innovation in a market economy is that there should be a prospect of 'super-normal' profit, and we cannot make much comment when 'super-normal' profit materialises. Even if the innovative machine-makers' profits turn out to be very high *ex post*, it is hard to comment on theoretical grounds. It may be that a small prior probability that profits would be very high was necessary to induce him to innovate in the first place — because the risks of failure may have seemed high at the time. It is true, of course, that appropriation of knowledge and the monopoly power it confers are very blunt instruments for inducing innovations. They may induce all manner of technological advances of high private profitability but negligible social value. Equally, they may permit levels of profitability largely in excess of what was required to induce the innovation — even on the most pessimistic assumptions by the most risk-averse firms. The difficulty is that it is extremely hard to say, after the event, whether such and such a level of profit was or was not necessary to induce a particular innovation in the first place, and consequently whether the future incentive to make risky (but conceivably desirable) innovations will be damaged by intervening in the market this time to reduce the profits a firm is getting from an innovation.

An underlying difficulty is that the information and data needed to test observed prices is usually inaccessible or unverifiable, or both. Second-hand machinery, for example, may turn out to give low rates of output and be privately unprofitable at the price paid for it, or indeed at any price above scrap-value. But these facts do not necessarily speak for themselves, even if they may create some presumptions. To make a judgment about the price which was actually charged, one requires knowledge about the circumstances (including claims made by the seller), which is commonly hard to get, if not totally inaccessible, and even harder to verify.

From a practical standpoint, these arguments lead to somewhat pessimistic views about verifying machine prices in general, and monitoring transfer pricing in particular.

III ORGANISATION OF 'TIED MARKETS' FOR MACHINERY

This pessimism about finding theoretical norms of practical use is neither a basis for nihilism about theory itself, nor need it lead to the conclusion that it is impossible to monitor transfer pricing.

Theory is practically useful — indeed essential — to policy, insofar as it gives the basis for arguments about why prices are what they are. It is always a problem for policy makers to judge whether the reasons are 'admissible' or not — but one cannot make the judgment at all if the arguments are not clear.

Nor does the lack of a theoretical norm mean that there is nothing to be done about transfer pricing. A more positive response is obviously possible. It is simply that the difficulty of evaluating prices in the abstract, means that policy makers should attach special importance to analysing the *organisation* of transactions. If we understand the organisational context of particular machine sales, it is often possible to say (a) whether a motive for 'overpricing' or transfer pricing of machines is likely to exist, and (b) whether necessary conditions exist for firms to accomplish such pricing objectives. If motive and opportunity exist, and there is also some evidence that machine prices are higher, say, than in some other transaction, there are grounds for demanding a particular justification for the prices that are actually charged. Of course, it is possible that the justification may be hard to test for all the reasons we have discussed — and some 'pure' judgments may be unavoidable; but it is possible at least to take a systematic approach to making judgments.

From the policy maker's point of view the problem is that many machinery transactions *are* done in contexts where both motive and opportunity exist for adjusting machine prices. This applies particularly to intra-firm machinery sales, and sales under licence agreements between more or less independent firms, where parent company or licensor is able to 'tie' the machinery inputs needed by the subsidiary or licensor.

The existence of 'tied markets' is not, in itself, evidence that over-pricing of machinery is taking place, since — in principle, at least — tying can have other motives. Dominant firms have an interest in the commercial success of their subsidiaries or licencees and may insist on their using specified machinery, so as to reduce perceived risks or safeguard the quality of output. Tying may also be unavoidable for technical reasons — when the dominant firm is the only source of equipment for a highly differentiated output. In general, though, tied markets often create conditions for transfer pricing, and motives exist for dominant firms to do it. What are the motives?

When recipient firms (licensors or subsidiaries) are oligopolistic or monopolistic, the overpricing of machinery is a method for a supplying firm to establish a lien on the future profits of the firm it is supplying.[6] The recipients' profits are reduced because of the larger investment cost it has to cover. When the recipient is an independent licencee, the matter is straightforward enough: overpricing machinery is simply an alternative method to others, like royalty payments, for example, for getting a return on the licence agreement. It usually has tax advantages (when royalties are taxable, for instance), and it generally has the advantage of being less risky than forms of return which depend on the future commercial success of the licencee's project. Suppliers may trade-off between higher but uncertain future gains and smaller but less risky gains from overpricing machines.

Things are somewhat more complex when the recipient is a wholly-owned subsidiary (or when the supplying firm has equity holdings in the recipient). In this case, overpriced machinery reduces net profits that would have accrued to the dominant firm anyway. Nevertheless, dominant firms may have good reasons for preferring to take profits by pricing up machinery: firstly, it reduces the amount declared for taxation in the recipient country; secondly, it evades restrictions on expatriation of profits. In addition, in the setting up of some joint ventures, the value of overpriced machinery may be used to determine the equity holding of the dominant supplying firm, which is increased in proportion to the degree of overpricing. This is an option on the use of untaxed pre-empted profits which dominant firms may choose to exercise, particularly if it offers the 'external economies' of increased control.

So much for motives that can lead to transfer pricing (except for some special aspects of second-hand machinery discussed later). We look next at how the organisation of tied sales creates opportunities for it.

The variety of tied-machinery transactions is considerable, and we cannot discuss all of them. We shall illustrate that it is relevant and useful to examine the organisation of transactions by a brief account of three types of tied-machinery transaction. These are transactions in which:

1. the dominant firm sub-contracts for the supply of machinery to the new undertaking;
2. the dominant firm is vertically integrated and produces the machinery itself;
3. the dominant firm supplies some of its used machinery.

The 'sub-contracting' case is mostly straightforward. When a dominant firm insists on sub-contracting particular machine makers, this is usually just a means of ensuring that particular types of machinery are used to reduce risks. There may, of course, be pricing problems — for example, if there is collusion between a licensor and his chosen machine suppliers, or if the machinery is an innovation appropriated by the licensor and produced on exclusive contract by the machine maker. Usually, however, the opportunities for transfer pricing when machinery supply is sub-contracted are not very considerable — and since the independent machine makers will ordinarily produce similar equipment for sale on open markets, there are some external checks on prices (be they ever so empirical).[7]

Matters are more complicated when the dominant firm is vertically integrated and itself produces machinery. Tied sales of this kind create opportunities for transfer pricing. These depend on the nature of the machinery. The scope for transfer pricing is obviously least if the machines are standard industrial equipment, sold widely on open markets by other machine making firms. The open market prices give some sort of check. More commonly, however, the vertically integrated firm's machinery is differentiated from machines on the open market.

Differentiation may be comparatively trivial: for example,

assembly-line equipment for consumer durables may be adapted in simple ways for particular products; or it may be profound: when the firm has appropriated a machine innovation. Assembly lines, for instance, *may* be highly innovative. Obviously, the more the machinery is differentiated, the greater the opportunities for transfer pricing.

The motives for overpricing discussed earlier work as well in the case of second-hand machinery as in the case of innovated or differentiated new equipment. Second-hand machinery, however, is particularly flexible in the opportunities it offers for transfer pricing in 'tied' sales, because of the difficulties of evaluating the price charged for it. The state of amortisation of the equipment is, as we have seen, hardly any guide to its value in use. Moreover, even if the equipment is known to be ready for scrapping — 'bought from the scrapyard' as it were — and yet is sold at a price above scrap-value, it need not follow that the price is in some sense unfair. Plainly this indeterminacy, plus the fact that the range within which the price of second-hand equipment may be expected to fall [P, P*] is in itself hard to specify empirically, leaves open many opportunities. So does the fact that any price monitoring agency (or buyer) is bound to have less knowledge about the real value of the equipment in use than the seller (the asymmetry problem).

So, opportunities for overpricing second-hand equipment in tied sales are often considerable, and motives for doing so can exist, as for any other machinery transaction.

However, even if there is no overpricing of second-hand equipment, tied sales of it to wholly-owned subsidiaries have some advantageous features in certain circumstances, because of anomalies of amortisation. Let us suppose a parent company 'sells' old vintage machinery to its wholly-owned subsidiary in another (high interest/lower wage) economy. Assume the equipment is fully amortised in the 'home' economy, and, to keep matters clear, assume also that a 'fair' price is imputed, lying somewhere between the second-hand pricing limits we have discussed — perhaps, even, at the lower limit. In this circumstance, there is an advantage to the parent company if the subsidiary is permitted by the company law of the recipient country, to amortise the newly installed, but used equipment at its purchase price. The effect of this double amortisation is that the subsidiary is able to accumulate amortisation funds out of pre-tax profits. Overall, double amortisation reduces the tax-burden on profits from what it would have been on any more rational calculus (viz., that a firm should not be able to cover a given outlay more than once). It does not depend on overpricing of equipment, but is nevertheless, an aspect of transfer pricing.

This question does not arise in tied sales to independent licencees. The licencee must obviously recover the resources it put forward to buy the machinery and so amortise it, even if it has already been fully amortised by its previous owner. In this case the amortisation charge is not a contribution to untaxed profit for the machine owner. The asymmetry arises because of the arbitrary conventions used for writing off equipment, in conditions of irreducible uncertainty about machine life.

IV CONCLUDING REMARKS

This paper puts two main arguments. The first is that economic theory provides little practical guidance about what machinery prices should be. Consequently, it does not provide norms for people who are concerned with transfer pricing problems. Secondly, the practical response to this situation is to examine how machinery transactions, especially 'tied' transactions, are organised in practice. The structural context of machinery transactions may indicate whether motives and opportunities exist for transfer pricing.

The discussion of the organisation of tied sales of innovative and second-hand equipment is meant to illuminate some of these motives and opportunities in two particularly important cases.

The actual business of evaluating the prices that are charged must be left to somewhat arbitrary empiricism — in the form of comparing whatever prices can be determined in various imperfect markets — and to making judgments about the arguments that are used to justify actual prices. Transfer pricing policy in machinery markets can only be based on an appeal to the notion of the 'most favoured customer' as a practical norm. It then requires an evaluation of reasons for departures from this norm in particular deals. There is arbitrariness about this, but it is decidedly better than nothing.

NOTES

1 See Salter 1966, for a classic discussion of conditions for replacement in a vintage model of technical change.
2 There are of course conditions in which optimality can be achieved with uncertainty, but they are very exacting (Arrow 1964; Debreu 1959). We shall not be concerned with them here.

3 More elaborate assumptions — though more realistic — do not add much to the point.
4 Suppose an innovation, costing present value £R to make, is perceived to have probability of successful commercial application of Π, and suppose that in the event of success, the innovator anticipates a stream of net profit whose present value is V. Then a risk-neutral innovator will undertake the project if $(1 - \Pi) R + \Pi V \geq 0$, neglecting the uncertainties attaching to R and V. If Π is small, we will obviously require $V > R$ for the project to go ahead. So the project will go ahead only if the innovator anticipates that his quasi-monopoly will yield some $V^1 > V > R$. If the innovation is successful, therefore, the innovator will get a return substantially above innovation costs. One of the practical puzzles about such high *ex post* returns is to know to what extent they can be justified by the risks involved in the innovation (in which case administrative restrictions on them may reduce *future* incentives to innovate), as opposed to being simply an 'arbitrary' outcome of monopoly power, i.e., $V^1 - V$ in the above.
5 This assumes similar machine life in the high and low wage economies.
6 If recipient firms are competitive, overpricing means that the monopolistic supplier mops up the consumer surplus that would have accrued through lower final output prices.
7 However, even though there are no pricing problems, there may be others — like exclusion of local machine makers or engineers, which curtails their opportunity for accumulating skills (see Cooper and Maxwell 1975).

BIBLIOGRAPHY

Akerlof, G.A. (1976), 'The Market for "Lemons": Quality Uncertainty and the Market Mechanism', Quarterly Journal of Economics no.360, vol. XC, no.3, August.
Arrow, K.J.K. (1962), 'Economic Welfare and the Allocation of Resources for Inventions', *Rate and Directions of Inventive Activity*, National Bureau of Economic Research, Princeton University Press.
Cooper, C.M. and Kaplinsky, R. (1974), *Second-hand Equipment in a Developing Country*, ILO.
Cooper, C.M. and Maxwell, P.I. (1975), *Machinery Suppliers and the Transfer of Technology to Latin America*, Organisation of American States, mimeograph.
Netherlands Economic Institute (1958), *Second-hand Machines and Economic Development*, mimeo, Rotterdam, May.
Salter, W.E.G. (1966), *Productivity and Technical Change*, Oxford University Press.
Sen, A.K. (1962), 'On the usefulness of Used Machines', *Revue of Economics and Statistics,* August.
Vaitsos, C.V. (1974), *Intercountry Income Distribution and Transnational Enterprises*, The Clarendon Press, Oxford.

PART THREE
Transfer Pricing and Control

(A)   General Strategies

10.
TRANSFER PRICING AND ITS CONTROL: ALTERNATIVE APPROACHES
ROBIN MURRAY

TRANSFER PRICING AND THE STATE

By transfer pricing I refer to the price assigned to goods, services and finance as they circulate within a planned system of production. We are concerned with transfer pricing in one such system — the private corporation — and I have referred to it as a 'planned system' because the range over which planned, non-independent relations take place does not always coincide with the range of formal ownership. Some large corporations, for example certain conglomerates, are formally single entities, but in substance are mere aggregations of independent parts which treat with each other as if they were autonomous entities. In other cases, a large firm may have a set of satellite firms which are nominally independent but effectively part of a single planned system bound in by detailed contracts. The prices at which 'commodities' circulate between them are planned prices. Since our concern is with transfer prices as distinguished from market prices, it is the zone of planned relations rather than the formal zone of ownership which we need to examine. By emphasising the planned system rather than ownership, I hope to provide another way into the discussion of what proportion of ownership is sufficient to qualify international trade flows as 'intra-firm trade'.[1]

Transfer pricing as defined above is associated with the growth of large firms. But it is striking that the literature on the subject substantially post-dates the early waves of corporate concentration. The first article, written by an accountant, appeared in 1929, and it was not until the 1950s that there was any extensive discussion in the managerial literature on intra-firm pricing, and not until the 1960s that international transfer pricing became an issue.[2] In part, this may reflect the fact that decentralisation (via divisionalisation and control through profit centres) became a more sensitive issue with the increasing possibility of centralisation that was opened up by the development of information and communication technology. In part, it may be the result of the

147

growth of overhead joint costs within the large corporation. Certainly the increased concern with international transfer pricing reflects the discontinuous post-war growth of international firms, and the sensitivity of governments, particularly in underdeveloped countries, to the possibilities open to these firms of by-passing exchange and other forms of control.

The literature is now substantial. There are perhaps 200 books and articles in the English language relating to the subject. I want to distinguish five different approaches which are apparent in this general body of work, paying particular attention to theoretical differences between them:

1. *Optimisation in a decentralised firm* — This approach has been concerned with the effects of different methods of transfer pricing on resource allocation within the firm treated as an economy. The concepts used are those of marginal analysis, and the problems discussed — particularly in the business economic and accounting literature — are those familiar to marginal micro-economics more generally: problems of optimisation with technological or demand interdependence, with differential transaction costs, with imperfect competition, and so on. Some authors, such as Hirschleiffer, even introduce the central management, as public finance theory introduces the state, to tax some departments, and give bounties to others in order to surmount imperfections.[3] The framework can quite easily be extended to a general equilibrium analysis with two stages of production. It may also be extended to an analysis of the implications of transfer pricing for international resource allocation, though there have been few contributions in this field.[4] At its most abstract, this general approach is distinguished by its concern to assess, against the background of a perfectly competitive economic system, the effects of differing 'imperfections' — whether they be indivisibilities, externalities, imperfect information, or 'arbitrary' state interventions — and the decision rules for transfer pricing which 'optimise' profits in these imperfect conditions.

2. *Optimisation in a centralised firm* — Whereas the first approach discusses transfer pricing within a divisionalised firm, a second body of business literature has concentrated on transfer pricing within a centralised firm. Here prices are not set *ex ante*, and decentralised divisions left to profit maximise in relation to them, but they are set to determine the distribution of income within the firm. With the decentralised firm, optimum transfer pricing may allow divisional profits to be taken as a measure of performance.[5] In the centralised firm profits are no such

measure. Rather, they are varied to determine the flow of funds within the firm, and minimise external levies on the firm as a whole. This is not an issue for domestic firms where there is freedom of capital movement within the country, and where taxation is levied on consolidated income. But it is, of course, a major issue for international firms. For this reason the discussion of transfer pricing in centralised firms has been largely confined to a lengthening literature on international financial management. This runs from general optimising models, like those of Rutenberg, to detailed tax avoidance manuals, such as that of Edwardes-Ker.[6] We should also include here the studies of international firms' practices, such as those carried out by Business International, Schulman and Arpen, though these are not confined to centralised firms.[7] Whereas the literature on decentralised firms concentrates on differing conditions in the private sphere of the firms' production and marketing structures, the literature on centralised firms mainly deals with optimising in conditions of differing state requirements: tax rates, exchange controls, tariff duties, financing obligations, and so on. As a number of authors have pointed out, these differences in external 'public' conditions imply quite different sets of transfer prices to those dictated by differing internal conditions, a difficulty which can be overcome by keeping two sets of books.[8]

3. *Reclaiming the market by account* — The first two approaches both consider transfer pricing from the perspective of corporate optimisation. The remaining ones look at the problem from the viewpoint of public policy. How should nation states, faced with these non-market prices, assess their validity for various areas of state control? One suggested method has been to try and calculate what a market price should be in these non-market situations. This has been the course pursued by customs and taxation departments in developed countries, by the OECD Committee on International Investment and Multinational Enterprises, and by some sections of the United Nations.[9] In the words of the Brussels definition of customs value:

> For the purpose of levying duties of customs, the value of any goods imported for home consumption shall be taken to be the normal price, that is to say, the prices which they would fetch at the time when the duty becomes payable on a sale in the open market between buyer and seller independent of each other.[10]

The problem has been how to determine such a normal price, and the literature and conferences which follow this approach have been concerned above all with establishing rules of thumb and guidelines for estimating supposed 'arm's-length prices'. They have also been concerned with harmonising these guidelines between countries, in order to prevent double taxation, and with developing double taxation treaties between countries to regularise such agreements. There are some similarities between this approach and the first one concerned with corporate decentralisation, though in this case the consideration is the extraction and distribution of tax revenue (or duties) internationally, rather than with optimising allocation within the firm. For both, however, there is some notion of a perfect market price which the authority — central management or state — should try and 'reclaim by account'.

4. *Reclaiming the market through competition* — An alternative approach is to restore free market prices by attacking the conditions of abusive transfer pricing, namely the monopoly power of international firms. This approach is associated with the Manufactures Division of UNCTAD, and is directed particularly at the use of transfer pricing to expatriate super-profits from underdeveloped countries.[11] If anti-monopoly legislation was more vigorously enforced internationally, and if the countries concerned restricted high rates of effective protection, monopolistic franchises, the use of restrictive contracts and licenses, there would be no super profits to transfer. This approach has not yet dealt with the problems of funding head-office deficit spending from third world 'normal profits', nor with international tax avoidance when such avoidance may be an important part of international competition,[12] but it certainly offers a distinct strategy for governments to follow in order to limit 'abusive' transfer pricing.

5. *Beyond the market to bilateral monopoly bargaining* — A growing number of authors have taken the monopoly analysis to transfer pricing further.[13] Their approach can be summarised as follows:

   (a) the growth of international firms has created large zones of administered economic systems, inside and outside of which the notion of a free market has little if any meaning.

   (b) their size and power is asymmetrical to that of many third world countries, and is based on the monopoly of technology and know-how, and a protected home market.

   (c) this power is used by the firms to transfer large amounts of surplus from the 'periphery' to the 'core' countries, where it is used to fund further research and development, and thereby reproduce their international monopoly of knowledge.

(d) it is impossible to simulate or reintroduce a free market in these circumstances; what can be done is to reduce some of the monopoly conditions which third world countries have themselves created (patent laws, restrictive contracts), and strengthen the power of states in their dealings with international firms (inter-country co-operation, as in the Andean Pact), consolidation of government departments dealing with foreign firms, development of alternative source of international supply, and of domestic technological capabilities.

(e) on the basis of the above, to bargain with international firms over the conditions of entry, the level of transfer prices, and of the tax offtake.

What is distinctive is that the model of perfect competition is abandoned, and the state's role changes from a guardian or imposer of competitive conditions, to an active intervener in a power struggle over the international distribution of surplus.[14] This approach is only tangentially interested in establishing guidelines for the fixing of arm's-length prices. Researchers have been eclectic in establishing bases against which to judge transfer prices. Moreover the relevance of some arm's-length prices — particularly those for technology — are disputed on the grounds that they represent a general monopoly of information preserved by international patent law. Rather, the main concerns have been with identifying the channels used by firms for expatriating funds, and gathering information on world costs and prices (thus eroding one of the key monopoly advantages of international firms), so that restrictions on financial outflows can be more effectively enforced.

Clearly the differences in these approaches is partly one of standpoint. The first represents the standpoint of the central management of a large corporation, the second that of the international firm, the third that of developed country governments, and the fifth that of the governments of the third world. At times the arguments advanced by each, the estimates of the significance of the problem, and the moral codes alluded to can be understood merely as self interest. But at their best, the approaches have theoretical positions which must be examined in their own right. The most notable distinction in this respect is between those approaches which take the free market as the base against which to assess transfer pricing, and the last approach which denies the possibility and even the validity of using a notional free market in this way, and instead argues for a perspective based on power: the state counterpart to the literature on international financial management and tax avoidance.[15]

TRANSFER PRICING AND THE DEVELOPMENT OF CAPITALISM

In order to assess the validity of these approaches, and the soundness of the positions that follow from them — particularly those relating to the place and form of state policy towards pricing — it is necessary to explain how the 'problem' itself arose. All the approaches identify the cause of the 'problem' with the rise of the large/international firm: hence the literature on the stages of corporate growth and the changing structure of the world market,[16] or on the expansion of overseas investment and intra-firm international trade.[17] These have been valuable additions to our understanding of the international economy, and have already forced reassessments of many of the old assumptions and problems of traditional international economic theory: the debates on comparative advantage and the terms of trade, on traditional trade and macro-economic policies, on the theory of regional integration policy, and so on.

I want to suggest an alternative way in to the 'problem' — which may also suggest an alternative way out. Instead of entering via the institutional form of the firm, I want to examine transfer pricing in terms of the changing place of the market in allocating resources or — to put it more specifically — in allocating social labour. In the early period of capitalism, the market was the dominant 'social nexus', the mechanism which bound society together. Commodities, particularly those produced by artisans, had unequivocal costs (predominantly living labour time) and they could be sold individually on the market. It is this feature of the marketability of commodities, rather than the competitive conditions existing on the markets, which is important. The market was *adequate* in measuring the inputs into the specific commodities which were purchased.

Even at this early period there were some goods and services which could not be adequately circulated by the market (as Adam Smith himself recognised). The administration and enforcement of law was one 'service' which could not be produced by private capital and sold as a commodity. Nor, for similar reasons, could armed force. These are examples of public goods from traditional economic theory. They are 'public' because the very character of the 'services' — impartial judgment, preservation of the rights of property — requires that command over them be separated from the power of money as expressed in market demand. The judge, in principle at least, should not sell his judgment to the highest bidder. A private police force would run the danger of being hired to appropriate the property of others, as much as defend what rights already exist. The character of the service 'contradicts' the sale of the service as a commodity. In these cases the market is inadequate as a mechanism for allocating social labour.

A second class of outputs for which the market is inadequate are those whose marginal cost of production, like the use of a road is effectively zero. There may have to be rules about usage, but the actual costs are the fixed costs of the initial investment. While a price can be placed on use in order to recover the fixed investment, that price will contradict the optimum use of the resource, since it will restrict use when the marginal cost of such use is zero. There are problems in short of selling as individual commodities, those things which have been produced jointly. Equally, there are problems with selling commodities individually whose consumption is joint. Here is a third class of outputs.

The above is sufficient acknowledgement to the literature on public goods in its concern with the problems of allocation in sectors where the market is inadequate. What this literature does not do is to place these 'awkward' sectors in historical perspective. Once we do this, it is clear that they have tended to increase with the development of capitalism. Fixed costs have increased, and with them the gap between average and marginal costs. Individual commodities are more and more the outcome of joint production. The cause of this trend is that increases in productivity have been won, in the long run, by increases in mechanisation, organisational scale, and in the extent of preparatory research and development. These are the fixed and joint costs of modern production. In their operation are to be found economies of scale.

The point about this long-run tendency is two-fold. First, the growing gap between marginal and average costs, in the short, medium and even the long run, makes the market problematic as the 'social nexus' for an ever-larger number of commodities. Second, *within* these zones of scale economy production, the market has already been surpassed.

Although each stage of industrial textile production could in principle be owned separately and related through price and free exchange, it has commonly been found much more efficient to collectivise ownership (for instance in the *joint stock company*), place the machines side by side, co-ordinate their plan of production, their throughput, pace, quality control, standards, and dispense with the market until the final product is sold. Buying and selling costs money. It takes time, and introduces uncertainty. The development of specialised instruments demanding co-ordination and synchronisation with others, and the increased possibilities for circulating information and enforcing control more efficiently than through the uncertain abstractions of the market, has meant that the labour of increasing numbers of people is now organised/allocated directly rather than through the mechanism of selling their products individually on the market. I call this the tendency to the direct socialisation of labour.[18]

What I have said is not new. But it is the emphasis which is important for our discussion. For as yet I have hardly mentioned institutions. I have not equated the state with public goods or with directly socialised labour, nor economies of scale with large firms or monopolistic competition. Rather, I have concentrated on the changes in the material characteristics of the processes of production and circulation, and in particular the increasingly problematic role of the market as the main instrument in the allocation of social labour. These changes underly the extension of the state in the capitalist economy, the growth of large and now international firms, and the development of new territorial structures such as the EEC. But if we enter the problem at the institutional level, we are in danger of neglecting the nature of the problem which all these institutions face, public or private, namely commensurability: how can the costs of individual goods and services be measured, and thus equated, with others in a period of increasingly socialised labour.

One thing which particularly concerns us is the changing role of price. If the market is rendered problematic, so necessarily is price. In the era of simple commodity production — or perfect competition, in the formulation of the textbooks — price performed a double function. First, it represented the real transfer of resources from the buyer to the seller, with which the seller could fund production afresh. Money was here a means of payment. Second, the price when compared to other prices served as a sign of both relative efficiency, and 'effective demand'. Money here acts as a unit of account. According to these quantitative signs, the composition of social production would be revised, resources would be shifted. According to the real flow of income embodied in the price, the most efficient producers would be favoured, and the least efficient squeezed. Price thus embodied within it two mechanisms, one of distribution, the other of steering.

What happens with those outputs for whose circulation the market is inadequate? Quite simply the unity of the two functions in price is ruptured. Their effects have to be achieved through other means. In the case of goods which cannot be sold, a new economic principle comes into play: the levy/bounty relation. The goods are now circulated freely, and their costs are paid by raising a levy (voluntary through donation, or forced through taxes or conscription). Since the area over which the levy is raised and the bounty distributed must be defined, there is a tendency for levy/bounty economies to become territorially exclusive.[19] This is the material basis for the nation state.

The levy/bounty relation still leaves open the problem of 'steering'. With states at least, the levy is forced: taxes are not paid according to the benefits the individual taxpayer voluntarily considers he or she is receiving from the state. The key mechanism that has developed as a 'steering' device in advanced capitalist societies is the institution of 'representative government', pivoting on the vote. But this is clearly a much cruder mechanism in the economy's own terms than individual purchasing on the market. Attempts have been made to overcome the problem by reinserting the quantifications of the market into the heart of the levy/bounty economy through cost-benefit analysis. Here individual prices are once more resurrected as signs and linked in to the free exchange sector of the economy (the world market for Little-Mirlees) as a base point for guiding, though not financing, the non-exchange economy. But such attempts must necessarily remain problematic since they seek to introduce prices into an area of the economy which is only organised as it is because price and the market were no longer adequate mechanisms for the circulation of their output.

Large firms are precluded from raising levies for their joint/fixed/overhead/social costs. They may either raise the necessary funds by a single indivisible sale, or by a subvention from an institution capable of levying (the state), or by adding a proportion of the general costs to each commodity sold, that is to say by fixing a price for general 'services' where no individual price unambiguously exists. This may meet the resources requirement of the firm, but it in no way meets the steering requirement. The development of socialised labour/general costs within the firm also serves to rupture the unity of price as distributor and sign which held in the prices of simple commodities.

We are now in a position to look again at the question of transfer pricing. There are two sources of difficulty addressed in the literature. the first — which concerns the managerial literature on transfer pricing in the divisionalised firm — is the problem of steering and incentives within a large organisation. The second — around which the international literature is arranged — is the problem of the allocation of income. The first is concerned with transfer pricing as part of a system of signals, the second with transfer pricing as part of a system of distribution.

TRANSFER PRICING AS SIGN

At this point we need only note one point about the question of pricing within a divisionalised firm. This is that most of the accountants and economists writing on the subject are attempting to 'reclaim the market by account', so that the system of allocation and incentives can operate in the same way as it would do if the divisions were in fact independent. But they are doing this in circumstances where price has, on our previous arguments, become a problematic sign. As Hirschleiffer pointed out, the market price is an adequate sign only when there is a perfectly competitive market together with technological and market independence. If there is technological interdependence, then Hirschleiffer admits there is no solution, and technological interdependence is the very circumstance which has so often led to the growth of the firm in the first place. Author after author examines different rules of thumb — pricing by marginal cost, average cost plus, final price minus, external 'market' price, inter-divisional negotiated price, and so on. Each rule is shown to be deficient because they do not encourage or reflect efficiency in at least some of the departments involved. It is not that these formulae are not adopted. The National Industrial Conference Board study of Interdivisional Pricing showed clearly that they are, since some formula has to be used if a firm is to run on a profit-centre basis.[20] But both accountant and businessman acknowledge their sub-optimality. As the firms who used 'market price' transfer pricing reported to the NICB: they adopted it so that they could satisfactorily appraise divisional performance, identify inefficient operations, and encourage cost reduction. The problem they found, was that it was often difficult to obtain a market price. Here, then, is the essence of the matter.

Few writers dwell on one implication of the impasse: that it may be advisable to abandon the attempt to recreate the perfect market with its neutral prices as a system of assessment and incentive within a single firm. But as Solomon concludes in his book, *Divisional Performance: Assessment and Control:*

> 'The profit spur is not the only way to maintain efficiency. Non-divisionalised businesses are not, invariably, markedly less efficient than those which are divisionally organised and so long as every effort is made to find and use other means of keeping the efficiency of service centres high, resorting to the profit motive for segments of a business where it is not appropriate is likely to do more harm than good.'[21]

Abandonment of the profit centre in favour of direct assessment of performance: this, at least, is one way out of the 'insoluble' problem posed by directly interdependent production for the traditional system of price as sign.

TRANSFER PRICES AND DISTRIBUTION

There is no such solution when it comes to the problem of transfer pricing as part of a system of distribution. For the internal corporate economy there is no difficulty. It owns income wherever it is declared, and it can move real money resources between its component parts at will. There is no necessary link within a firm between the amount declared as income or profit by one part, and the amount available to it for reinvestment.

The problem occurs when there are differential outside claims on income of the component parts. These claims may come from shareholders, workers or governments. In all these cases it matters how the firm distributes profits/income between its affiliates, for on this will depend the total drain of income from the firm as a whole. This is the issue involved in international transfer pricing.

From the firm's point of view the issue is entirely practical: how to adjust transfer pricing to minimise tax, maximise subsidy, reduce exchange and other risks, and so on. It is not just how much profit is declared, but how far net assets are 'exposed', or where liquidity is stored. Since the price of goods is no longer a privileged conduit for the movement of money in the firm, other channels can be used. All forms of intra-firm relations can be classed as transactions and can be given a price: advisory services, blue prints, factoring, insurance, general management, capital goods maintenance and of course the loan of money. Or lump sum charges can be made for brand names, or head office overheads, or future research and development, or simply 'goodwill'. Each command that is made can be given a price, each phone call, letter, meeting attended — any aspect of normal intra-corporate interchange can be set up *as if* it were a transaction. The firm will choose those channels which achieve its ends for the interaffiliate allocation of income, at least cost. This is the subject of the ingenious business literature on international financial management and tax avoidance.

What cannot be claimed is that the resulting international distribution of income is in any way optimal, as some proponents of international business have done. The model in terms of which optimality is judged is that of utilitarian trade theory and the perfect market. The intervention of states to disturb equilibrium prices can only serve to distort, and thus anything (such as transfer pricing) which undermines the power of the state to distort (through tariffs, withholding taxes, exchange controls) will also help to restore optimality. Now, quite apart from the many objections to the free-market optimality model itself — notably those concerned with scale and economies of agglomeration — the undermining of the state's power to tax at the same time undermines a key tenet of this traditional model, which holds that the surplus which has been maximised as the result of the free market can then be redistributed to those who have been extruded from the accumulation process, notably the unemployed or peripheral areas outside the agglomerations. Even were we to assume a tendency for central states to consistently and sufficiently redistribute surplus to the margins of the world economy, the existence of transfer pricing as a means of tax minimisation raises the question of whether the surplus can be appropriated from the sphere of private capital in the first place. The very limits set by international firms to state power to 'interfere' with the perfect market, are also limits to state power to redistribute the results of this perfection.[22]

For international firms, therefore, international transfer pricing is an operational rather than a conceptual problem. For states it is both. The keystone of the levy/bounty economy — the power to levy — is challenged. The power of international firms to shift the location of their declared profits induces individual states to create conditions which will encourage profits to be declared within their borders. It sets state against state, heightening the anarchy of the international economy.

Inter-state competition may take the form of a down bidding of tax rates, duties and controls. The extremes are found in tax havens. They tend to be small, with little production, a small population, weakly organised labour, and a restricted state budget (with low, even zero, military expenditure). With little if any income tax, the main duties tend to be initial start-up dues, and some indirect taxes on expenditure. The infinity point of tax havens is represented by the reef of Minerva.[23] Larger countries have created low-tax enclaves, entrepôts of labour, finance and trade — the export processing and free-trade zones that have spread through competition to more than fifty countries in the semi- and less-developed world. These countries can gain through transfer pricing, gaining necessarily at the expense of others. But it is a non-zero sum gain: what one gains, the other loses more of.

A second type of competition takes the form of tax enforcement, and the more effective control of transfer pricing. While there are areas of collective interest between high-tax countries wishing to restrict the minimising effects of the low, there is also an individual rivalry, since what one high-tax country gains, another may lose. On commentator even sees policy towards the control of transfer pricing as an instrument in the arsenal of trade war.[24] We must keep this discordance in mind when considering both the reasons for tax havens continuing to exist, and the different remaining approaches to transfer pricing control.

Let us recall that the third approach I discussed at the beginning tried to solve the indeterminacy of international profit distribution by resort to the notion of arm's-length prices. This was true of the leading accepted guidelines on customs valuations, and on tax determination by revenue authorities. The problem in both cases is how to establish such a price. The Customs literature shows how problematic contemporary prices, particularly for international trade, can be. It is no longer merely a question of a specified price — say 10p — for an unequivocal commodity: a bag of nails. First, the commodity has to be specified. It may be unique, as in the case of capital goods, new or second-hand. It may be part of a package whose individual use, and therefore value, will depend on its relations to other parts of the package. It may carry with it trade marks, or other distinctive features. In all these cases — cases which increase with time — it will be difficult to establish what a comparable article would be.

Second, the price has to be specified: the currency and its rate

U.S. Selection of Valuation Standards

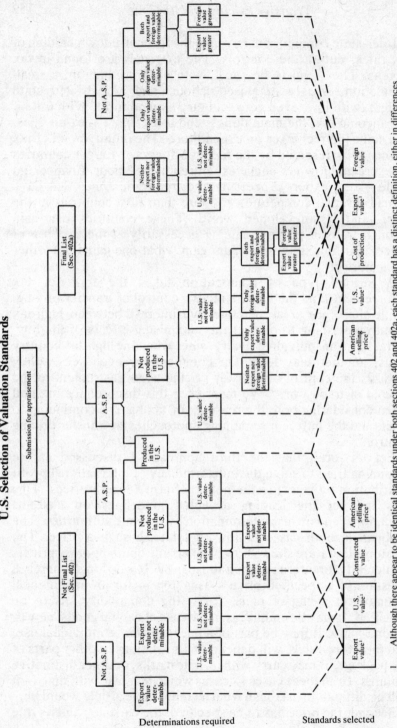

1   Although there appear to be identical standards under both sections 402 and 402a, each standard has a distinct definition, either in differences in wording or interpretation.

Note   The determinations and order of selection of standards for articles subject to A.S.P. valuation under sec. 336 of the Tariff Act of 1930, but not of exchange, the time period of payment, the extent of discounts and rebates; the terms of delivery, the transportation and insurance costs, the market in which a comparable price might be sought. All these considerations render the setting of arm's-length prices by means of other market prices difficult, if not impossible. The Valuation Standards used in the US as of 1973 reveal the difficulties (see diagram). The following are possible 'comparable' prices to which appeal is made: the export value of similar goods in the exporting country either sold or merely offered for sale; the price at which the export good is offered for sale in the domestic market of the exporting country (the foreign value); the price at which similar imported goods are freely sold or offered for sale in the US market (the US value); the price at which similar goods produced in the USA are sold or freely offered for sale in the US market (American Selling Price or ASP). In each case allowances have to be made — added or subtracted — to get the import price, and these deductions are themselves the subject of alternative specification (the US value for section 402a goods, for example, must have deducted from it a commission not exceeding 6%, or profits not exceeding 8% and general expenses not exceeding 8%).[25]

Each of these possible criteria for determining a free-market price can produce very different results. The US Tariff Commission found that to value all goods under Section 402a (where the principal difference was that prices were those offered for sale rather than 'sold or offered for sale', plus the specified percentage reductions) would, according to the guidelines of Section 402, cut import duties by 5%. The Hearings into the International Grain companies, and specifically into alleged claims of price rigging of international markets, in part hinged on whether the grain quotes were for lots sold or merely offered for sale.[26] The EEC have objected strongly to the use of the American Selling Price standard, and said that the complete removal of tariffs as part of the Kennedy Round would only take place if the ASP was abandoned.[27] These examples show the problematic character of a market-price approach to value in international trade, particularly in an era of differentiated products, monopoly restrictions and international firms. As the International Chamber of Commerce commented on the retrogressive method of establishing market prices (a sales-price minus), the results could only be established by a set of completely arbitrary decisions which would result in a bargain between fiscal authorities and the importer into which the concept of the definition of value does not enter.[28]

As far as customs practice is concerned, the US Tariff Commission study reported that US customs rarely used the price of identical or similar goods as a basis for their calculations. The main standard is the purchase price of the goods under discussion (75% of the value of all *ad valorem* imports). The other standard (used in the remainder of the cases) is that based on the cost of production of the goods in question.[29] What is striking in the customs literature, however, is the relative lack of discussion on how these costs are determined. The Dutch require that a royalty be included in the declared value of the good (where it stands to be paid), and the Brussels Definition of Value specifies (Article III) that the value of the right to use a patent, design, or trade mark in respect of imported goods should be covered in their price.[30] Other than these ways of taking account of technology costs, and 'goodwill', there is no public detailed discussion that I have come across on the problems of overhead allocation, embodied know-how, contribution to future R & D and other joint costs.

Inland Revenue literature has been more explicit on costs. Whereas customs valuation has been seen as a problem for all forms of international trade — with intra-firm trade being considered as a form of uncompetitive relation likely to induce a departure from free market prices — the Inland Revenue's concern with international values has from the first been linked with international firms and transfer pricing. As with the guidelines on customs valuation, most developed-country revenue departments take an arm's-length price as the basis of comparison. Maurice Collins' paper submitted to the UN Expert Group on Tax Treaties sets out the approach and procedures clearly. What is evident is that, while the formula for estimating market prices are similar to those used by customs authorities (uncontrolled market price, unrelated third party price, resale price minus, cost plus), there is a less specific discussion than in the customs literature as to which market is the appropriate one (overseas, domestic, export, import, home) and a more detailed consideration of costs.[31]

What is also notable is an uneasiness with all the methods for large classes of taxpayers. Maurice Collins, for instance, suggests that uncontrolled market prices may be suitable for assessing natural produce or mass market manufactured goods but that 'there is clearly a wide range of goods where evidence of such uncontrolled sales is lacking'. The resale price method is easiest to use where the goods are simply re-sold by the purchaser, and least easy to use 'where the goods are processed and incorporated in a manufacture before being resold'. With the cost plus method there are problems of estimating the appropriate profit mark-up, the allocation of joint costs such as start-up advertising, depreciation of capital equipment and administrative overheads. On allocating indirect costs, he writes that 'it does not appear that any general rules can be devised, and the only practicable solution seems to be to adopt a case by case approach'.[32]

This lack of a clear, general set of guidelines is evident in all developed-country experience. In Germany, the courts noted that customs and tax departments' estimates of an arm's-length price for the same transaction may differ, and that there is no basic way in which they can be made to coincide, other than mere factual compromising of the parties. The French Note on transfer pricing of May 1973 acknowledges that the nature of the imported product 'often makes it awkward to use terms of comparison'; that the apportionment of joint research, production, purchasing or sales costs raises 'very difficult problems whenever definite mandatory rules for such apportionment do not exist'; and that turnover, gross proceeds and asset value are all possible bases for use in such apportionments. Similar problems have arisen in the administration of US arm's-length guidelines. In the words of the USIRS: 'US experience has demonstrated that, even with detailed guidelines, the safe-haven rules, and substantial disclosure requirements, an arm's-length profit margin or mark-up is still often an elusive phantom'.[34]

The USIRS put their emphasis on the difficulties of information. The point I want to bring out is the conceptual difficulties. As we saw in the case of private business practice, the problem is that much of the circulation of goods, skill, and knowledge within a firm can no longer be unambiguously priced. What seems an adequate price from one point of view is unsatisfactory from another. This does not apply to all intra-firm transactions. There are some, such as those mentioned by Maurice Collins, where the 'market' price guidelines do give a meaningful basis for comparison. But the more integrated the economic system, the larger the proportion of joint costs, R & D, central administration and capital equipment, the wider the gap between average and marginal costs of production, then the less adequate will be the very concept of the market and an arm's-length price for 'commensurating' costs and results by commodity and division within a firm.

My argument is that these areas of interdependent production are increasing. They carry with them, as a corrolary, an increase in the size of firms, and this very size may further influence the external market price system through different forms of market power. We would thus expect to find the problem of transfer pricing more acute, and more difficult to pin down through comparison with external market prices, the larger the firm.

Arpan found just such a correlation in his study of non-US systems of transfer pricing: the larger the parent firm, the more likely it was to use a cost-oriented system of pricing. The reasons given by the large corporations in question were: (a) that product differentiation often meant that there was no close market equivalent; (b) that their cost systems were more complex than small companies, with larger joint costs, and given sophisticated auditors they could present highly complex and confusing cost formulae to government agents; and (c) they have a significant influence on the market price itself.[35] These points refer to a correlation of size and cost based methods of the corporations themselves, and it is interesting that both the Business International and Conference Board studies report a predominance of cost-oriented systems in US international firms. The fact that large businesses are forced to dispense with market-based systems for their own internal pricing reflects the underlying developments in integrated/non-market systems of production.

Because of this, Revenue Departments are likely to have as much difficulty in using price based formulae as the firms. In the US Treasury Report of the International Cases involving Section 482 it was found that the uncontrolled sales method was used in 46% of the cases of adjusting the transfer pricing of goods. The resale method was used in 5% of the cases, the cost plus in 18% and 31% of the cases were settled by other methods. However, they reported that fewer than 30% of all potential pricing adjustments were successfully made (compared to 53% for intangibles, 67% for interest, 52% for services, 84% for the allocation of expenses, and 89% for the allocation of net income), and that more than half (56%) of the adjustments *not made* had used the uncontrolled sales formula. In fact, only 21% of adjustments made used this formula, 11% used resale price, 28% cost plus, and more than 40% of successful adjustments used a variety of other formulae.[36]

These data suggest that even the USIRS, well-staffed, with sophisticated methods, has found it extremely difficult to make reassessments of transfer pricing of tangibles stick. They have had more success with adjustments of interest and the pricing of invisibles and services, but less because there is an objective market price (financial interest is perhaps an exception here), than because it is relatively more straightforward to apply a rule on allocation of a stream of services or know-how than it is to compose the price of individual commodities.

In discussing developed-country guidelines and practices I have not wanted to argue that allocations cannot be made. Indeed, they clearly have to be made. What I have tried to establish is that there is no unambiguous way of allocating profits between subsidiaries of an integrated international firm, there is considerable latitude, and the choice of method will reflect the interest of the body doing the assessing: the firm, a customs department, the inland revenue department, a less developed as against a more developed country, a trade union.

There can be no way of 'reclaiming the market by account' unambiguously for many of these cases. The underlying model of the perfect market, with its implications for free circulation, welfare optimisation, and 'just prices' can in these circumstances no longer be invoked, in spite of its magnetic presence in the literature we have been discussing. Rather, what is at issue is a struggle over the distribution of profit between private capital, governments and workers on the one hand, and between different governments on the other.

This is recognised by the resort of revenue departments to the method of allocating world income. This method was used in 7% of the successful adjustment cases reported by the US Treasury, and has also been used in a number of well-known cases in the US — those involving Pittsburgh Plate Glass, Johnson Bronze, the Lufkin Foundry and Machine Co. and the Eli Lilly case. Moreover, as Edwardes-Ker notes in his tax-avoidance manual: regardless of theory, 'there seems little doubt that, providing a reasonable profit is made in a country by a subsidiary, the local tax authorities are far less likely to query its intra-company pricing arrangements than if little or no profits are made'. The reality is that most revenue departments are not primarily concerned with re-establishing notional free-world market prices by whatever means. They are interested in laying claim to a portion of world profits as their share of the levy. The arguments advanced on the basis of a supposed system of free prices will play a part in this struggle over distribution. But they can no longer claim — even within their own terms — the status of a privileged criterion for the allocation of income over and above other criteria based on equity or market power.

The third approach rests on the propositions that:

(i) free market prices can be established;

(ii) that those free-market prices are the legitimate basis for allocating international profit between tax authorities.

The fourth approach by implication accepts these propositions but argues that the re-establishment must not be by account but on the basis of anti-trust action. It is here that approaching the problem via the nature of the social nexus rather than institutions in the market becomes important. For my argument on the social nexus implies that it is the growing indivisibility in production which is the material basis for large firms, and, in some periods, for large firms which are also monopolies. In spite of the magnificent quixotic thrusts of North American and EEC trust busters, we have seen how confined are the limits on decomposing these great aggregations of contemporary integrated production systems. The confines are set by the impetuous drive to increase productivity, and the tendency to interdependence of production systems as the requirement for achieving these increases of productivity. No national anti-trust authority can ignore these twin necessities. To attempt to reimpose short-term competition by breaking up large firms, and/or shearing them of their short-term monopolistic advantages, would be to undermine, in any particular national instance, the potential of long-run international competitive success. I would not of course deny the room for anti-trust action which clipped rather than sheared. But as a major answer to the problem of transfer pricing, the reintroduction of competition as traditionally conceived is as contradictory in terms as the reintroduction of the market in zones of the economy where price has lost its voice.

POWER AND PRICE

The fifth approach — which I have distinguished as an administrative, bargaining approach — shares with the operational business literature the virtue of micro-realism. Rooted in the perspective that it is the world market, dominated by the monopoly power of large firms and the developed country states, which has led to the severe poverty and unemployment that exists in the third world, this approach is geared to preventing the continued drain of profit by mobilising and consolidating what power the underdeveloped country states have got. For them there is no 'just' price; rather the relevant price is the minimum (imports) or maximum (exports) that they can obtain in the face of the power of the international firms and their domestic states.

It is here that the theoretical issue becomes particularly sharp. If one of the features of modern socialised production is that fixed costs tend to be high and marginal costs low, then in principle a firm should be willing to sell its product as long as it earns a normal rate of return on its marginal costs. Given that a national market can be largely isolated from other markets, and that a low price will not then reduce overall world revenue for the firm, the underdeveloped countries as marginal markets could in principle expect to enjoy one of the benefits of being a 'latecomer', namely low prices.

For firms, this fact of modern production is most uncomfortable. To produce more efficiently they have to invest more in research, development and heavy machinery, but are then in a weak bargaining position with consumers who owe no allegiance (in the jungle of the real market) to sunk costs. The states of advanced capitalist countries (where these sunk costs tend to be incurred) have developed four ways of protecting their firms from this contradiction between the nature of modern production processes and the reality of the market. They have taken on some of the fixed costs themselves and funded them out of levies. They have left the firms with the fixed costs but lowered their levies (depreciation allowances, capital grants, investment credits — all effectively amounting to a grant of bounty from the state). They have provided tariff protection so that fixed costs can be recovered by sales in the home market, and exports in the world jungle can then, if necessary, fall to marginal cost plus without driving the firm out of business (this is the basis of Otto Bauer's famous fortress theory of the nation state). Finally they have provided monopoly power for a fixed period of time in the form of patent rights or trademarks. Fixed costs are thus either funded by the state, or the firm is given a monopoly zone in time and/or space to recover them. There is no immediate reason why an underdeveloped country — which rarely plays host to such fixed investment — should participate in state protection or funding of sunk costs. If the jungle principle is strictly followed, foreign firms should be allowed to cover their international marginal cost plus a normal rate of return. That is to say, costs allowed would be the total costs of production of the underdeveloped country facilities, plus any incremental cost that the international firm had incurred elsewhere as the result of its investment. For a particular commodity, the price would be composed of average local costs, plus marginal foreign costs.

Applying this to transfer pricing, imported intermediates would be valued at their marginal, not average, costs, which effectively means they should be valued at dumping prices. Machinery, too, should be valued at its marginal cost — in spite of suggestions by tied aid agencies that average cost is the relevant benchmark. Know-how, and formulae, should be valued at their marginal cost, which is usually close to zero. On this basis, the high marginal profits created in the third world — which are normally transferred under average pricing codes — would be realised where they were created and taxed accordingly.

Various average cost pricing formulae have been advanced against this: average international cost at historic value, average international cost at replacement value, and average expanded reproduction cost. The first argues that firms should be paid what they have invested. The second, that they should be paid what they will have to invest to maintain the same rate of output; and the third, that they should be paid to allow for an expanded rate of output. All of them assume that the firm should have sufficient returns to reproduce itself. In some instances a third world country might see itself as having an interest in funding the continued existence of international firms, but it should then be seen for what it is: a contribution towards future expenditure rather than a payment for what has been incurred in the past.

In the era of socialised production, accounting, like price, becomes increasingly ambiguous, and the very standards such as those argued currently in inflation accounting debate can be seen to represent different interests.[38] So, too, with cost. Each time a joint cost or a sunk cost is discussed, we will often find the argument turning on conflicting material interests. This is why it is so important to be clear about the nature of cost and what it represents.

To take one recent example, that of the pricing of intermediates of the drugs Librium and Valium by Roche Products. The UK Monopolies Commission produced figures which (leaving out UK selling and administrative expenditure) suggested an international marginal cost of production of the two drugs of respectively £76 and £77 per kilo. The Commission accepted the principle of some contribution to joint costs, which in the case of R & D they felt for practical reasons could not take the form of payment for sunk costs, but a portion of current R & D expenses. They made it clear that this allowance was to ensure that the company maintained its research, and not that it should fund a 'cumulative increase in research cost'. This is equivalent to international average historic costs, or 'simple reproduction' costs and amounted to more than four times the marginal cost. Roche Products argued their case in part on the basis of average international replacement cost: 'The research costs you have got to recover, which are not the research costs on that drug, have gone up, perhaps, by twice'[40] hence the need for a higher current price. Some protagonists of Roche, in arguing for a price which gives an incentive for expansion, were effectively advancing an argument for 'expanded reproduction' costs. This stood at ten and twenty-five times marginal cost for the Librium and Valium respectively. What will determine the price granted will be the interest a country has in any of these outcomes: the provision of the drugs alone, or their provision with various levels of continued existence for the international firm who makes them.

Thus, the fifth approach starts from the principle of allowing international firms to cover their marginal international costs, together with any allowances for further expansion. Sunk costs are recognised only in so far as allowing them is necessary to encourage expansion in the future.

On the import side, therefore, the argument is that the incremental profits should be declared where they are realised, for it is either local labour which has produced the profits, or — if there is local protection — the excess profits are effectively value appropriated from elsewhere in the economy. In either case, profit has been produced locally and should be taxed locally.

On the export side the argument is somewhat different. Here the key concept is rent. In major international raw materials and primary production there commonly exists what in most versions would be seen as a differential rent. In many sectors this rent is appropriated almost entirely by the international firms, and accumulated largely outside the primary export economy. Costs allowed by firms in the transfer export price may in these cases not even cover national marginal costs. (Frank Ellis has found the banana price in Central America on occasion so low that it does not cover the wage bill.[41]) In these cases, the fifth approach would argue that the relevant method is to allow the firms the international marginal costs plus normal rate of return on their upstream operations, deduct that from the world market price, and appropriate the rent for the holders of the land (usually the government) as in traditional economic theory. This method was that used by Jamaica in its calculation of the appropriate tax to levy on bauxite exports, though they agreed to distribute the rent equally by stage of production rather than appropriate it entirely to themselves.[42]

With both imports and exports, the transfer price will be fixed not so much at a notional arm's-length but at an actual fist's-length. Whereas the third approach was interested in individual costs in order to estimate a notional free-market price, the fifth approach is interested in market prices in order to estimate individual costs. And it is here that the difficulties remain. For the cost figures relevant for estimating both international marginal costs and international rent are privatised within the international firm. The accounting ambiguities of modern production make the matter more difficult, for the costs relevant to the bargaining country are not some objective costs that can be independently established. They are the costs as the international firm sees them. Frequently bargains of this kind, which may start on issues of pricing principle, finish as disputes about costs, discount rates, allowances for risk, and so on, whose actual magnitudes only the firm knows.[43] While for the third approach the problem is pricing the unpriceable, for the fifth approach it is one of ascertaining the costs of the costable. While in practice the US IRS and the Colombian Division of International Price control may follow similar procedures, what I have tried to establish is that the contradiction between the growth of directly socialised labour on the one hand, and the continuation of the market as the dominant social nexus on the other, is expressed in the very terms of the problem of transfer pricing, and in the differences and incongruities of the conceptual attempts to deal with it.

CONCLUSION

This paper has argued both a method and a case in relation to control. The method is an historical one, the case an interpretation of transfer pricing's history. Together they provide the basis for a critique of the main approaches to the control of transfer pricing by the state.

One set of approaches was distinguished by its attempt to restore the market to zones where it no longer existed. Some sought to do this 'ideally', by calculating what prices would be were free-market relations to hold for intra-firm trade. Others proposed to do so in practice, by anti-trust action against large multinationals. The main weakness of both these approaches is that they abstract from the historical forces that have caused transfer pricing to become an issue in international trade. The long drive for productivity which has marked the history of capitalism has had a two-fold consequence: (a) an increase in sunk and overhead costs to incremental production costs; and (b) an increase in the planning or synthesis of labour outside the market — what I called the 'direct socialisation of labour'. One result of these tendencies has been the growth of large multinational firms. Another has been the displacement of the market as an adequate mechanism for organising labour within the firm. Because the 'restoration' approaches to transfer pricing remain at the level of the appearance of the problem — large firms on the one hand, the absence of arm's-length prices on the other — their proposals for control take no account of the underlying causes of the phenomena. They envisage large firms without oligopoly power, high productivity without large firms, or market relations within large inter-dependent units where the conditions for adequate price relations are absent. They wish, in short, to have the content without the form. As a result, both approaches are seriously limited in practice.[44]

The bargaining approach suffers from a different limitation. The writers accept the existence of the form but do not fully come to terms with the content. In posing the question solely as one of distribution between states and firms, they run into the difficulty of the disparities between the private units controlling international production (multinationals), and the regulative units (governments), which are restricted to the national sphere of circulation. Yet in transfer pricing disputes, as in so many fields of economic activity, power in circulation reflects power in production. Oligopolies have market power because of their productive power. The two cannot be divorced. So there is a real issue as to whether states which have no base in production can generate the power to control firms who do. Partly, it is a question of information. This is privatised by firms, and commonly requires a knowledge of the production process itself to 'read' it adequately. It is also a question of economic power, irrespective of information. Though states have considerable *formal* regulative power, firms have the *real* economic power. It is the threat of withdrawal and redundancy or the promise of new investment which is often enough to restrict government departments in their negotiations over transfer price adjustments.

This same economic power relates also to political power. The connection may be direct, as when multinationals support particular politicians or political movements, and finance pressure groups conducive to their interest. But it may equally be indirect, when local political forces argue against transfer pricing control because their own economic interests are dependent on those of the‾multinationals. In either case, the political cannot be seen as exogenous to the economic. In a sense it is produced by the economy, or, put another way, the economic is itself political. Regardless, therefore, of the technical capacity of a state to control transfer pricing, the economic power of multinationals may be translated into a political restriction on state officials using what regulative powers they have.

All this is not to say that the bargaining approach cannot lead to substantial redistribution. It has clearly done so, particularly as far as rent on primary commodities is concerned. The experiences of Jamaica or Panama reflect in part the development of social forces opposed to the unhindered operations of multinationals, and in part the development of theory (since theory is also political) and bargaining skills within government departments themselves. What I am saying is that the question of transfer pricing control cannot be abstracted from broader questions of economic policy, since that economic policy will in part determine the relative political power on which the outcome of control programmes so heavily depends. By divorcing distribution from production, the bargaining approach is in danger of losing these wider connections. It tends to assume what has to be proved, namely that it is possible to control international firms through intervention confined to the sphere of circulation (monitoring prices and financial flows).

If, then, the bargaining approach has highlighted some of the limitations of control strategies based on *exchange*, it has at the same time illustrated the shortcomings of an approach confined to *distribution*. If these theoretical shortcomings are confirmed in practice, it suggests that the only effective strategy of control would be a long-run policy of state control of *production*. This would once more unite the sphere of public distribution (the national levy-bounty economy) with that of production (directly socialised labour). It would dissolve the problem of international transfer pricing into one of arm's-length price negotiations between state enterprises and the world economy. The latter would still involve the questions of information and of economic and political power that we have discussed in relation to transfer pricing; but the evidence of the countries which have followed such a strategy is that they approach negotiations with considerably greater strength than they had when state power was confined to circulation.[45] It may well be that only by state control of production can the distributional goals of the bargaining approach be effectively realised.

NOTES

1 The issue is discussed in: Gerry Helleiner, 'Intrafirm Trade and the Developing Countries: Patterns, Trends and Data Problems', in this volume.

2 For the developments in transfer pricing literature, see Jeffrey S Arpan, *International Intra-Corporate Pricing: Non-American Systems and Views*, Praeger 1971, Chapter 2.

3 Jack Hirschleiffer, 'Economics of a Divisionalised Firm', *Journal of Business*, XXX 3, April 1957, pp.96-108.

4 One exception is Copithorne who has argued that transfer pricing does not affect global output and prices of the firm, only the distribution of revenues within the firm. See L.W. Copithorne, 'International Corporate Transfer Prices and Government Policy', *Canadian Journal of Economics*, IV, 3 August 1971.

5 For reasons why profit is not necessarily a good measure of performance, see H.C. Verlage, *Transfer Pricing for Multinational Enterprise*, Rotterdam University Press, 1975, Chapter 4.

6 David Rutenberg, 'Manoeuvring liquid assets in a multinational company: formulation and deterministic solution procedures, *Management Science*, Vol.16, No.10, June 1970, pp.B671-84. Michael Edwardes-Ker, *International Tax Strategy*, In-Depth Publishing, 2 vols, 1974. Other valuable books include: D.B. Zenoff and J.Zwick, *International Financial Management*, Prentice Hall, 1969, the volume edited by A.L. Stonehill, *Readings in International Financial Management*, Goodyear, 1970, and the Harvard study by S.M. Robbins and R.B. Stobaugh, *Money in the Multinational Enterprise*, Basic Books, 1973.

7 Business International, *Solving International Pricing Problems*, New York, 1965: James Shulman, *Transfer Pricing in Multinational Business*, PhD dissertation, Harvard, 1966, and a more accessible article by the same author, 'When the Price if Wrong by Design', *Columbia Journal of World Business*, II 3, May-June 1967, pp.69-77; Arpan, *op. cit*.

8 Edith Penrose noted a firm who kept three sets of books, one for internal management, one for the tax authorities, and one for the shareholders. See her book, *The Large International Firm in Developing Countries: the International Petroleum Industry*, Allen & Unwin, 1968, p.44, note 1.

9 See the paper by G.N. Carlson and G.C. Hufbauer, 'Tax Barriers to Technology Transfer', Office of Tax Analysis US Treasury, Paper no.16, Nov. 1976, and also the survey in Edwardes-Ker, *op. cit*.

10 The Brussels Definition of Value is reprinted in Verlage *op. cit*. pp.92, seq.

11 Colin Greenhill developed this approach at the UNCTAD/IDS conference on Intra-firm Trade, November 1977. See the video-tape report on the conference. There are indications of it in the UNCTAD paper to that

conference, 'Dominant Positions of Market Power of Transnational Corporations: Use of the Transfer Pricing Mechanism', ST/MD/6 1977 but it is not spelled out there explicitly.

12 See, for example, the testimony of Walter Sauders, Vice-President of Cargill Corporation, the international grain traders, to the Senate Hearings on Multinational Corporations: 'Taxes are a critical cost element in our business. Unlike firms involved in manufacturing operations, commodity traders possess no unique advantages like patents, trademarks, brand franchises, technology or product superiority which enable them to absorb higher tax costs. We all buy and sell the same commodities, dealing with the same sellers and the same buyers. To compete on equal terms, we had to seek tax costs no greater than those accessible to established foreign owned competitors.' US Congress, Senate, Committee on Foreign Relations, Sub-Committee on Multinational Corporations, Multinational Corporations and United States Foreign Policy, 94th Congress, second session on International Grain Companies, 18, 23 and 24 June 1976, Part 16, p.101.

13 The leading contributors to the monopoly approach have been Constantine Vaitsos (see in particular *Inter-country Income Distribution and Transnational Enterprises*, Clarendon Press, Oxford 1974) and Norman Girvan, 'Corporate Imperialism in the Caribbean Bauxite Industry', in his collection of essays, *Corporate Imperialism: Conflict and Expropriation*, Sharpe, 1976, pp.98-159, though many other authors have developed this approach to multinational corporations without so detailed a discussion of transfer pricing. We should also note the large body of work produced by the Transfer of Technology Division at UNCTAD which has been based on this perspective.

14 Peter Fitzpatrick's paper in this volume brings out the legal side of this alternative view very well.

15 A sixth approach was suggested by David Evans during the UNCTAD/IDS conference on Intra-firm Trade. He argued that disregarding the points about monopoly and non-marketability within international firms, the price system itself reflected a particular set of social relations which were themselves open to question. The issue was at the centre of the debate between traditional utilitarian international economic theory and the 'new' approaches to trade: neo-Ricardian, Unequal Exchange, and the Marxist social value school. What was clear from this debate was the problematic nature of market prices as in any sense just or desirable from the point of view of labour. David Evans himself suggested that the Marxist Circuits of Capital Theory could enlighten the transfer pricing debate, by isolating those sections of the circuit where exchange between independent parties did take place (purchase of labour power, raw materials and means of production, and sale of the final commodity) from those where it did not (circulation of use values within a firm for further processing). In as much as it was the latter aspect of circulation which was under discussion in the transfer pricing debate, then the arguments about non-commensurability were particularly strong. See his note: 'Intra-firm transactions and the circuits of capital: a note' in UNCTAD/IDS Conference, *Intra-firm Transactions and their Impact on Trade and Development, a Report of the Proceedings*, prepared by Frank Ellis and Susan Joekes, November 1977.

16 In addition to the authors mentioned in note 13, see also the article by Stephen Hymer, 'The Multinational Corporation and the Law of Uneven Development' in Charles Kindleberger (ed.), *The International Cor-*

poration, MIT, 1970.

17 See Gerry Helleiner, *Intra-Firm Trade and the Developing Countries*, Macmillan 1981, and Constantine Vaitsos 'Transnational Enterprises and Latin American Integration', UNCTAD, Geneva, 1978.

18 On the changing character of the social nexus under capitalism, see the work of Alfred Sohn-Rethal, notably: 'The Dual Economics of Transition' in the Bulletin of the Conference of Socialist Economists, No.2.2, 1972, reprinted in the Conference of Socialist Economists collection, *The Capitalist Labour Process*, CSE/Stage 1, 1976, as well as his longer book, *Intellectual and Manual Labour*, Macmillan, 1978. On the connection of the socialisation of labour to international firms, see my paper, 'Underdevelopment, International Firms and the International Division of Labour', in *Towards a New World Economy*, Rotterdam University Press, 1972, pp.161-247.

19 In some cases where it is possible to make distinctions other than through area, for example through skin colour or language, the territorial element may be less significant, but it is striking that in such circumstances the state still has problems of confining 'bounty' without some form of spatial separation.

20 National Industrial Conference Board, 'Interdivisional Transfer Pricing' in *Studies in Business Policy*, no.122, 1967.

21 Quoted in Verlage, *op. cit.*, p.187. It is interesting to note that most of the non-US firms studied by Arpan had no profit centres, see Arpan, *op. cit.*, p.75.

22 The relation between the forces of the world market, and the institutional power of international firms and states is discussed more fully in my paper cited in note 18.

23 The Republic of Minerva is a small reef off Fiji and Tonga. The *Financial Times* (20 November 1972) stated that certain people in California and Nevada had enrolled as Minerva's first citizens and that a Reno doctor, Dr. David Williams, the Secretary of the Interior of Minerva's four-man provisional government, intended to start dredging operations to build up the reef to between 10 and 15 feet above sea level. The *Financial Times* reported that Dr. Williams admitted that the reef is 'not really livable as it is', but that once the dredgers had been in, 'people will be free to do as they damn well please'. The *Financial Times* also reported that the Tongolese were not particularly friendly and that King Taufa'ahau Tupou of Tonga had personally stormed the reef in full military regalia to raise the flag of Tonga, replacing the Republic flag which had been 'bravely' flying on the reef. This is reported in Edwardes-Ker, *op. cit.*, Chapter 32, section 3, p.26.

24 Edwardes-Ker, in particular Chapter 5.

25 On the US Valuation standards, see 'Customs Valuation, Report of the US Tariff Commission to the Committee on Finance and the Sub-Committee on International Trade', US Senate, 14 March 1973.

26 See International Grain Companies hearings (note 12), and the various discussions surrounding the Trick memorandum.

27 Verlage, *op. cit.*, p.91.

28 *Ibid*, p.86.

29 Tariff Commission Report, *op. cit.*, p.78.

30 See reprint in Verlage, *op. cit.*, p.93.

31 See Maurice Collins' paper 'Suggested Guidelines — payment for goods — technology — services', originally submitted to the UN Expert Group on

Tax Treaties between Developed and Developing Countries, Geneva, October-November 1977.

32　*Ibid.*, pp.5, 7 and 13.
33　Verlage, *op. cit.*, pp.110, 115, 116 and 117.
34　United States Internal Revenue Service, 'Multinational Companies, Tax Avoidance and/or Evasion Schemes and Available Methods of Curb Abuse', in this volume.
35　Arpan, *op. cit.*, p.79.
36　US Treasury Department, 'Summary Study of International Cases involving Section 482 of the Internal Revenue Code', Washington, January 1973, Tables 2 and 8.
37　Edwardes-Ker, *op. cit.*, Chapter 5, Section 7, p.16.
38　On the debate in Britain, see the interesting paper by Grahame Thompson, 'Capitalist Profit Calculation and Inflation Accounting', Open University, October 1977.
39　The Monopolies Commission, 'Chlordiazepoxide and Diazepam', HMSO, 1973, para.223, pp.65-6.
40　*Ibid.*, para.192, p.56. See pp.53-6 for a summary of the whole Roche argument.
41　Frank Ellis, 'Export Valuation and Intra-Firm Transfers in the Banana Export Industry in Central America' in this volume.
42　Norman Girvan, *op. cit.*
43　I have discussed the principles of pricing and the issues of risk, discounting, and sunk costs in relation to the debate in the UK on the pricing of North Sea Natural Gas. See 'Pricing North Sea Gas: Case Study and Commentary', London Business School, 1969.
44　It is interesting to compare this 'restoration' approach of governments with that of businesses. The latter seek not so much the revival of the market but the creation of systems of internal control which do not depend on price.
45　The importance of the control of operations as a means of securing information is clearly brought out in K.M. Lamaswala's paper on copper in this volume. For political and technical considerations see J. Faundez and S. Picciotto (eds.), *The Nationalisation of Multinationals in Peripheral Economies*, Macmillan, 1978.

11.
TAXATION AND THE CONTROL OF TRANSFER PRICING
FRANCES STEWART

This paper considers how LDCs may use the tax system to reduce the extent of transfer price manipulation by TNCs and to minimise the losses caused by it. Somewhat surprisingly, most attention, in the recent literature and in LDC efforts to control the phenomenon, has been devoted to administrative means of investigating and eliminating these practices. Yet the tax system provides an obvious mechanism of control for two reasons. First, because among the many reasons commonly suggested for transfer price manipulation, TNC desire to minimise world tax liability ranks very high.[1] Secondly, because in large part, the losses caused to any LDC as a result are tax losses. Hence, if these could be avoided, the significance of transfer price manipulation would also be substantially reduced. Changes in the tax system to avoid such losses would not remove the need for administrative action, but they would lessen it, and also give administrative action powerful support.

The activities of a TNC subsidiary in an LDC are subject to a variety of taxes in the LDC: these include tariffs and taxes on inputs, indirect taxes on output, and taxes on the income (profits, royalties, management fees) generated by the activities. The total tax liability of the company depends not only on these taxes, but also on the tax treatment of the income when remitted overseas. Tax incentive for transfer price manipulation occurs when total tax liability is reduced by 'under' or 'over' declaring profits in one country, and correspondingly 'over' or 'under' declaring profits elsewhere. If profits are underdeclared in the LDC, the LDC suffers a tax loss, which is one significant reason why LDCs wish to prevent transfer price manipulations. In addition, as a result of transfer price manipulation, they lose control over transactions with for example their exchange control regulations and restrictions on dividend remittances being invalidated.

The actual net incentives for TNC subsidiaries to manipulate transfer prices for tax reasons are rather complex depending on:[2]

177

(i) the existence of tax havens, with near zero tax rates on profits, and the possibility of routing profits via tax havens;

(ii) the tax rates on profits in the investing countries, to which the income is being remitted, their system of double tax relief, and tax rates and allowances for corporate income in the host LDC;

(iii) the extent to which the TNC headquarters in DCs have unused allowances against which they could write off tax; and

(iv) tax rates on royalties and management fees, taxes and tariffs on imports and exports in both host and investing countries.

Given that the various investing countries have differing systems of double tax relief, differing tax rates, etc., that our knowledge of tax havens and the possibilities they offer is limited, and that LDCs have no control over tax systems other than their own, it might appear perhaps that LDCs face an impossible situation in trying to change their own tax systems to deal with transfer pricing. Hence, the tendency to rely on administrative action.

But the administrative approach, while an important supplement to the tax approach, involves very great difficulties. This is partly because of the administrative resources involved, partly because of the real difficulties in identifying arm's-length prices. The US administration has encountered very significant problems in establishing arm's-length prices.[3] Kopits[4] concludes a survey: 'with the exception of the US, most countries have neither the willingness nor the administrative machinery to enforce arm's-length prices.'

However, closer examination of the tax situation in LDCs suggests that they may offset many of the losses associated with transfer prices and reduce incentives for its practice by changing their own tax systems, irrespective of the tax systems elsewhere. Two approaches are possible: the formula apportionment approach and the uniformity approach. Both aim to ensure that the actual tax paid on TNC activities to the LDC tax authorities are the same, irrespective of transfer price manipulation; the formula approach achieves this by taxing TNC activities on some formula-determined postulated profits, rather than declared profits. The uniformity approach would achieve it by levying uniform tax rates on all relevant items so that the TNC pays the same total taxation whatever prices it uses. With either approach the LDC total tax revenue would be the same irrespective of transfer prices.

FORMULA APPORTIONMENT TAXATION

Taxation based on formula apportionment taxes company profits in any country on the basis of what the profits *would be* if they bore the same proportion to worldwide overall company profits, as the company's employment or sales or turnover or investment in the country, or some weighted average of the possible variables does to worldwide company employment or sales or turnover or investment. There is, then, no incentive to manipulate transfer prices for the sake of avoiding taxation within the country which is using the formula apportionment basis.[5] Problems about this approach are: (i) problems about which is the 'correct' basis to use. Since the ratio of profits to any of the variables is likely to vary, there is no 'correct' formula if the aim is to secure the best proxy for 'real' (though undeclared and unknown) profits. According to how the formula is calculated, companies will have an incentive to increase/reduce their contribution in relation to the different variables. In choosing the formula, therefore, attention needs to be paid to which aspects of company activity the country wishes to encourage and which to discourage. (ii) difficulties in obtaining information about the worldwide profits, turnover, etc., essential for the application of the method.[6] Disclosure requirements vary between countries: some companies are likely to have headquarters in (or to shift to) countries in which disclosure requirements are inadequate for a proper application of the method.[7] It has been suggested that this type of taxation is not possible without international disclosure requirements and international tax administration.[8]

While this conclusion may be exaggerated, it does seem that current disclosure requirements are likely to be inadequate to operate a formula apportionment approach in a satisfactory way. Nonetheless, it might be an improvement on the current system, and the adoption of the approach might itself lead companies to improve disclosure to avoid excessive taxation. Formula apportionment deals with the problem of transfer price manipulation in intra-firm transactions, but not with transactions between unrelated enterprises. When technology is transferred to third parties (or joint ventures) taxation may be avoided by charging inflated prices for machinery and inputs, supplied along with the licence for knowhow on which royalties are paid.

UNIFORMITY OF TAX TREATMENT

An alternative approach is for tax authorities to treat all relevant items uniformly. The total amount of taxes that a TNC pays an

LDC government is the sum of taxes on its inputs (notably tariffs on imported inputs), indirect taxes on output, and taxes on income, including corporation tax and withholding taxes on royalties, management fees, interest, etc. When a company manipulates transfer prices, it reduces the value of one element and increases the value of another. If the tax rate on each element is the same, then no loss of tax revenue occurs and the incentive to practise transfer price manipulation is reduced. For example, in many cases companies appear to charge relatively high royalty fees in order to reduce the quantity of profits subject to corporate tax. But if the tax rate levied on royalties and corporate profits are the same, this will not affect total tax payments. The Andean Pact introduced a provision treating royalties as corporate income for this reason. More significant elements of price manipulation relate to prices of imported inputs. If the tariff rate on imported inputs is the same as the corporation tax on profits, then manipulations which overprice imports and underdeclare profits will not affect total tax revenue. Another major source of transfer price manipulation is the underinvoicing of exports.[9] To prevent this causing a tax loss, the value of exports must be *deducted* from the value of profits in calculating profits tax liability. With this provision, underinvoicing of exports will reduce declared profits, but will not affect taxable profits. Consequently, the total tax revenue will remain the same irrespective of invoicing practices.

One way to achieve the required uniformity is to bring the tax rates in line so that the combined tax rates on each item are broadly similar. This would mean setting tariff rates on imported items at the same rate as the sum of corporation tax plus withholding tax on remitted profits; and royalties would either be amalgamated with profits for tax purposes, or the withholding tax on royalties plus any other taxes (e.g., turnover taxes, levied in, say, Algeria), should be set at the same rate. Another way of achieving the uniformity would be to redefine the tax base so that all the relevant items were included — viz. the corporation tax would be replaced by a tax on profits plus royalties plus remitted management fees plus imported items less exports.[10] The tax would be similar to a turnover tax which excluded payments to local labour and exports.

This uniformity of tax treatment would not mean that manipulation of payments would stop because (a) of incentives in other parts of the world — for example, in relation to DC taxation — for particular types of payment; and (b) other motives for manipulation which would continue. But it would mean that the consequent loss in tax revenue would be prevented — which is a major reason for concern about such manipulation. The uniformity approach would reduce countries' freedom to alter the relative taxes on different items. This would probably not matter much, since to a large extent the freedom is illusory, given manipulation possibilities which often make the use of relative tax rates to achieve policy ends ineffective. In any case, countries have tended to use the relative tax rates in the wrong direction, encouraging over capital-intensive and import-dependent types of projects. Moreover, governments would maintain the ability to alter relative costs by use of subsidies, which is normally a much more effective means of achieving desired consequences.

It is likely to be argued that taxing royalties at the same rate as corporate profits, would involve an unjustified burden of taxation on royalties, which according to some,[11] are already taxed very heavily by LDCs in relation to the net of cost return. This argument assumes a high cost element in technology supplies to LDCs. Yet, in practice, most of the technology supplied to LDCs has already been written off against taxation by royalties paid within DCs. Hence, royalty payments from LDCs represent a taxable surplus. Any argument about the need for high surplus on some technology items to finance the failures and provide a general incentive to R & D is inappropriate in the context of LDCs. DC R & D is undertaken for their own rather than LDCs markets, and much of it results in technology which is inappropriate for LDCs, and which in many ways the LDCs would be better off without.[12] In any case, under the present system, payments described as 'royalties' and taxed accordingly are not the sole return for technological transfer; the gross return may include some of the profits on overseas investment and some of the price of parts/equipment supplied. Thus, to assess whether the technology is being fairly taxed requires an assesment of taxation on all these elements.

The transfer price problem arises not only with respect to transactions within the TNC, but also in many transactions between unrelated parties, where one company supplies an LDC company with more than one item, and receives more than one type of payment. In such cases (e.g., where machinery and parts are supplied as well as know-how), payment for one item may be artificially attributed to another, for tax or other reasons. The uniformity approach would prevent such transactions causing revenue loss, in the same way as for intra-firm transactions. It is important that any attempt to tighten up in relation to TNC transactions also affects transactions between unrelated parties: otherwise, the effect may be to induce a switch away from intra-firm to inter-firm transactions to avoid the consequences of the tightening up. In this respect, the uniformity approach is to be preferred to the formula approach.

RATES OF TAX

The new approaches to taxation suggested above are designed to avoid tax loss as a result of transfer price manipulation, and also to reduce the incentive to practise it. The approaches are consistent with any rate of tax. Since the main aim is to reduce tax loss, it is worth considering other ways in which this might be achieved. Many LDCs offer foreign companies very generous tax incentives, which take the form of tax holidays or investment allowances.[13] While tax rates in LDCs are broadly similar to those in DCs,[14] because of the incentives, effective tax rates are often much lower. As a result, the LDCs suffer a considerable loss in revenue compared with what they might achieve with higher effective tax rates. In very large part, this loss in tax revenue simply accrues to the revenue authorities in the DCs. This occurs where the DC tax rate is higher than that effective in the LDC, where the credit method of exemption for tax relief is given and where the DC allows no tax-sparing relief.[15] Since the main[16] investors in LDCs — the US and the UK — use the credit method of relief, and since the US never, and the UK rarely, allow tax-sparing, many of the incentives provided by LDCs increase the revenues of the DC tax authorities, rather than the after-tax profits of the companies. To avoid this unnecessary loss, it would seem sensible for LDCs to introduce effective corporate tax rates no lower than those ruling in the DCs from which the bulk of their investment comes, and to provide investment incentives, if any, in the form of subsidies rather than tax relief. In any case, there is overwhelming evidence that LDC tax incentives have been ineffective in attracting foreign investment, which has come (or not come) for other reasons.[17]

CONCLUSIONS

Transfer price manipulation arises in transnational activities because the companies' activities cover more than one tax jurisdiction, and because of differences in system and tax rates between the various jurisdictions. One way of dealing with the problem is to work for closer cooperation between tax jurisdictions, and eventually towards an international system of taxation for international companies. But prospects of achieving this seem very remote. Not only is there a fairly marked lack of cooperation between tax authorities in DCs and tax authorities in LDCs (as compared, for example, with tax authorities in different DCs), but the existence of tax havens imposes a wedge between the investing and host countries. The most that can be expected in the near future in the direction of international cooperation is more agreement on standards of accounting and disclosure, more double tax treaties involving mutual assistance in monitoring, and perhaps, a concerted attack on the privileges enjoyed by companies in tax havens. Developing countries, therefore, will have to tackle the transfer pricing problem on their own. This paper has proposed ways in which they might change their own tax systems so as to reduce the tax loss caused by transfer pricing, and reduce the incentive to practise it. It is likely that transfer pricing abuses will nonetheless continue, and that administrative means will be required to back up the tax changes. But if the tax changes were put into effect, transfer pricing would cease to cause a significant loss of revenue.

NOTES

1   See, e.g., Vaitsos 1974, Lall 1973, Kopits 1976.
2   For a more detailed discussion see Stewart 1981.
3   See e.g., O'Conner and Russo 1973.
4   Kopits 1976.
5   A formula apportionment basis is adopted by some states in the US for company transactions across states. The proposal to introduce it for the taxation of multinationals is discussed by a Group of Eminent Persons (*The Impact of Multinational Corporations on Development and on International Relations*, ST/ESA/6, New York 1974).
6   As Shoup 1974, has suggested, there may be no unique worldwide profit given fluctuations in exchange rates.
7   In some countries, companies are required to publish their consolidated world accounts, but this is rare outside the Federal Republic of Germany, the UK and the US.
8   One should distinguish between standardised international disclosure requirements and international tax administration. The former may be a realistic aim in the medium term.
9   See the evidence in UNCTAD 1977.
10   Suggested in the ILO Kenya Report, Technical Paper 17.
11   E.g., Carlson and Hufbauer 1976.
12   Discussed at length in Stewart 1977.
13   See Lent 1967 and Reuber 1973 for a description of tax incentives.
14   See Kopits 1976 and Lent 1978.

15 I.e. credit for tax relief given under special incentive schemes.
16 In 1971, the US accounted for an estimated 52% of total foreign private
    investment in LDCs, and the UK for 15%.
17 See e.g., Aharoni 1966 and Reuber 1973.

BIBLIOGRAPHY

Aharoni, Y. (1966), *The Foreign Investment Decision Process*,
    Boston.
Carlson, G.N. and Hufbauer, G.C. (1976), 'Tax Barriers to
    Technology Transfers', US Treasury Department, OTA
    paper 16.
ILO (1972), *Employment, Incomes and Equality, A Strategy for
    Increasing Productive Employment in Kenya*, Geneva.
Kopits, G.F. (1976), 'Taxation and Multinational Firm Behavior:
    A Critical Survey', *IMF Staff Papers*, 23.
Lall, S. (1973), 'Transfer Pricing by Multinational Manufacturing
    Firms', *Oxford Bulletin of Economics and Statistics*.
Lent, G.E. (1967), 'Tax Incentives for Developing Countries',
    IMF Staff Papers, 14.
—— (1978), 'Corporation Income Tax Structure in Developing
    Countries', *IMF Staff Papers*, 25.
O'Conner, W.F. and Russo, S.M. (1973), 'A Study of Corporate
    Experience with Section 482', *The European Tax Review*.
Reuber, G.L. *et al.* (1973), *Private Foreign Investment in
    Development*, Clarendon Press.
Shoup, C.S. (1974), 'Taxation of Multinational Corporations', in
    *The Impact of Multinational Corporations on Development
    and International Relations*: Technical Papers Taxation,
    ST/ESA/11, UN, New York.
Stewart, F. (1977), *Technology and Underdevelopment*, Mac-
    millan.
— (1981), 'Technology Transfer: A Consideration of the Role
    of Taxation,' in T. Sagafi-nejad, R. Moxon and H. Perlmutter,
    (eds) *Controlling Technology Transfer*, Pergamon.
United Nations Conference on Trade and Development (1977),
    'Dominant Positions of Market Power of Transnational
    Corporations: Use of the Transfer Pricing Mechanism',
    ST/MD/6.
Vaitsos, C.V. (1974), *Intercountry Income Distribution and
    Transnational Corporations*, The Clarendon Press, Oxford.

12.

CONTROL OF TRANSFER PRICES IN INTERNATIONAL TRANSACTIONS: THE RESTRICTIVE BUSINESS PRACTICES APPROACH

C.R. GREENHILL and E.O. HERBOLZHEIMER

GOVERNMENT CONTROL AND TRANSFER PRICING

Transfer price manipulations have an impact on many areas of a national economy: on market structures, balance of payments, domestic capital formation, i.e., funds available for reinvestment, and tax and customs revenues. For example, by overpricing imports to a subsidiary, the parent company is able to prevent or limit, directly or indirectly, a subsidiary's export ability, or circumvent controls on foreign profit remittances by tapping-off excess profits. On the other hand, by underpricing imports to a subsidiary, custom duty payments are likely to be less and the subsidiary can engage in predatory pricing behaviour with the aim of eliminating competitors in order to obtain or reinforce market dominance. The potential for such manipulations is already great and increasing as a result of the continued concentration of economic power in the hands of transnational corporations in both developed and developing countries, and the significance of intra-corporate transactions in total world trade,[1] reflecting the horizontal, vertical and conglomerate nature of their activities.

Several governmental departments have an interest in this issue but their interests are not necessarily in harmony with each other. A customs authority, for example, is generally not concerned with import prices being higher than they should be, since these result in higher duty payments. Tax departments and foreign exchange control authorities, on the other hand, are likely to be concerned since such prices lead to lower profits and therefore lower tax collection, and higher than necessary payments for imports. The contrary exists where import prices are artificially low. The extent to which transnational corporations will under- or overinvoice imports and exports will depend upon the vigour with which controls are applied by the different authorities and on the corporation's overall strategies.

Transfer price manipulation in a foreign trade transaction is likely to elicit different responses by the two Governments in question. While authorities in the importing country could well be

185

disturbed by an overcharge on the import of a particular good or service, authorities in exporting countries will welcome higher export receipts. Such a situation clearly entails actual or potential conflict of interest between countries in control of transfer prices and is perhaps a major reason why little regulatory action has so far been taken.

The most effective way of dealing with the transfer pricing issue is to focus attention on the cause of manipulations and the economic conditions permitting them. This is the restrictive business practices approach. The cause of transfer price manipulations is to maximise global profits of the transnational corporation. The basic economic condition permitting transfer price manipulations is the existence of monopolistic or oligopolistic market positions for the parent and/or subsidiary in the relevant market. Such a market position generally results in monopolistic profits, enabling the subsidiary and parent to over- or undercharge for goods or services supplied. Therefore, the most effective means of controlling transfer pricing manipulations is to control monopolistic or oligopolistic market conditions. One means is to change the market structures by encouraging greater competition in the market. Where this is not possible, another means is to control the behaviour of the market dominating enterprise. One of the principal indicators of an enterprise holding a dominant market position is its ability to fix prices, maintain resale prices or systematically apply predatory, discriminatory or excessive prices.

RESTRICTIVE BUSINESS PRACTICE LEGISLATION AND TRANSFER PRICING

The approach to the control of restrictive business practices and in this context to the question of transactions between related enterprises differs widely from one country to another.[1] Few countries have, in their restrictive business practice laws, provisions dealing specifically with transfer pricing. Transfer prices have been controlled under broad provisions relating to pricing practices. This is largely due to the fact that the problem was not clearly recognised when most countries were drafting such legislation.

Only limited action has been taken, either in developed or developing countries, to control such abuses. This is not to say that such practices have not been evident, but rather that governments have tended to ignore them. Recently, however, governments experiencing balance of payment and inflation difficulties have shown new vigilance by using their already existing powers to control transfer price manipulations.

Irrespective of the approach adopted to the control of transfer prices, the effectiveness of such control has been limited. The first reason would seem to be the difficulties faced by authorities in determining 'fair' or 'reasonable' prices. There can be wide variations, at any one time, in the prices of products frequently traded, whether or not in similar quantities and on similar terms of sale. In many cases the products or services have no market prices as such, since they are traded only between related parties. The second reason is the difficulty of obtaining from firms the data necessary to reconstruct prices on the basis of actual costs. For the developing countries the problems are accentuated, for often information necessary to determine the reasonableness of transfer prices has to be obtained from abroad.

The following is a brief review of the legal position in a selected number of countries, including a few examples of investigations undertaken by restrictive business practice authorities. The extent to which these provisions have been applied to the control of restrictive business practices is not known, since the vast majority of the cases are settled out of court.

DEVELOPED MARKET ECONOMY COUNTRIES
(a) *United Kingdom*
Transfer prices are controlled under the section relating to monopolies of the 1973 Fair Trading Act. In evaluating monopolies account is taken of intra-firm relationships, including those of transactions in goods and services. For the purposes of the Act, a monopoly exists in the supply of goods and services or exports if at least one-quarter of all the goods or services of that description in the UK: (a) are supplied or produced by one and the same person or by members of one and the same group of inter-connected bodies corporate; or (b) are supplied to one and the same person, or to members of one and the same group of inter-connected bodies corporate. Pricing practices of monopolies are investigated by the Monopolies Commission.

The most publicised case involving manipulation of transfer prices was the investigation undertaken by the Commission into the supply of tranquilisers (librium and valium), on the UK market.[3] The principal supplier of the products in question was Roche Products, the UK subsidiary of the Hoffman-La-Roche group. The group 'has virtually a monopoly position, being derived from its success in product innovation and from patents on the active ingredients of both medicines. This patent monopoly is reinforced . . . by the effect of established brand names in a market where there is a low degree of price competition and price sensitivity'.[4] Distortions in transfer pricing occurred principally in two different areas: (a) the overcharging of prices on 'tied' inputs supplied by the parent company, and (b) excessive charges to the UK subsidiary for central and head office expenses. Indirect profit transfers from 1966 to 1972 from the UK subsidiary by the above means was estimated at £22 million, in contrast to a declared profit of only £3 million.

The prices of the active ingredients provided by the parent company to the UK subsidiary were substantially higher than those quoted on the international market: the prices for these ingredients, if purchased from independent sources in Italy, would have been £9 and £20 per kg. compared with those charged to the Roche subsidiary by its parent of £370 and £922.

Furthermore, based on its own cost estimates, the Commission determined that the rate of return on capital was far above the rates for the UK manufacturing industry. Accordingly, it requested the subsidiary of the Roche Group in the UK to reduce the price of librium by 40% and that of valium by 25% of the selling prices prevailing in 1970.

Following the action in the UK, courts in Australia, the Netherlands and New Zealand also asked the subsidiaries of Hoffman-La-Roche to reduce sale prices of librium and valium in these markets. In Denmark in 1976, the Monopolies Control Authority imposed maximum prices for the tranquilisers of Hoffman-La-Roche, Dumex (Denmark) and Pharma A/S (Norway). The decision was reversed by the Monopolies Appeal Tribunal in February 1977, but pharmaceutical prices are currently being examined by the Monopolies Control Authority following a request by the Danish Parliament for its suggestions concerning price controls in the pharmaceutical sector.

(b) *The Federal Republic of Germany*
Transfer prices are examined by the Federal Cartel Office (FCO) within the framework of Section 22 of the 1957 Act Against Restraints of Competition. This Section deals with the supervision of enterprises in dominant positions of market power. It was only after the strengthening of the provisions of this Section, following the second amendment of the Act in 1973, that specific action was taken on transfer prices. Such prices have been examined in the context of enterprises' justification of costs of production and therefore final market prices. In determining the

reasonableness of market prices, the 'as-if competition' principle is applied, i.e., the prices obtainable if competition had existed. The prime concern would seem to have been with overpricing by foreign parents of goods or services purchased by subsidiaries in the Federal Republic of Germany, which may have led to excessive market prices.

The two investigations by the FCO in which transfer prices have been examined conerned the Hoffmann-La-Roche prices of valium and librium and those of the major international oil companies in respect of gasoline, diesel oil and light fuel.

In the former case, the FCO initiated proceedings in 1973,[5] and ordered Hoffman-La-Roche (Roche Grenzach) to cut its selling prices by 35 and 40% respectively for valium and librium on the grounds that it had abused its dominant market position by charging excessive prices. It noted that in a number of other European countries the prices charged for valium and librium were considerably lower than those in the Federal Republic. The transfer prices charged by the parent were found to correspond to ninety times the Italian competitive price of valium and 47 times that of librium. The company appealed to the Court of Appeals but in 1976 the Court confirmed the decision of the FCO.

Folowing price increases for gasoline, diesel oil and light fuel oil, the FCO opened proceedings against the major oil companies in the Federal Republic of Germany for abusing their dominant market position. However, during its investigations, it encountered difficulties in obtaining information on transfer prices for crude oil and other charges. All except one of these companies claimed that they could not provide the required information since it was held by group headquarters located in other countries. A procedure was initiated against British Petroleum's subsidiary in the Federal Republic of Germany with a view to prohibiting it from charging prices in excess of those valid at a certain date. The FCO order of immediate enforcement of this decision was subsequently reversed by the Court of Appeals. In its decision the Court agreed that, in the light of the considerable profit increases of the parent company:

> 'There was a suspicion that this enterprise had improved its profits as a result of the increase in the product prices; however, it said that the reasons given to prove the abuse were not conclusive. The Court, however, confirmed the possibility of conducting investigations into whether foreign affiliates of the company had caused an abuse affecting the domestic market by charging excessive crude oil prices and direct a request for information to the foreign affiliate, possibly through the

domestic subsidiaries. In view of the changed market situation leading to a reduction in oil prices, the proceedings have been suspended, or declared to be settled as to the merits'.[6]

(c) *Japan*

Under the Antimonopoly Act of 1947, agreements which 'fix, maintain or enhance prices' are considered 'unreasonable restraints of trade' (Section 2[6]) and are prohibited. This prohibition also covers agreements in international transactions (but not in domestic transactions) between related enterprises involving: (i) a Japanese corporation and its subsidiary established under foreign law; or (ii) a foreign corporation and its subsidiary or branch in Japan.

Transfer pricing manipulations are further controlled in the Japanese law under the section dealing with abuses of market power or 'unfair business practices'. Among the practices which are defined as amounting to an unfair business practice is 'dealing at undue prices' (Section 2[7]).

(d) *Canada*

In Section 32 of the Combines Investigation Act, agreements which restrain or unduly restrict competition in manufacture or trade (including those which 'enhance unreasonably the prices' of products) are prohibited. The law further states clearly that agreements between related enterprises are also subject to this prohibition unless the enterprises are 'controlled' (defined in terms of sufficient voting rights to elect the majority of directors of the company) by the same person or company.

(e) *EEC*

The pricing policies for transactions between related enterprises may be examined by the Commission under Article 85 (dealing with restrictive agreements) and Article 86 (dealing with abuses of dominant market power) of the Treaty of Rome. When a subsidiary is considered as economically independent of its parent, transfer prices could be controlled under Article 85; but when the subsidiary is considered as economically dependent, then the enterprise as a whole can be charged with abuse of a dominant position of market power under Article 86 if its transfer prices result in discriminatory or excessive market prices within the EEC.

One particular case concerned the inquiry by the Commission into the behaviour of oil companies in the Community during the period of the oil crisis (October 1973 to March 1974). The main aspect examined was crude oil prices including the 'transfer prices charged by oil companies in respect of crude oil sold to their refineries and refined products sold to their distributing subsidiaries'.[7] There are no details on the outcome of this case.

DEVELOPING COUNTRIES
(a) *Brazil*
Under regulations giving effect to Law No. 4137 of September 1962 on the control of abuses of economic power, one of the most commonly investigated practices in Brazil has been predatory pricing and price discrimination. These investigations have frequently involved foreign corporations operating in Brazil and the prices charged for intra-firm transactions. One such investigation involved Yamaha Musical do Brazil, a subsidiary of Nippon Gakki Company. The latter is alleged to have underpriced imports into Brazil thereby enabling the subsidiary to sell below cost with the objective of monopolising the market. Similar cases are reported to involve Ericsson in the tele-communications sector and Cargill in the grain sector.[8]
(b) *India*
According to the provisions of the Monopolies and Restrictive Trade Practices Act, 1969: 'a monopolistic trade practice will be deemed to be prejudicial to the public interest if, as a result of such practice, the cost of production or . . . the price or profits charged is unreasonably increased or if competition is unreasonably limited or reduced . . .' In this context, the Monopolies and Restrictive Trade Practices Commission has enquired into three cases of monopolistic trade practices by transnational corporations because of their very high profit earnings. The main objective of such enquiries appears to have been to submit these corporations to 'costing discipline', in particular as regards service charges by the parent companies, and to 'price administration' in order to curb the high level of prices by correlating them with costs.
(c) *Pakistan*
The Monopolies and Restrictive Trade Practices (Control and Prevention) Ordinance No.V, 1970, prohibits any practices between a subsidiary and a parent company which are likely to benefit one such undertaking to the prejudice of the other. The Monopoly Control Authority is empowered to order such action, 'as may be necessary to restore competition in the production, distribution or sale of any goods or provision of any services'.

INTERGOVERNMENTAL CO-OPERATION IN THE CONTROL OF TRANSFER PRICE MANIPULATIONS

Control of transfer price manipulations by transnational corporations is difficult without co-operation among states. The effects of such manipulations transcend national frontiers and information on how the transfer prices have been established is frequently located outside the country wishing to control them.

Governments' desire to control particular manipulations is unlikely to be identical since, as mentioned earlier, what is of concern to one country is unlikely to be the concern of another. As a result, conflicts of interests are likely to occur where co-operation is needed to obtain information. Enterprises may themselves refuse to supply information on the grounds that it is located abroad and therefore outside the country's jurisdiction. However, even if the enterprises are willing to provide such information, foreign authorities may not allow this to happen. Legislation exists in a number of countries providing powers to prevent the transmission abroad of information held in these countries — for example, in Australia, Canada, the Netherlands and the UK.[9]

So far, there would seem to have been only limited co-operation among governments on control of transfer price manipulations and, in particular, on the supply of information and consultations about possible conflicts of interest. What is needed is international agreement on two fronts; firstly, that all forms of transfer price manipulations should be prohibited; and, secondly, that enterprises and governments should assist one another to this end.

An initial step has been taken in this direction following the decision of the General Assembly of the United Nations in 1978 to convene, under the auspices of UNCTAD, a United Nations Conference on Restrictive Business Practices to negotiate a set of principles and rules for the control of restrictive business practices having adverse effects on international trade, particularly that of developing countries and the economic development of these countries. The basis for the negotiations at this Conference, is a text drawn by UNCTAD's Third *Ad hoc* Group of Experts on Restrictive Business Practices which had held six sessions during the period 1976 and 1979. The Conference met in November/December 1979 and reconvened in April 1980 to complete its work.

At the expert group level, a variety of pricing practices were identified for control, including predatory, a discriminatory and excessive pricing of products and services. With respect to the pricing of transactions between parents and subsidiaries, experts from developed market economy countries proposed that enterprises should refrain from: 'using discriminatory pricing transactions between affiliated enterprises as a means of abusing a dominant position of market power and affecting adversely competition outside these enterprises'. On the other hand, developing countries proposed a wider application of the provision, namely, that enterprises should refrain from restrictive business practices through: 'The use of pricing in transactions between affiliated enterprises to over-charge or under-charge for products or services supplied.'

In an attempt to reconcile these two positions, the President of the Conference proposed the following:

> '(ii) discriminatory (i.e. unjustifiably differentiated) pricing or terms or conditions in the supply or purchase of products or services, including by means of the use of pricing policies in transactions between affiliated enterprises which over-charge or under-charge for products or services purchased or supplied as compared with prices for similar or comparable transactions or by means of excessive pricing of products or services'.

Concerning the need for enterprises' co-operation in providing information, and for co-operation between states on this issue, a number of provisions were previously agreed at the expert group level. These include:

> 'Enterprises should consult and co-operate with competent authorities of countries directly affected in controlling restrictive business practices adversely affecting the interests of those countries. In this regard, enterprises should also provide information, in particular details of restrictive arrangements, required for this purpose, including that which may be located in foreign countries to the extent that in the latter event such production or disclosure is not prevented by applicable law or established public policy. Whenever the provision of information is on a voluntary basis, its provision should be in accordance with safeguards normally applicable in this field.

> States should, on request, or at their own initiative when the need comes to their attention, supply to other States, particularly of developing countries, publicly available information, and, to the extent consistent with their laws and established public policy, other information necessary to the receiving interested State for its effective control of restrictive business practices.'

NOTES

1 The most recent estimates of US imports showed that in 1977, 48% of all imports (54% in the case of manufactures) into this country were purchased by buyers related through ownership (5% or more equity stock) to the sellers. The estimate for 1975 was 45% (Source: UNCTAD computations on the basis of information supplied by G.K. Helleiner and R. Lavergne of the University of Toronto from data provided by the Foreign Trade Division of the US Bureau of Census).

2 For a review of restrictive business practice control in developed and developing countries see C. Greenhill, 'UNCTAD: Control of Restrictive Business Practices' *Journal of World Trade Law*, vol.12, no.1, 1978, pp.68-70.

3 United Kingdom Monopolies Commission, *Chlordiazepoxide and Diazepam*, HMSO London, 1973.

4 *Ibid.*, p.50.

5 Budeskartellamt G. Beschlussabteilung 36-432190 - T-37/73.

6 OECD, Annual Reports on Competition Policy on OECD Member Countries, 1975, no.2, Paris, p.53.

7 Fifth Report on Competition Policy of the EEC Commission, 1977, p.15.

8 Annual Report 1979, on 'Legislative and other developments in developed and developing countries in the control of restrictive business practices', prepared by the UNCTAD secretariat (TD/B/750) para.163.

9 'Dominant positions of market power of transnational corporations: use of the transfer pricing mechanism', study by the UNCTAD secretariat, United Nations, Sales No. E78.II.D.9, p.5.

(B) The Mechanics of Control

13.
TWO LEGAL MODELS IN THE CONTROL OF TRANSFER PRICING
PETER FITZPATRICK*

INTRODUCTION
I will argue that the control of transfer pricing by less developed countries (LDCs) is unnecessarily restricted by the legal model on which this control is based. This model I call a 'private law' one. I try to show that it inhibits governmental responses to transfer pricing and that it does not recognise other legitimate interests in the transfer pricing situation such as the interests of workers. I also describe and explore a possible alternative called the 'public law' model. The legal aspects of changing from the private to the public law model are then considered. I conclude by looking at objections to use of the public law model.

THE PRIVATE LAW MODEL
The private law model reflects law under competitive capitalism. It is a market model of law. Legal actors exchange in the market and in so doing they are considered free and equal in capacity. The terms of exchange are a matter of voluntary agreement. Law simply acts as a facilitator in providing the frame for exchange. It provides contract as the legal form of exchange and it provides stable and universally applicable rules around which the legal actor can orient his or her conduct. Contracts and the rules are upheld by the state through impartial courts which apply traditional principles and standards, and through officials who enforce the decisions of the courts. In this way the state is seen as being above the legal actors. But intervention goes only to the upholding of the frame and it does not disturb the freedom of legal actors to contract on their own terms within the frame: the private law model has no concern with the substantive fairness of exchange. To maintain this space within the frame, as it were, the state is also bound by law. It cannot intervene to affect the legal subject adversely unless this intervention is justified by law.

This account is, of course, sketchy. It is largely an account of an ideology, but of an immensely influential one. The element of exchange is essential to competitive capitalism and the private

197

law model reflects this reality. But with the private law model this element of exchange is generalised so as to appear the dominant or even sole economic nexus. In this way relations of production, which are based on inequality and economic coercion, are hidden or disguised by relations of exchange which are based on equality and freedom. A worker in an LDC is hardly in any 'real' sense equal to the transnational corporation (TNC) that employs him but, as we shall see, the law assumes a basic equality between them — to the benefit of the TNC.

THE PUBLIC LAW MODEL
With the growth of monopoly capitalism, the state has assumed more supportive and even directive functions in relation to the economy. In performing these functions, the state takes on wide, discretionary powers under flexible legal provisions. The legal actor does not just operate economically outside the state, orienting his conduct around stable and universally applicable rules; rather — if he has effective power or is otherwise recognised by the state — he bargains with the state for particular outcomes within the context of these flexible legal provisions. Instead of impartial adjudication, the outcomes more immediately reflect policy and clashes of material interest. As an example, in LDCs the public law model often typifies legal provisions giving officials broad powers to impose conditions on the exploitation of natural resources.

THE APPLICATION OF THE PRIVATE LAW MODEL TO TRANSFER PRICING
By way of giving some concreteness to the discussion, I will first look briefly at a relatively neglected area. Concern with transfer pricing from the perspective of the host country usually focuses on the interests of the government. Yet there are numerous other interests in the host country affected by the disposition of the surplus generated within the transnational corporation. For example, joint-ventures between TNCs and national investors (including the LDC government) as well as 'fade-out' requirements are becoming much more common. Overpricing equity contributions from the TNC discriminates against the other shareholders who have given (more) adequate value for their shares since the TNC will be draining-off capital-related profits at their expense. But legally the price for the capital contribution is determined by the contract to supply it — a contract between the TNC and the joint-venture, the latter often being controlled by

the TNC. Since, in line with the private law model,
concern with the substantive fairness of contractua
will normally not disturb this price. (Some countrie
have a form of official valuation for non-moi
contributions). Somewhat similarly, a worker
employed by the TNC has no legal basis on which
transfer pricing transaction even though transfei
depress domestic profits and low profits will ofte.. ᴜᴄ ᴜꜱᴇᴅ to
justify low wages. These are all matters which, in terms of the
private law model, can be accommodated in the contract of
employment between free and equal parties — the worker and the
TNC (or its domestic subsidiary.)

Examples could be multiplied, but I shall look now at the more
complex case of the interest of LDC governments in transfer
pricing and in its use to evade tax and exchange control laws.
Even when officials are given broad powers in the form of the
public law model — such as a power to determine a price 'in the
national interest' for exchange control purposes — they tend to
create and rely on narrower standards that are more typical of the
private law model. In terms of the private law model, generally,
what is apparent here is the rather direct dependence of legal
standards on the idea of a market. The most common formula of
control is that of an 'arm's-length price' — officials are
empowered to substitute the price that would have applied if the
parties had not been related. At best the formula may be invoking
a price that is or is assumed to be determined freely in the market.
But in its terms the formula does not necessarily go this far since
prices between unrelated parties can be subject to monopoly
influences. Other legal formulae can be somewhat less abject.
Some refer a 'normal price' to 'free market conditions' and
others, perhaps ambiguously, refer to the 'open market' and the
'fair market value'.

With these formulae and approaches the general and underlying
assumption is that price in most cases will be determined by the
market, and law need only intervene to correct the occasional
deviant case by reference to the market price — law supplements
the market. Yet for many exchanges between affiliates there will
be no comparable market price. In this situation 'price' becomes
very much a dependent and manipulable element in the
international voyages of surplus value. Quite apart from this,
there remains the question of price 'distortions' in the market
which can be reflected immediately in the formulae. Indeed it may
be argued that the predominant dynamic of the world economic

ystem is increasingly monopolistic in its effect so that, in relying on a price determined within that system, a government will often be directly subordinating its interests to the monopoly power of TNCs and others. More particularly, it can be argued that the world economic system inherently discriminates against LDCs and that this discrimination will be reflected in 'price' even in a 'free' market.

There are several detailed implications of relying on the private law model that I will bring out later but I will draw just one more general implication here. The private law model sees the state and law as being 'above' the legal actor. The legal actor or 'the individual' must even be protected by law from the powerful state. In terms of the private law model, the TNC is a legal actor 'equal' with any other. But the private law model cannot reflect agglomerations of corporate power. More specifically, it is a truism that many TNCs are more powerful economically than many LDCs. Indeed, some LDCs have been not unfairly called 'branch countries', so dependent are they on TNCs for their very existence and identity. At the very least TNCs, as legal actors, are qualitatively different from domestic legal actors in that they have considerable room to manoeuvre in the international arena and so pose great and often insuperable problems for a government that seeks to control them. In the international perspective the private law model becomes increasingly absurd. Faced with an 'overmighty subject' in the TNC, governments inhibit their own response to transfer pricing in narrow legal formulas and, as I illustrate later, in jurisdictional fetters and in legal presumptions meant to protect the weak legal actor against state power. Further, the governmental response is weakened in organisational fragmentation among disparate legal-administrative categories that usually only focus tangentially on transfer pricing; such categories include natural resource regulation, general investment conditions, corporate organisation, revenue collection and exchange control.

As something of an excursus, I should mention efforts of the private law model to sustain itself in the attempted control of monopoly. This matter is also relevant in that, as Vaitsos' work strongly suggests, transfer pricing and certain monopoly practices are connected.[1] There are laws — including some attempting to affect international corporate networks — which confront the issue structurally by prohibiting and even providing for the breaking-up of monopolies. But it is now manifest that, overall, such laws are a spitting into the wind. More peripherally and more sensibly, other laws prohibit particular abuses of a monopoly position such as various kinds of tied arrangements. Often, however, monopoly laws do not apply to transactions within the TNC's corporate network, such transactions being considered internal to the enterprise. From the LDC perspective this is probably the situation where these laws are most needed.

THE APPLICATION OF THE PUBLIC LAW MODEL TO TRANSFER PRICING

The thoroughgoing adoption of a public law model should provoke a government to maximise the effectiveness of its response to transfer pricing or, in a broader perspective, to maximise its share of the surplus value generated within the TNC. The government would not subordinate or restrict itself in formulae of 'the arm's-length' or even 'free market' varieties but, rather, would assume an unfettered discretionary power to control transfer pricing. Other legal restraints would be done away with or appropriately modified, and I will instance these later. In other words, the government would, in terms of the public law model, intervene to secure the best price and in so doing it would be concerned not to have its position rigidly limited at the outset. For this purpose, the government would want to concentrate its technical bargaining strengths and knowledge and not have them scattered, as now, over the numerous and disparate legal-administrative categories that I mentioned pre-viously. The need for 'co-ordination' in this is frequently stressed and almost invariably ignored. Organisational fusion is needed, unless there are valid and weightier factors keeping these categories administratively separate. There would not appear to be any. This organisational division is an anachronism in the 'developed' world where it originated, but it has been passed on in a largely unmodified way to LDCs where it is even more inappropriate.

In a public law frame, transfer pricing would no longer have the appearance of being even formally contained in limiting legal categories. It would have to be seen as part of the wider concern to maximise returns from the TNC. This factor plus, again, the need to maximise the application of relevant skills and knowledge, indicates that the control of transfer pricing should be fused legally and administratively with the negotiation of conditions generally with TNCs, and with the monitoring of their behaviour. A related practical point is that since transfer pricing can undermine the initial terms negotiated with a TNC, the potentiality for transfer pricing and apt countervailing measures should be taken account of at the outset.

LEGAL ASPECTS OF CHANGING TO A PUBLIC LAW MODEL
I will now look in more detail at the legal aspects of changing to a public law model, and generally of maximising the governmental response to transfer pricing.

1. *The formular element*
As I have mentioned, there would be a change from constraining forms of the arm's-length variety to the broadest form of discretionary power.

2. *Information for government*
Effective intervention by the LDC government under the public law model depends on adequate information, and such information will be largely under the control of the TNC. The LDC government, to comprehend transfer pricing, must have the most detailed knowledge of the structure, operations and accounting 'rationality' of the TNC. The government has to be able, as it were, to stand in the shoes of the (senior) officers of the TNC who make the decisions about transfer pricing. The UK and the US governments insist on 'equality of information' with government contractors through 'truth in negotiation' legislation or similar contractual terms, and perhaps this can provide an apt precedent here. As an aspect of organisationally focusing bargaining strengths, there would have to be a change in confidentiality laws which restrict information given to the government for some certain purposes, such as taxation, to use for that purpose.

3. *Information for citizens*
Interest in transfer pricing under the public law model may extend further than purely governmental concerns. Workers in the host country have a rather direct interest in the surplus value spirited out through transfer pricing. I have already referred in some detail to the position of national shareholders in the joint-venture and 'fade out' situations. Domestic consumers of the TNC's product also have an interest, for prices could be lower if transfer pricing were contained. Domestic suppliers to the TNC will often be negotiating prices related to the profitability of the TNC's national presence — a profitability that transfer pricing can ostensibly depress or obliterate. Unfortunately, many LDC governments, including some 'strong states' at that, would see their interests as being more compatible with those of the TNC than with those of workers or even those of national shareholders. Sometimes the LDC government provides workers with infor-

mation and some assistance for the purpose of wage negotiation. Exceptionally, national shareholders can obtain a special statutory audit to check on their interests. But most commonly these people and others have to rely on information that is publicly available under corporate law. Such information sometimes runs to a standard form of group accounts, but more often the information does not go anywhere near this far. Sanctions for failure to provide information can be derisory and the obligation not effectively enforced.

All this will usually fall very short of what is needed to uncover transfer pricing practices. At the simplest, workers, national shareholders and others with specified interests could be informed of prices negotiated or adjusted by the government for its own purposes. Going further, access could be given to information that would help these people identify and evaluate transfer pricing practices independently, or at least enable them to raise appropriate questions in their dealings with the TNC. Both these proposals come up against standard notions of commercial confidentiality and governmental secrecy. In contrast, the 'freedom of information' law in the US gives considerable access to government information. Some laws giving access to information held by the government enable a government official to withhold information for some such reasons as these. This expedient cannot accommodate the conflict that can exist between, say, workers and, on the other hand, the LDC government and TNCs. One way of minimising this dimension of the problem is to put more emphasis on general public disclosure. In the host LDC, most activities of TNCs are matters of profound public effect — a point that the public law model can serve to concretise. The Canadian Corporation and Labour Unions Returns Act of 1962 provides an interesting model of how far public disclosure relevant to transfer pricing can go. A modified form of disclosure would be to require officials charged with the control of transfer pricing to report publicly and annually on the performance of this function.

4. *Jurisdictional limits*

There are numerous legal rules characteristic of the private law model that inhibit an LDC government's assuming jurisdiction over a TNC, and that are incompatible with the thoroughgoing application of a public law model. With the TNC being able to use its international spread to manoeuvre around the requirements of 'fixed' nation-states, the LDC government should maximise the potentiality of its response to the situation. (The extraterritorial legal aggressiveness of the US government can provide lessons and justifications here.) For a start, the LDC government, when bargaining, confronts the full power and whole identity of the TNC; the negotiated terms, information requirements, penalties for transfer pricing and national legal obligations in general should be capable of enforcement against any part or parts of the corporate network constituting the TNC. Any two corporations within the network will usually be treated in law as two distinct legal subjects, and it will usually be the case that legal obligations will only be applicable to and enforceable against the domestic subsidiary of the TNC. What can be provided for here is a 'lifting of the corporate veil', as it is put in English law, to make obligations enforceable throughout the corporate network. Such a provision would have to be sufficiently broad and flexible to cover the variety of ways in which transnational corporate networks get tied together. A refinement on this line of argument can be illustrated in the power some developed-country governments have to require a resident parent to make available information about a non-resident subsidiary; it would add some balance to the situation if an LDC government could penalise a resident subsidiary for failure of a non-resident parent to provide information or indeed for failure of the parent to ensure the performance of obligations in the context of the host country. A related point is that rules conferring jurisdiction on courts in the host countries are often too narrow to cover the whole corporate network of the TNC; for example, jurisdiction based on 'residence' within the host country could well cover only the TNC's local subsidiary. These jurisdiction rules should be broadened to encompass the whole transnational corporation. Somewhat akin to jurisdiction rules are precise definitions of the circumstances in which transactions between affiliates can be questioned; these are used by TNCs in structuring transactions so as to 'avoid' controls on transfer pricing.

5. *Procedural presumptions*

There are certain procedural principles symptomatic of the private law model which can inhibit a government's response to transfer pricing. Typically, the government has the 'burden of proof' in any prosecution or other legal case it initiates, but with the public law model it should not be so hindered. Similarly restrictive is the interpretative presumption applied by the courts to 'read down' or 'strictly construe' (as it is put in English law) laws that are somehow adverse to the 'rights' of the legal subjects such as tax laws. This presumption also influences official behaviour in applying the law since the courts will usually be its ultimate interpreters.

6. *Governmental sanctions*

Governments often are considerably restrained about sanctions against transfer pricing — although some countries have introduced substantial penalties. From the perspective of the public law model and because transfer pricing can so fundamentally affect the terms on which a TNC's presence in the host country is considered acceptable, there should, in cases of serious abuse, be broad powers for the host government to re-negotiate the conditions under which the TNC can operate; ancillary to this would be powers to revoke any relevant governmental licences and to install official management.

7. *Remedial action by citizens*

A fundamental issue is whether workers, national shareholders and others should be able to take action (or whether action should be taken by the government for their benefit) aimed at correcting past depredations — whether, for example, these people could obtain some type of compensation for value already drained off through transfer pricing. Or should the TNC in relation to these people (continue to) be allowed 'to get away with it'? This raises issues of substantive fairness that are alien to the private law model but which receive no specific resolution with the public law model. Whatever action people such as workers and national shareholders can take, a certain plurality of interests concerned with transfer pricing can serve as a check on and spur to government action against transfer pricing.

OBJECTIONS TO THE PUBLIC LAW MODEL

It was objected at the Conference when the earlier version of this paper was delivered, that the public law model would give rise to such 'ad hocery' and basic instability that it would be administratively unworkable. But the public law model does not rule out the use of administrative routinisation. Quantitative significance and qualitative variation of transactions would in most cases reveal whether examination *de novo* or resort to precedent was in order. Moreover, it will sometimes be the case that applying a public law model will lessen the need for administrative involvement in regulating transfer pricing. With this model, legal regulation of particularly significant investment would involve taking account of the widest range of factors and would involve the working out of a particularised 'package'. In this process it may be better to restrict the scope within which transfer pricing can operate rather than seeking to control it on a broad front. For example, the package could involve a tax base alternative to net income, such as a royalty-type tax on physical production or a turnover tax.

Another objection raised was that the public law model involves greater discretion than the private law model, and would be more open to corruption. Bourgeois legality is not exactly strong in LDCs and it would be surprising if the private law model served as anything like a bulwark against corruption in relation to the control of transfer pricing or in relation to anything else. Central concepts in the private law model of the arm's-length variety sometimes bear so little or no relation to any constraining reality that they impart a considerable, if somewhat random, discretionary element.

Finally, corruption must be seen as an aspect of influence on government generally. Many governments would not have the capability or the desire to apply a public law model to transfer pricing. Indeed the use of the public law model to control TNCs often merely gives an appearance of power and masks a subordination of government to the TNC. An LDC government could only use the model successfully if it had a significant degree of autonomy in its dealings with TNCs. But I would argue that the model is a real possibility and that, even where the level of foreign investment is considerable, many LDC governments are now showing such a significant degree of autonomy. (In this they may be serving privileged elements within the LDC, but I do not take this as an adequate argument against the more effective control of transfer pricing). All this is not to say that for governments lacking significant autonomy reliance on the private law model is preferable — rather, they should confront the prior issue of the nature and extent of their involvement with TNCs.

NOTES

* In reworking this paper, I have benefitted greatly from the discussions and presentations at the 1978 Conference, especially from Robin Murray's paper on 'Transfer Pricing and the State'. Apart from the Conference, I also very much appreciate the help Julie Southwood gave me and Pearce Rood kindly supplied some useful information about the law relating to transfer pricing.

1 Constantine V. Vaitsos, *Intercountry Income Distribution and Transnational Enterprises*, The Clarendon Press, Oxford, 1974.

14.
THE INTERNATIONAL ECONOMICS OF THE INFORMATION INDUSTRY AND THE DEVELOPING COUNTRIES
G.K. HELLEINER

INTRODUCTION
In order for individuals, firms or nations to profit fully from exchange they must have adequate information to permit them to assess the available alternative terms and forms of exchange. Developing countries are notoriously ill-equipped in this respect, and their relative disadvantage shows vividly in their limited capacity to assess the appropriateness of the prices with which foreign suppliers or buyers present them. Their assessment difficulties relate not only to transfer pricing control but also to effective import shopping and export marketing in arm's-length relationships.

Political independence in the Third World, and the more recent attempts to de-link economic relationships — through national-isations, the exercise of greater control over exports and imports, unpackaging, etc. — alter, in a fundamental way, the organisation of the relevant information flows and processing systems. Whatever their other characteristics, colonial relationships in the political sphere and parent-subsidiary relationships in the realm of economics offered 'internalised' rather than arm's-length, market-type forms of informational (and other) organisation. The move 'from status to contract' in North-South relationships implies a need for the development of new informational systems and means of interaction. Where developing countries are now independently buying or selling on world markets they must develop effective means of search in the manner of any arm's-length shopper or seller. Where intra-firm trade still persists in their international transactions, such search is required instead for the purpose of monitoring or controlling transfer pricing.

At present, information flows to the developing countries' decision makers through a wide variety of channels and media. It arrives through 'inhouse' collection and communication on the part of overseas commercial representatives, attachés, or agents; it is assembled through trade journals, specialised consultancies,

207

the services of brokers and dealers, the messages of salesmen and foreign aid or trade bureaucrats, and various informal contacts. Rarely is its assembly and dissemination systematised on an ongoing basis as it typically is in large commercial enterprises (e.g. Strassman 1976, Nanus 1978). The basic informational resources — in the form of libraries, data banks, and the like — available to the poorest countries are typically hopelessly inadequate: frequently taking the exclusive form of published sources arriving sporadically by sea mail to understaffed libraries. For those 'in the trade', published sources, even 'hot from the press', are typically too obsolete to be useful for daily decision making. The telephone and telecommunications, while more expensive, are frequently *essential* instruments of communication.

It is necessary to assess the capacity of the informationally weak to acquire, usually at arm's length, and to process the information which they now require to make independent decisions which are in their own interest, rather than in the interests of the total information (and other) systems of which they were previously part. Difficult decisions must now be taken on how much to spend, and in what ways, in order to improve the informational 'efficiency' of national decision making.

INFORMATION, MARKETS AND ECONOMIC THEORY

Intra-firm trade is itself the product, in part, of some peculiarities of economic transactions which are made under conditions of informational uncertainty, and of imperfections in markets for information. There are thus strong pressures working against 'delinking' and in favour of internalised international trade; they can be expected to encourage intra-firm trade in newer Third World-based firms as well as in the old-fashioned transnationals. In order both to understand the difficulties of shifting to more arm's-length economic relationships, and to assess the possibilities for the mobilisation of information for the control of transfer pricing where internalised trade remains, it is important to understand the economics of information.

Until very recently the study of information and knowledge has occupied 'a slum dwelling in the town of economics' (Stigler 171). It should not, therefore, be surprising that the implications of information economics and politics for the poor of the world have received so little attention. In no part of the current debate over global political and economic problems is the importance of information more dramatically evident than in the search for new forms of mutually agreeable relations between transnational corporations and poor nation states.

The information industry can be defined in different ways. Marschak (1968) regards it as that which provides the services of 'inquiring, communicating, deciding'. Inquiring is a matter of data gathering or production; communication involves means of encoding, transmission through a variety of channels of differential speed, reliability and cost, and decoding; deciding has to do with the software which renders what is available usable by decision makers. Broad definitions would include virtually all white-collar employment, and in particular, the educational system. In one study, employing a broad definition, it is estimated that the information industry accounts for over 40% of US employment (Porat 1977), and is at the very centre of the notion of 'post-industrial society'.

Information and knowledge can take many different forms. Considerable attention has been devoted in recent years to the developing countries' dependence upon imported knowledge in the form of technology; and to the imperfections of technology markets, the inappropriateness of much of what is available to them, and the need for developing increased indigenous technological capacity. Rather less attention has been devoted, however, to the more general question of '*market* information' or 'commercial intelligence', upon which the effective functioning of arm's-length systems of exchange depends; this, at a time when increased resort to arm's-length exchange is an accepted part of Third World aspirations. The latter kind of information is obviously relevant to the new interest in the control of transfer pricing.

This type of information cannot be entirely separated from knowledge of the underlying technical change, demand shifts, and the like. The distinction between 'market information' and other types of knowledge is nevertheless a real one. A consideration of the economics of market information must address such matters as the economics of alternative organisations, and the economics of search, as well as the peculiar properties of information markets. Political-economic analysis obviously must extend still further to include interest articulation, power and other organisational issues.

Fully-informed, rational economic man still can be found in elementary economics textbooks where 'his cool, consistent mind quickly and costlessly scans the myriads of alternatives facing him' (Shubik 1967, p.358). In popular mythology, his principal habitat today is in large business organisations and, above all, in the transnational corporations. But, increasingly, theorists are investigating models of a more realistic world in which one typically finds instead 'the uncertain decision-maker acting under severely restricted conditions of information embedded within a communication system upon which he is becoming increasingly dependent' (Shubik, p.361).

Market information is not a free good, available to all. It can be considered as a product like any other which can be acquired at a cost — either by 'making' it oneself or by acquiring it from another. In the standard literature on the economics of search (Stigler 1961) it consists of information on the range of available price alternatives in a real world in which, because of transactions costs of various kinds, the 'law of one price' is all too rarely encountered; and assumptions as to the distribution of prices and the costs of searching lead to decision rules for both buyers and sellers on how much to search or how much information to offer through advertising. Matters become more complex when the searcher does not even know the degree of price dispersion, for then he cannot know how much to search; the ignorant, e.g., the tourist in a foreign land, can expect to pay more when he buys, and receive less when he sells. But market information involves much more than this static and unidimensional fact of price dispersion. Prices and their degree of dispersion are constantly changing in response to innumerable influences upon demand and supply; market information, therefore, becomes obsolete very quickly. More important still, information as to the likely (though obviously still uncertain) future state of prices becomes a necessary input to market decision making; even better, if one possesses the capacity to process it independently, is information concerning the major underlying influences upon future market behaviour, for this permits one to make one's own judgments independently of others' possible biases or 'opportunistic' behaviour. Information of this more qualitative kind is clearly much more difficult to quantify or even theorise about.

Of equal importance to price information, particularly when goods are not homogeneous, is information as to the *quality* of items to be acquired. Search must therefore take place on the intensive (quality) margin as well as on the extensive one. In some instances the suitability of goods to the buyer can only be tested through use; such products have been termed 'experience' (as opposed to 'search') goods (Nelson 1970).

Among the means of reducing qualitative informational

uncertainties in a complex world are the development of 'customer relationships', brand loyalties, 'reputation' and 'goodwill'. In conditions of great informational uncertainty, cautious buying (or selling) behaviour is understandable: the familiar — in terms of existing relationships, geography, language, etc. — may be chosen even when the cost, objectively speaking, appears high. As information improves, the breadth of shopping (and marketing) increases. Thus what geographers call 'information space' (Törnqvist 1977 pp.156-7), the nature of information networks, can play an important role in the determination of the direction of both domestic and international flows of goods and services. The internalisation of trade inside firms is a major device for reducing informational uncertainty.

Those who do not themselves obtain information in the volume or form they require in the course of their general activities must acquire it from others. While such acquisition does not always occur on markets, it is analytically helpful, as in the case of technology, to consider it as if it did. Information markets, like technology markets, have peculiar properties.

1. Information is not an exhaustible product; that is, it is not 'used-up' through employment or dissemination. Many can possess it at the same time. Its provision to others, even if transactions costs are zero, may nevertheless involve one in losses, and there may be private advantages in not sharing it. On the other hand, substantial costs may also be sensibly incurred for the provision of information to others — e.g. through advertising. (Indeed, there may be advantages in passing on *mis*information; and that fact necessitates a greater capacity to assess information acquired from 'external' sources.)

2. The cost of transmitting information which has already been produced (transactions cost) is not zero, and can be expected to vary greatly as between different types of information and different means of transmission. Transmission systems have their own factor-intensity and scale requirements, and it is likely that the lowest-cost systems require substantial capital inputs and scale. The latter create barriers to entry to certain transmission systems, and it follows that different actors will have differential access to low-cost media.

3. The returns from the production of information are generally not fully appropriable; that is, it is often possible for others to realise gains from the use of information which you 'produced' without your being able to obtain a share of them. There are no laws or conventions, such as those governing patents and

trademarks, which protect intellectual property rights in this area. It follows that great quantities of information are transferred through low-cost or even totally non-commercialised channels, sometimes quite informal ones. (Some kinds of information are not easily transferred, such as those learned best by doing; and others are successfully kept secret.)

4. Information is a product of extremely rapid obsolescence, an attribute which also impedes its effective transfer among unrelated decision makers.

5. Like technology, its quality is impossible to judge accurately until one possesses it; many of those with the 'best' supplies are themselves, consciously or unconsciously, biased about its content. Given the advantages to be gained from the conscious provision of misinformation, one must be particularly careful about its reliability.

6. Information is frequently only available (at reasonable cost) in packages or indivisible lumps which, not being tailor-made, include goods and services other than those actually sought. These indivisibilities may relate to the size of the information package itself, to the packaging of the required information with goods or other purchases, to the minimum period of time over which it is to be offered, etc. It is often a by-product of some other activity.

7. On the supply side, the production of information seems likely to be characterised by economies of scale, economies of experience (learning by doing), and positive externalities; the cumulative effect of acquiring information over wider areas and over longer periods of time is to render one better at acquiring more. 'Since the cost of collection of information is (approximately) independent of its use (although the cost of dissemination is not), there is a strong tendency toward monopoly in the provision of information: in general, there will be a "standard" source for trade information' (Stigler 1973). Where information is not supplied by independent specialised firms, these influences promote oligopolistic tendencies in the industries dependent upon it.

8. Still on the supply side, the production, storage and processing of information is highly skill-intensive and capital-intensive.

Incomplete information, and resulting risk and uncertainty, have become central to major theories of economic organisation, both at the macro- and the micro-level. At the macro- or societal level, the debate between advocates of central planning and decentralised market systems has long centred on questions of data collection and distribution. Hayek, in the pre-computer age, believed that the sheer size of the data collection, communication and processing requirements for effective centralised decision making made it unfeasible, whatever other merits or demerits it might have. Markets are themselves, he argued (1945), the most efficient and effective information systems. Needless to say, the new technologies of the electronic age today require a different formulation of such arguments. The efficiency with which macro-systems of economic organisation employ available data for the purposes of allocation of resources continues to be a matter for (pure) economic theorising. These investigations have not as yet adequately addressed the implications for 'social efficiency', (in which 'efficiency' is defined not in terms merely of Pareto optimality but in terms of income distributional objectives as well), of the *differential and asymmetric* access to information of actors within the system.

At the micro-level, the modern theory of the firm itself, and certainly the theory of mergers and vertical integration, have been built in substantial part upon assumptions with respect to the availability and quality of information. In a recent symposium on the very frontier of the 'economics of internal organisation' its organiser remarked on the 'striking' fact that all of the papers were 'critically concerned with information in some form or other' and could be regarded as explorations into 'a variety of informationally constrained resource-allocation problems and institutional responses that characterise firms, organisations, and groups' (Spence 1975, p.164). The replacement of the market through integration or merger takes place, among other reasons, as a result of 'transactional failures' in markets (Williamson 1971), failures traceable primarily to problems in the processing of information. Dunning (1977, p.403) refers to them as 'cognitive imperfections' (see also Hirschleifer, Malmgren, Marschak, Spence and Williamson).

According to these theories, in circumstances of great complexity and uncertainty there may be limits to individuals' or small firms' capacities to receive, store, retrieve and process information faultlessly, or to transmit information to one another effectively ('bounded rationality'); in such circumstances internalisation of what would otherwise be arm's-length transactions or learning by doing may be the most effective means of organising activity and realising scale economies.

Moreover, where there may be reason to doubt the total veracity or completeness of information being supplied by one's (arm's-length) source, particularly where 'small numbers bargaining' rather than active competition (which is to some degree an automatic 'policeman') is found, it may be necessary to internalise one's information sources to prevent what has been termed 'opportunism' (i.e. 'an effort to realise individual gains through a lack of candor or honesty in transactions', Williamson, Wachter and Harris 1975, pp.258-9). Internalisation may also reduce the incidence of 'information impactedness' stemming not so much from opportunism as from inherent difficulties of specifying contractual arrangements.

Both the cost of information and its quality may be influenced by the institutional arrangements through which it is collected, communicated and processed. In general, modern micro-theory concludes, 'A situation in which anonymous agents deal with an impersonal market is not conducive to efficiency with imperfect information' (Spence p.171). Internalisation of transactions through merger or integration is the mechanism through which private actors seek to overcome these problems in a market economy. Governmental institutions and planning systems are obvious alternative means of organising information assembly and use in order to seek more efficient overall outcomes.

At the international level, the potential for governmental institutions is limited by the weakness of the world 'political system'. The transnational corporations are far ahead of governments in their utilisation of the most modern information systems. They possess the capital, skill and scale to produce, transmit and process information with maximum efficiency; and they have long since overcome the major imperfections of market exchange by internalising their informational (and other) flows.

IMPROVED INFORMATION FOR DEVELOPING COUNTRIES

There is a clear need for the development of better systems of market information for the use of the developing countries, particularly the poorest and weakest among them. But the basic characteristics of the information industry, its markets and its present institutional manifestations, severely challenge the ingenuity of developing countries seeking to improve their access to international market information. On the one hand, the development of an indigenous informational capacity faces especially in its early stages, the disadvantages of small scale limited experience, and limited positive externalities, together with its need for substantial capital and skill inputs. These constitute significant barriers to entry. On the other hand, to acquire information through arm's-length purchase is to face the difficulties of quality assessment, rapid obsolescence, inappropriate packaging, others' market power and probably high cost. Whether information is to be 'made' or bought, the difficulties of appropriating the product, the gains to be realised through its diffusion, and the potential for scale economies and positive externalities, all suggest the potential productivity of governmental rather than decentralised private activity in this sector.

Within individual developing countries there is undoubtedly some potential for improvements in existing systems for gathering and interpreting market information. By no means all information is firm-specific, sector-specific or ministry-specific; yet it is frequently collected in parallel efforts through different sources in a wasteful and repetitious manner, even within the same governmental system, without adequate domestic distribution or use. Information is often acquired at great cost from foreign sources when it is already readily available at home (or from cheaper foreign sources known to other domestic users). It may be possible to realise at least some scale and other economies through greater rationalisation of existing information systems; and this is likely to involve conscious governmental policy to that end.

It is likely that the developing countries, especially the poorest, will still have to purchase many of their information requirements from abroad. This is as true of information required for the control of transfer pricing as of that for more efficient arm's-length shopping or marketing. The available sources of information for the possible use of developing countries concerned with transfer pricing abuse are varied, and differ with the sector concerned. There are not many sellers of across-the-board information on market prices.

It may be worth considering a specific instance in which a private firm in the information industry at present does provide such *general* services to a number of African governments, from the standpoint of its 'efficiency' relative to possible alternatives.

The activities of General Superintendence, (actually Société Générale de Surveillance, SGS), on behalf of the eight African countries which employ its services, illustrate some of the limitations of present market arrangements in the information sector. Here is a firm of substantial scale and experience, drawing upon considerable reserves of capital and (especially) skill, to provide certain limited packages of rapidly dating information to its clients. Specifically, it undertakes to check the quantity, quality and price of imports, the latter being compared with 'prices commonly charged for this product and related services in the applicable market and conditions'. The information it supplies consists of a 'yes' or 'no' on each shipment it inspects. In return for this service it is paid a fee averaging roughly 1% of the value of the shipments. The quality and value of its services to these clients is extremely difficult to assess, since its reputation in the field of its specialised activity may alone be sufficient to deter large numbers of exporters from practices they might otherwise attempt to employ against ill-informed buyers, even if the quality of the information it actually provides is dubious. It could also be influenced by conflicts of interest, particularly where, as in the case of its relatively small African clients, it has more important interests and business relationships to protect.

Moreover, it does not begin to provide the full shopping information which buyers really require. In the first place, it confines its role to making comparisons with other shipments purely at the national market level. (British and American tax authorities are considerably more stringent in their assessments of the 'reasonableness' of prices for traded goods.) Secondly, it does not even transmit the market information it collects; it simply offers a dichotomous verdict (yes/no) on individual shipments. This modest price information is not typically sold to private clients since, significantly, they prefer to do their shopping themselves. SGS is unlikely to do more for their African clients because of their need to preserve the value of their information, and their image of independence and objectivity. A commercial firm must, after all, seek to appropriate as much as it reasonably can from its investments.

What this service provides, then, is a generalised check upon some forms of 'opportunism' on the part of those with whom African buyers transact at arm's-length, including foreign firms whose shipments are made on an intra-firm basis. The possibility of some opportunism on the part of the information firm itself remains, but it is presumably believed to be smaller. It does very little to improve commercial information of the more important sort, e.g., price information, which is at the core of the economics of search. Nor, therefore, does it provide an adequate information base for the effective monitoring of transfer prices.

The commercialisation of information generates some obvious social inefficiencies. If a commercial firm in the information industry, such as SGS, learns that a *particular* exporting firm is unreliable or 'opportunistic' in its dealings with weaker trading partners, or that *particular* shipments are qualitatively flawed, or that the price dispersion with respect to a *particular* product in its particular 'applicable market' is thus and so, it never pays it to make this information widely available. Although the cost (whether private or social) of transmitting such information widely would be minimal and the social gains potentially great, it will not happen because there are no private gains to be appropriated from such a practice. Only those who specifically pay for the provision of such information will receive it, and even they will receive no more than is specifically required under the terms of their contracts. Thus, if a shipment of grain is found to be infested, the probable effect of the information industry will be to redirect it from a country which pays for its services to another which is less well-serviced or informed; indeed, if the exporter himself knows of the infestation he may well redirect it in advance to countries which are not as well serviced by the information industry.

The cost of transmitting such information, once acquired, is seemingly very small. If a private firm does not do it — for reasons which are readily apparent — why do governments which have acquired it not do so? Once one client of the commercial information firm has paid its service charge, why should it not pass the resulting information on at minimal further cost to other interested and friendly parties? Could not at least some of the information be paid for only once, instead of — as in the case of SGS' eight African clients — eight times? In part, the answer may lie in the problem of the 'free rider': it is difficult to arrive at mutually agreed means of financing activities which are in everyone's interest when individual parties know they will derive benefits from the service anyway. In part, it may lie in the technical difficulties of transmitting relevant data, since certainly the problems of shipment-by-shipment checking will remain, and the supporting infrastructure for such information storage and transmission is weak or non-existent in Africa today.

Probably most important, however, is the fact that although SGS has information which, if widely shared, could be much more productively employed, it provides it only in a form — dichotomous decisions on individual shipments — which severely limits not only its use but also its transferability.

It is time, then, to consider how an alternative information system might work. Could the considerable expenditures (1% of their total import value) undertaken by SGS' African clients be better employed in some collective information activity of their own? Or, if not, could the information that they already acquire at least be more effectively utilised in their common interest? What is at issue is not necessarily a matter of across-the-board import substitution of SGS so much as it is a matter of considering in which sectors and activities they are really best suited to supply their services.

Evidently, SGS does not provide much price or market information to its African clients, although that information is certainly collected. A major positive externality of the policing function thus remains unrealised, essentially because of SGS' own business calculations. If buyers controlled the organisation they would most certainly utilise all of these possibilities more effectively.

Cooperation and exchange of information among information-poor countries has gone much further in the exporting sector — through producers' associations and the like — than it has in importing. I do not mean to minimise the difficulties — both technical and political — of working out such new schemes for economic informational cooperation. Nor should one underemphasise the enormous headstart and genuine advantage enjoyed in these matters by large, experienced firms such as SGS. It may be that for the present one can do little better than to continue to employ them for many purposes. One suspects, however, that better terms might be negotiated through coordinated bargaining; African-government business already accounts for about 10% of SGS' total turnover (*Financial Times*, 2 February 1979).

Further investigations of alternatives, and the exercise of a little institutional imagination are certainly due in the informational sector. There can be no defence of unthinking adherence to the *status quo* in the face of its obvious and manifest limitations. The question in this specific instance is whether there may be scope for governmental action to take advantage of the potential for positive externalities and scale economies realisable through the exchange of information. By so doing they might begin to counter the advantage enjoyed at present by large, experienced commercial firms operating in quasi-monopolistic circumstances. More generally, failure to develop new information systems for the developing countries, to permit them more effectively to control transfer pricing and to shop efficiently, may mean not only the perpetuation of the inefficiencies and inequities of present international exchange but also their worsening, as a result of internationally unbalanced technical change, in the foreseeable future.

NOTE

*   I am grateful to Robin Murray and Reginald Green whose comments on an earlier version have considerably sharpened the argument; neither are to be implicated, however, in the contents of the present paper.

BIBLIOGRAPHY

Darrow, Joel W. and Belilove, James R. (1978), 'The Growth of Databank Sharing', *Harvard Business Review*, November-December.

Dunning, John H. (1977), 'Trade, Location of Economic Activity, and the MNE: A Search for an Eclectic Approach', in Bertil Ohlin *et al.* (ed.), *The International Location of Economic Activity*, Macmillan, pp.395-418.

Hayek, F.A. (1945), 'The Use of Knowledge in Society', *American Economic Review*, vol.35, no.4, September.

Helleiner, G.K. and Cruise O'Brien, R. (1980), 'The Political Economy of Information in a changing International Economic Order', *International Organisation*, Autumn.

Hirschleifer, J. (1973), 'Where Are We in the Theory of Information', *American Economic Review*, vol.63, no.2, May.

Malmgren, H. (1961), 'Information, Expectations and the Theory of the Firm', *Quarterly Journal of Economics*, vol.75, August.

Marschak, J. (1968), 'Economics of Inquiring, Communicating, Deciding', *American Economic Review*, vol.58, no.2; reprinted in D.M. Lamberton (ed.), *Economics of Information and Knowledge*, Penguin, 1971.

McHale, John (1976), *The Changing Information Environment*, Westview Press, Boulder.

Nanus, Burt (1978), 'Business, Government and the Multinational Computer', *Columbia Journal of World Business*, Spring.

Nelson, P. (1970), 'Information and Consumer Behavior', *Journal of Political Economy*, vol.78, March-April.

Porat, Marc Uri (1977), *The Information Economy: Definition and Measurement*, US Department of Commerce, Office of Telecommunication.

Shubik, M. (1967), 'Information, Rationality and Free Choice in a Future Democratic Society', *Daedalus*, vol.96, pp.771-78; reprinted in D.M. Lamberton (ed.), *Economics of Information and Knowledge*, Penguin, 1971.

Spence, Michael (1975), 'The Economics of Internal Organization: An Introduction', *The Bell Journal of Economics*, vol.6, no.1, Spring.

Stigler, George (1961), 'The Economics of Information', *Journal of Political Economy*, vol. LXIX, no.3, June.

Strassman, Paul A. (1976), 'Managing the Costs of Information', *Harvard Business Review*, September-October.

Törnqvist, Gunnar (1977), 'Comment' in Bertil Ohlin *et al*. (ed.), *The International Allocation of Economic Activity*, Macmillan.

Wachter, Michael L. & Harris, Jeffrey E. (1975), 'Understanding the Employment Relation: the Analysis of Idiosyncratic Exchange', *The Bell Journal of Economics*, vol.6, no.1, Spring.

—— (1975), *Markets and Hierarchies, Analysis and Antitrust Implications, A Study in the Economics of Internal Organization*, Free Press, New York.

Williamson, Oliver E. (1971), 'The Vertical Integration of Production: Market Failure Considerations', *American Economic Review*, May.

15.

TRANSFER PRICING, ITS RELATIVES AND THEIR CONTROL IN DEVELOPING COUNTRIES: NOTES TOWARD AN OPERATIONAL DEFINITION AND APPROACH

REGINALD HERBOLD GREEN*

On a cloth untrue
With a twisted cue
And elliptical billiard balls . . .

— Gilbert and Sullivan

We have only two rights in the present economic order — to sell cheap and to buy dear . . .

— President Julius Nyerere

Even the longest journey begins with the first step.

— Chinese Proverb

TOWARD OPERATIONALITY

Relatively little of the literature on transfer pricing is directed to operational questions of defining, identifying and controlling transfer pricing as they confront a medium — or small — sized peripheral economy or its institutions (e.g. central bank, board of external trade, public sector external trade bodies). This paper seeks to outline elements of an operational approach to transfer pricing for such states and institutions.

It assumes that some key decision takers wish to stop some transfer pricing losses. Without that there can be no serious action. That assumption is a mild one. An alert bribe taker or a mildly assertive compradore is likely to meet it. Any regime seeking dependent, junior partnership with TNCs is likely to want to know more about, and exert greater influence over, at least some of their transactions. Neither a strong nationalist bourgeoisie nor a dominant decision-taking group committed to a transition to socialism is a necessary condition.

221

TOWARD A WORKING DEFINITION

Transfer pricing is usually defined in terms of transactions between or among members of the same corporate group, e.g., TNC subsidiaries in different countries. Further, most literature centres on goods, with only minor attention to services. A somewhat broader definition is useful for operational purposes.

Transfer pricing exists whenever, for reasons related to inadequate national[1] knowledge or bargaining skill, a country or a nationally controlled enterprise pays too much or receives too little for goods and services bought or sold.

This definition turns on knowledge and bargaining ability. It excludes ownership and most structural power. It is both broader and narrower than TNCs. It is broader because it includes all transactions between controlled units as well as among domestically- and externally-located branches of foreign groups. If relative knowledge, bargaining ability and institutional capacity to collect and use the first through the second are the basis of transfer pricing, then transfer pricing (or its close relatives) can affect sales and purchases to or from unrelated parties.

On the other hand TNCs possess power which goes well beyond elements which can be controlled simply by knowing their nature and mobilising decision-taker will and national power to overcome them. Pure oligopoly power is more than transfer pricing in any operational sense. Knowing what alternatives exist and what degrees of inequality there are in 'bargains' struck can help chip away at the edges but not necessarily much more.

If the aim of control is to augment or economise on the use of foreign resources, it is immaterial whether the parties are jointly owned. Relationships are not limited to ownership and a series of contracts can produce joint gains to independent foreign companies analogous in kind and impact to joint ownership. Defining ownership/control in an operational way and determining whether it exists is far from simple. Minority, indirect ownership can give control; management or sales or technical service contracts can give most of the power of 100% subsidiary ownership.

Even if the local seller/buyer is independent of the external party, it may pay too much or get too little because it lacks knowledge (e.g. of normal prices or of alternative markets/sources), bargaining expertise, or institutional capacity. Corruption in the narrow sense can result in transfers at abnormal prices and can often best be caught by price monitoring.

If a foreign-owned sisal plantation sells to an independent merchant at a low price and he in turn sells another product to a third company in a third country associated with the sisal plantation, there is a transfer-pricing loss even though the visible parties are quite separate. If a national import firm is unaware of typical instant coffee prices, discounts for quantity, and varying prices/qualities of different suppliers it can pay 100% above the 'going rate'. If a tea estate sells through a small regional auction market dominated by a handful of buyers whose prices are usually 30% below London market prices, there is *prima facie* evidence of transfer pricing. Each of these is a real case.

Large transactions (singly or in total value) among related, foreign-controlled firms require special scrutiny. They will usually have a high payoff/control cost ratio and intra-firm or intra-group transactions are especially likely to be made at prices other than those which would occur in a competitive market characterised by equal knowledge and freedom of choice. If TNCs and their affiliates are dominant in key sectors of exports, imports or production, their transactions are a logical starting point for studying, monitoring and controlling transfer pricing and its extended family.

Services allow even more scope for transfer pricing than goods. There are fewer open markets, normal prices or identical products. For example, a selling agreement between a meat packer/tinner and a TNC provided for a 15% sales commission when 2-5% was 'normal'. A national processing company with a foreign managing agent shifted from being a modest debtor to a major creditor (five months' sales) to the main purchaser (identical in this case with the managing agent) charging no interest on the large, permanent book credit. Both are cases of abnormal pricing at least partly related to lack of knowledge and/or ability to bargain.[2]

Interest rates paid to foreign sources of finance by similar local companies (or the same company after negotiating with a new source) vary in ways which suggest inadequate knowledge of how to keep the total interest costs to a minimum.[3] Branch banks pay their overseas parents fixed proportions of 'central overheads' for services suspiciously similar to those correspondents provide each other without direct charges.

Transfer pricing in this operation oriented definition does not include unequal exchange (whether neo-Ricardian, neo-Marxian or neo-oligopolistic in definition) nor general imbalances of economic power other than imperfect knowledge. These are much broader issues and require different decisions and operational approaches. OPEC is not usefully considered as a transfer price control exercise.[4] For opposite reasons, pure fraud — e.g. payment on forged invoices, shipment of empty boxes — is also excluded.

To define *transfer pricing losses as excess foreign exchange paid or inadequate foreign exchange received* is to use a proxy variable. The true cost is to Gross Domestic Product. However, the cost takes the form of inadequate earnings on exports (directly reducing GDP) or excessive payments on imports (reducing the real command over goods given by GDP). For identification, estimation and control purposes the foreign exchange cost estimate seems logically adequate and operationally more convenient.

In some countries the loss that is estimated is tax revenue. This is a loss to GDP but hardly the whole loss. Losses to domestic factors of production and to domestic consumers are — or may be — of concern to decision takers. The first step would seem to be to claw the loss back into GDP and then to analyse what allocations among domestic wages, producer prices, domestic price reductions, profit increases, tax revenues and foreign enterprise profits (remittable or otherwise) are desirable, possible and prudent. The broad-front foreign exchange protection approach includes the tax protection one; the tax approach does not include other components of real GDP loss.

WHAT TO DO?

Transfer pricing, as defined, results *primarily from inadequate knowledge* on the peripheral state or economic unit side. Its monitoring and control must begin with knowledge building. Until that is done there can be no clear idea of the scope of the problem either as to types of goods and services or total costs in lost export proceeds and needless import bills. A checklist includes:

1. collect data on spot and future prices, normal contract terms, market patterns and structures, main purchasers and sellers (and their special characteristics) for main goods and services;
2. build analytical capacity to interpret data to create norms or ranges for comparison with actual transaction;
3. develop negotiating ability using analysed data to obtain better results in bargained contracts;[5]
4. legislate to require production of data, enforce rulings on

acceptable prices, require contract revision, collect penalties and block contracts inherently contrary to the 'public interest';[6]

5. create institutions to plan, control (e.g. central bank) and operate (e.g. Commodity Export Corporation) transfer price monitoring and control;

6. ensure that these institutions are under national control — preferably by citizens, second best by individually recruited expatriates in a national institution, as a last resort by external contractors with no conflict of interest;

7. where practicable confine transactions subject to transfer pricing to competent domestically owned institutions (public or private[7]); in other cases build monitoring/control structures.

Each component is critical. Each can be expanded into a full paper — indeed, would need to be by any group designing a national programme. However, perfection is not required; after first steps on each, the system can be put into operation. Initial successes and problems will often be better guides than institutional or individual research as to priorities for improving control capacity.

CONTRACTING OUT — THE USES AND LIMITS OF SPECIALIST FIRMS

A number of states — particularly, but not only in Africa — have contracted out transfer pricing control to specialist firms, especially General Superintendence of Switzerland who handle import price checking and inspection for eight African states from Tanzania to the Ivory Coast. This is not in principle (nor, it appears from user comments, in practice) a very satisfactory solution. It may on occasion be a useful first step.[8] When, for what purposes and for how long are such firms worth hiring?

Data available to a specialised company based in Europe with branches in most major trading countries is more up to date and more relevant to commercial transactions than that collected by most central banks. Collecting quotations and price lists is easier from a European base than from 'the end of the world', as American Express describes Dar es Salaam, Tananarive, Colombo and Port Louis. However, this coverage is limited to goods which are precisely defined. It rarely includes detailed cross-comparison of alternate sources. In General Superintendence inter-country comparisons are not made; the territorial branches of the company do not exchange information. For goods with complex quality characteristics the margin of error can be wide — a company agent in West Africa estimated the range for detecting pricing abuse as 20% for tropical timber exports. No services coverage (beyond insurance and freight on inspected goods) appears to be provided, but shipping, interest and insurance rates could probably be checked by existing specialist company methods.

Most serious, use of the company does nothing to build national data collection and analysis capacity. Such firms prefer contracts covering all imports or all trade, and this hinders commodity by commodity build-up of national capacity.

Personnel presents analogous gains, limits and costs. The specialist has a structure and staff in being (several thousand, in the case of General Superintendence) and can readily recruit a few additional personnel to service a new contract. On the other hand, the quality and range of analysis is often limited or suspect. So is their knowledge of particular product- or country-related issues. Again, the firm substitutes for local staff and may delay a decision to give priority to specialised person power allocation and training.

Quality of results varies. Pure fraud (e.g. shipping scrap metal as machinery) is readily detected by pre-shipping inspection. Exact conformity of contents to documents is not — e.g., one knocked-down vehicle assembler over six months received about 20 kits each with an inspection certificate of correctness and each with one or more parts missing. Prices utterly out of line with normal ones where there is an open market will be caught, e.g. Sh 100 a case for French sardines of a given brand when the list price is Sh 50. So will prices for any goods out of line with the same supplier's price to another buyer — a test of some potency, given the growing number of General Superintendence clients. Anything less easy to check may slip through. In one case crude oil shipments at 25% above the going rate to the importing country from other firms were passed. There was no cross checking of prices of the same product from different sources. Indeed, a meretricious explanation by the seller which could readily have been disproved by anyone with expert knowledge (as it eventually was by national sources) was accepted at face value. For specialised transactions, e.g. a complete factory, the specialist firms do not claim expertise and could do little checking the value of individual shipments in the absence of overall contract evaluation and a detailed cross-check of total shipments with contract lists of components and capacities.

Cost may be the least of the constraints but is not negligible. In the early 1970s, 1% of all imports was the going rate (for lesser coverage much higher rates were quoted). Since about half of all imports were goods for which no open market existed and another quarter bulk commodities on which a domestic check could have done as much (or as little — *vide* the oil case) the cost on transactions on which gains could be expected was 4%. Frauds and gross overcharging detected probably, but not necessarily, cover the cost.

Intra-TNC transactions in goods without a standard open market price, e.g. components, many branded products, much machinery, semi-processed goods, some major commodities, are an area in which specialist firms are of limited value. Nobody can learn what the price of a knocked-down Landrover should be by adding up list prices of spares.[9] Nor can it be done by collecting general wholesale price lists — the contract prices with assemblers are treated as confidential. However, the Landrover case illustrates gains from checking even on goods for which no exact substitutes or open markets exist. Prices for comparable kit shipments to different purchasers were discovered by General Superintendence to differ widely. Whether the end result was to reduce peak prices or also to raise the lowest, leaving its clients taken together in the same situation as before but with uniform (versus unequal) losses from transfer pricing, is unclear.

Possibly a *mixed approach* is the most workable initial strategy for a small peripheral economy with limited data sources, analytical capacity and personnel:

(a) use General Superintendence for pre-shipment physical inspection. *Ex Post* claims on arrival are slow, costly to pursue, uncertain of result, and do nothing to meet consequential losses of lacking the right goods at the right time. This is taking a leaf from the TNC's book — the bulk of GS's work is such checking for them!

(b) identify key products (e.g., copper in Zambia, cashew nuts and petroleum in Tanzania), key firms (e.g., aluminium smelter in Greece), key sectors (e.g. insurance in Ghana and Nigeria) and build a national capacity to collect and analyse data and to monitor their transactions. If the results show severe transfer pricing, attempt to create a regulatory frame and/or intervene in the exchange process by taking part in negotiations or creating a national commercial unit to break the chain of foreign enterprises.

(c) use a firm like General Superintendence for broad front

price monitoring until (unless) nationally-owned enterprises have built up commercial data and analysis capacity to the extent that their proposed purchases are rarely queried by GS price checks.

In fact, the Greek and Colombian experiences have concentrated on a key product/key company approach. Some of their estimated gains appear optimistic, but actual achievements seem substantial despite lack of systematic *ex ante* intervention in negotiations or institution building to break the foreign enterprise chain in the circuit of exchange. No parallel broad-front exercise has yet been mounted. Zambia has concentrated on one key product (copper) and moved straight to the national commercial enterprise form, backed by use of GS on the broad front import side. Tanzania has placed domestic emphasis on building commercial expertise of public enterprises (which have a near monopoly of external trade) and the competence of central units (Bank of Tanzania, Treasury) to intervene in major contract negotiation, again using GS on the import side. Both African cases appear to show positive results from the domestic and GS programmes.

Given personnel and institutional limits, Colombia and Greece were well advised to start selectively. Tanzania and Zambia could only achieve results on any front by selecting specific targets. It is not clear whether Greece and Colombia would have been well advised to use General Superintendence as a complement. That depends on how rapidly they can generalise their coverage, and whether using GS would have slowed such generalisation. For Tanzania and Zambia, the problem is how to broaden nationally-run monitoring and control, and to phase out the price (probably not the physical) inspection services of GS.

Two types of limited contracting-out may have permanent value. One is specialised procurement. An independent purchasing body, e.g., the Crown Agents, may have the expertise and knowledge to secure savings in excess of its, say, 2½% commission. This is a question of fact not theory. The larger the country's purchases of the goods in question and the broader its own data collection net, the less the value of a specialist buyer and vice-versa. The danger is hiring a buying agent who is apparently independent but has special relations with one or more suppliers, e.g., many confirming houses. In one extreme case a managing agent of a road haulage company supposedly doing 'best price' equipment procurement was (as those hiring it knew!) the local sole agent of a particular lorry manufacturer with whom it had at least indirect ownership links.

Major one-off contracts require specialist knowledge. That knowledge varies from case to case: e.g., used printing machinery, a secondhand sisal twine plant, an obsolete (in Europe) tyre moulding line, a $30 million highway contract, a $100 million plus dam and power house. Only a handful of developing countries have, today or in the foreseeable future, costing and pricing expertise in each of these fields.[10] The way to fill the gaps is with a hired consultant. How wide a brief he needs depends on the complexity and scope of the purchase. At one extreme, transfer price control becomes an aspect of costing feasibility and engineering studies (and of their use in testing tenders and negotiations) and of consulting/supervisory engineers. A successful example is Akosombo Dam in Ghana where Kaiser Engineering's fee was probably under a tenth of costs saved.[11]

NOTES ON METHOD
To talk of goals without identifying method, and to conduct analysis without relating it to practice does not get one very far. If the goal is to monitor and control transfer pricing by acquiring and deploying specialised knowledge, the rational decision taker, operating manager or bureaucrat will, quite properly, ask 'How?'.

Detailing method here to the degree an actual national exercise requires is not practicable. The length would be inconsistent with a digestible paper. The main points would be submerged in detail, and the generally applicable in the specific applications. Any complete exercise is — in volume — 75-90% specific to one country, and thus rather boring to practitioners whose central concerns relate to a different state. The author is competent to write on method in detail for only two countries — Tanzania and Namibia — in programmatic terms for perhaps three more — Ghana, Zambia, Sri Lanka — and in overall strategy terms with some specific national emphases for perhaps another dozen. Beyond that range he can at most offer broad guidelines as to method for the use of those who do possess specific country priority and operational competence.[12]

Data can be collected in several ways. For many commodities various published services, e.g., Reuters, give spot and forward prices on major markets. For some products, specialised journals, e.g., the *Petroleum Economist*, allow calculation of pre-profit landed cost — in the petroleum case to ±2%. General published series, e.g., UN, IBRD, GATT, are of value in comparing past country results with global levels/trends to identify areas for detailed study. They are too late and too general for use on individual current transactions. The same holds true of many specialist journals which also tend to mask divergences among transactions by giving list or average prices.

Nationally-owned commercial banks can collect prices and sources of price data from overseas correspondents. This can be particularly useful for large transactions which need to be concluded speedily and where published quotations are an inadequate guide.[13] Commercial offices in embassies should — but apparently rarely do — collect a broad range of price lists and quotations on an ongoing basis. Nationally-owned trading companies can (and in their own interests should) keep in touch with a broad range of potential suppliers and buyers. This source has the advantage that trading company specialists are better able to identify what products are really about the same and what effect quality or size of order differences should have.[14]

A dummy company can be used to cross-check prices being paid or received by TNC subsidiaries against those offered to a new customer or supplier. There are two limits: the dummy will become known; and odd lot dumping or spot buying offers may not be a good guide to standard prices for secure sources of supply.[15] For special initial checks this approach deserves wider use than it has had.[16] The spot use of 'own' bids through an intermediary, or sample direct sales to users bypassing normal channels, can give similar data on the degree of buyer collusion and probable levels of intermediary surplus shares;[17] e.g., if coffee sales direct to European roasters yield about 15% more than auction prices in an African country, internal freight is 2%, shipping and insurance 8%, interest 2%, administration 1%, then transfer pricing — as defined — is not a serious problem. Here, the actual costs are 13%, and a 2% margin for risk and knowledge is not exorbitant. Were the divergence 30%, the reverse conclusion could be drawn.

Some data can be reconstructed. For bauxite it is possible to work cost structures backwards from aluminium prices and, thereby, to get alumina and bauxite prices to carry a reasonable proportion of total aluminium industry world profit. For specialised components, e.g., car doors, an engineer and a cost accountant can reconstruct costs accurately enough for a rough check on how reasonable existing prices are. Simpler methods can also be used. Over four years the New York cashew kernel price rose 120%, shipping costs rose 200%, general wage and price levels in the processing country 50%, but the (near monopsonist) buyer for the processing units insisted that the raw nut price could not be raised appreciably without bankrupting the processors. The data showed that a shift from a 1 to 6 to a 1 to 14 ratio of raw nut to kernel prices was not necessary to cover increased shipping and processing costs. That conclusion radically altered the bargaining stance (and price secured) by the (oligopsonist) seller.[18]

Services pose special problems. Distribution of service expenses by banks, and selection of types, levels and sources of reinsurance by insurance companies, can alter foreign exchange costs, domestic profit levels and user charges substantially. In one African country in the early 1960s, 'Head Office Charges' to local branch banks were about half pre-tax profits. Following nationalisation, the new commercial bank found only about a tenth of that amount could be related to services not normally exchanged 'free' among correspondent banks. Correspondent relations did entail doing services and maintaining deposits, but the branches had larger deposits with (and services to) head offices than correspondents require. A domestic insurance company managed by a foreign reinsurance firm maximised reinsurance in general and reinsurance with the foreign managers/owners in particular.

Arm's-length pricing is no guide in services; surrounding conditions are too complex and data on 'comparable' transactions too hard to come by. Requiring local incorporation gives a coherent set of data on foreign exchange outflows and makeup, but not necessarily much more. Intervention from outside in cost allocation, reinsurance strategy and tactics requires detailed, specialised knowledge of banking and insurance. Removing or reducing conflict of interest, e.g., using an insurance broking not a reinsurance firm as a partner, and/or creating national institutions to control policy from the inside, seem more promising than pure regulation. For any approach, hiring an experienced international banker and a senior insurance corporation executive with experience in reinsurance (almost by definition non-citizens in small, peripheral economies) is the logical first step in building a relevant data bank and contacts for updating it.

Analysis is vital. Straight reading off is rarely possible. Knowledge of market structures, price fluctuations, normal discounts, variation (at the relevant times) between one-off and regular supply/purchase contract prices, and of relevant quality differentials is often required to interpret raw data. One needs to avoid the colonial agricultural expert's mistake of trying to secure West Indian prices for West African cocoa without realising that the first was a highly flavoured blending product, constituting 2-4% of volume, and the second a base product, comprising up to 90% of cocoa used in quality and 100% in utility chocolate products.

How long it takes to build analytical capacity depends partly on the industry (petroleum, oddly, is moderately easy at present, tinned foods quite difficult, specialised machinery a nightmare), and partly on how detailed a checking is desired. The latter varies with the probability of major percentage transfer pricing and with the absolute volume of trade. A full-time specialist on grain, dairy products and cooking oil is a good investment for a poor country for which these comprise 10% of imports in normal and 40% in drought years. A specialist in domestic electric appliances — if these are .25% of imports and .02% of exports — would be a misallocation of scarce personnel, and probably not save enough to cover his or her expenses.

Analysis should result in 'norm' or 'yardstick' prices. For major routine imports and exports these should be constructed and updated regularly. For specific transactions unusual in type, size or probable degree of transfer pricing, and for major long term selling or supply contracts, special analytical exercises will be needed. It is desirable to create procedures for regular, routine handling of the bulk of transactions (possibly on an *ex post* basis) so that concentrated attention can be given to the special cases and issues clearly falling outside the ordinary.

The 'norm' price route may work for shipping and some insurance contracts. Quoted rates, data on negotiated rates and some relevant seller cost-structure data can be compiled to yield plausible charge ranges within which to negotiate (e.g., with liner conferences as the Interstate Standing Committee on Shipping of Tanzania, Zambia, Uganda and Kenya does) or divergence from which would cause querying a contract (e.g., export insurance on primary product shipments). In banking and insurance companies it is unlikely that 'norm' prices can be set. Analysis should focus on key decisions, e.g., reinsurance strategy, the nature of allowable head office or associated company charges. Individual transactions can be checked *ex post* against strategic guideline limits.

Action steps include:
1. using 'norms' or special studies to select sources/markets

and/or to negotiate on prices;
2. identifying and following up new, better-priced markets and/or suppliers;
3. identifying and acting on indications that new market structures (e.g., diversifying buyers, selling direct to processors, bidding oneself at commodity export auctions) would reduce transfer pricing;
4. re-negotiating or voiding contracts characterised by massive transfer pricing;
5. building up a checklist of firms, countries, institutional structures and contract provisions closely associated (in a particular country's experience) with transfer pricing abuses to inform national buyers, sellers, controllers for subsequent transactions.

INSTITUTIONS: COORDINATION AND OPERATION

A method needs to be embodied in an institutional structure. Actual institutions will vary significantly both as to title and function from country to country, but some requirements are general.

A *single coordinating centre* is needed. Since the primary purpose of transfer pricing monitoring and control is increasing inflows/decreasing outflows of foreign exchange, a strong case exists for locating it in the Central Bank. This is reinforced if, as is common, the Bank has analytical capacity, experience in external transaction data collection and analysis, and operates an exchange control system.

Locating control in tax or trade institutions has severe drawbacks. Customs authorities are rarely commercially oriented and very often little concerned with prices on non-dutiable exports or imports. Their — quite proper — concern for revenue gives a built-in bias toward accepting excessive valuations for imports. They cannot be expected to deal with invisibles nor to see the overall pattern of external leakages of which transfer pricing and its extended family are a part. Income tax authorities are, in practice, concerned with tax lost, not with the balance of the profit which should have been available for payments to domestic producers or workers or for reinvestment. They have no expertise in indirect taxes. Trade authorities often have little commercial expertise, have a built-in desire to protect local firms not always consistent with challenging high import prices, and lack capacity to deal with invisibles or company tax and surplus allocation.

A satisfactory alternative may be a special section in a Treasury or Ministry of Planning. These are central bodies which are concerned with tax revenue, surplus generation and allocation, price patterns, foreign exchange and ownership/control structures. Their ability to use existing data flows and to exert influence on enterprises and governmental units is usually relatively high. Admittedly their degree of operational, commercial orientation is uneven but so is that of Central Banks.

A strong point for Central Bank versus Treasury/Planning location is avoiding overcentralisation. A case for putting every major analytical/operational unit in a Treasury/Planning Ministry can be made, but the results are unsatisfactory — elephantiasis appears. If a sound alternative institutional base (one which normally relates closely to the Treasury/Planning nexus) is available, it should be selected. Specific contexts may reverse this rule of thumb. They cannot so readily justify the choice of a tax authority as coordinating unit because the partial approaches and weak commercial orientation seem integral to taxation units.

Data collection should comprise a coordinated programme with copies of all data sent to the coordinating unit. Actual *collection should be decentralised*, with users, e.g., national trading companies, commercial and investment banks, collecting and applying data directly related to their operations. Similarly, while basis analysis leading to norm setting and divergence identification can often be carried out best by the central unit, this could complement specific analysis by operating units in respect to prices and products of direct concern to them. Major exercises, e.g., grain contracts under an emergency drought relief procurement programme, a bulk sale contract covering 80% of a major export, should be handled jointly:- e.g. by Central Bank, Grain Corporation, Ministry of Agriculture, and Treasury, in the grain case.

Wherever practicable *operating responsibility* — getting the right price — should be decentralised. This is easiest in public sector enterprises with citizen management, and hardest in TNC affiliates with foreign management.[19] The coordinating unit cannot be involved in each transaction. For large transactions, highly subject to transfer pricing, e.g., a TNC affiliate selling a semi-processed export to other group members, the coordinating body needs to take part in negotiations and to have *ex ante* veto power.[20] For very large transactions, especially those involving negotiated prices, pooling of data, analysis and bargaining skills is appropriate.

Policing powers can be handled via import/export licensing (which, when used to conserve foreign exchange, should be located in the Central Bank together with classic Exchange Control.)[21] Norms can be checked against prices on license applications, and divergence of more than a set per cent set aside for further information and checking. The *power to demand data* (with legal power to enforce the demand) should be analogous to exchange control.

Penalties and sanctions can also be modelled on exchange control. Transfer pricing control really is exchange control: a more important part of it than the classic side. One power is to require renegotiation of, or to block transactions in cases of, extreme transfer pricing. For example, in 1974 a Central Bank discovered that half a year's output of its third ranked export had been sold forward at prices 25% below the then current spot prices. Reasonable evaluation of the data suggested rising prices. As it turned out, the prices on delivery dates were up to 60% below spot prices.[22] It blocked performance of the contracts under the standard exchange control provision that no exports could be allowed unless the bank was satisfied a commensurate remittance of foreign exchange would be made.

Coordination includes reviewing work of operational units and seeing that specialised personnel training programmes are available. Review is especially critical if the operational unit may have mixed interests, or if its staffing position is weak. Available evidence suggests[23] that national firms are significant losers through transfer pricing and need data, personnel training and supervision.

Structuring external trade is a broader issue than transfer pricing. Control is, in principle, easiest if all major import/export transactions are via public sector corporations, hardest when many external transactions are internal to foreign company groups and intermediate when all are by private domestic firms. However, a public sector monopoly over external trade would rarely be created solely to control transfer pricing. Specialised firms in areas of particular concern may be. Units such as Zambia's Metal Marketing Corporation (responsible for copper, which comprises over 90% of the country's exports) and the grain supply unit of Tanzania's National Milling Corporation might be created to control transfer pricing even in a context of substantial private sector external transactions, including TNC subsidiaries or joint ventures. Marketing Boards for export crops, while initially created for rather different reasons, have often come to play a transfer price control role, albeit with uneven success.[24]

Legal instruments required are neither unusual nor, in broad terms, complex. Standard British model exchange-control regulations can, with quite moderate amendment, be used to require disclosure, impose prior approval, provide for government involvement in negotiations, allow regulatory body frustration of contracts, and impose penalties. There are broad bodies of legislative precedents for nationalisation, confinement of selected transactions to specified bodies, central regulation of, and involvement in, the planning/budgetary processes of state enterprises. Intelligent consideration is required of specific needs and constraints, with a competent draftsmen clearly informed on the substance his legal formulation is intended to convey, and the ends it is to achieve. Any country can meet these conditions if decision takers seriously want legislation embodying and supporting specific goals.[25]

Broader legal problems include recognition that the *state is not an impartial arbiter outside economic activity but an actor in it, with definite interests, responsibilities, weaknesses and weapons.* Law is one of the ways to use 'sovereignty' (one of the state's major weapons) to bear on particular transactions or decisions, or on particular struggles. Law is not a set of rules of the game abstracted from concern with who wins or loses. Rules do have a major influence on actual outcomes. The state is concerned with the outcome as well as with the way it is reached.[26]

A related problem is the concept of administrative law as a tool of, and framework for, state strategy implementation. This concept is inconsistent with the view that such laws are written on tablets of stone. (What is the abiding moral, natural justice or class basis of details of exchange control legislation?) Equally, however, it is inconsistent with breaking administrative law wherever it is inconvenient in a specific case. The absence of a coherent framework for deciding, and predictable decisions in respect to, routine cases, entails high costs of time, personnel and money for government and enterprise alike. Administrative laws should be used so long as they serve their purposes; when they do not, amendment is needed.

These are not trivial issues. The idea of the state as impartial referee checking compliance with rules set by some absolute, autonomous standard is implicit in much legislation and legal discussion. The view that laws are immutable or almost so is scarcely less common, even if less frequently stated explicitly.[27]

Staff and costs for a national monitoring/control system can only be assessed in relation to a specific country, institutional pattern and coverage. For Tanzania, perhaps 15 high and 50 medium qualification personnel in the Central Bank, 5 high and 10 medium in other government bodies (Treasury, Planning, Indirect Tax, Income Tax, Attorney General's, Board of Trade) and 25 high and 75 medium in, say, a dozen public sector financial and commercial enterprises, would be required to provide reasonably complete local data collection, analysis, monitoring, negotiation and enforcement. Direct salary cost might be $720,000 ($4,000 each), supporting staff $130,000 and associated expenses (office, travel, literature, etc.) $650,000 — a total of $1,500,000.

This is not comparable to the General Superintendence bill of approximately $4 million for two reasons: it excludes international specialised data collection or analysis not feasible in Dar es Salaam, and requiring overseas offices and/or specialised consultancies; and it excludes physical pre-shipment inspection. If the first cost $500,000 and the second $2 million, then out-of-pocket costs would be comparable. However, the Tanzanian system could have four advantages:

1. it includes exports which the actual GS service does not;
2. it could cross-compare sources in different countries, which GS does not;
3. commercial bargaining expertise can secure price reductions (or increases) beyond levels at which invoices would be rejected out of hand as unreasonably priced;
4. a system operated by Tanzania gives greater self reliance and can be used more flexibly than a hired contractor.

INTERNATIONAL COORDINATION AND INTERNATIONAL AGENCIES

Transfer price monitoring and control must be primarily national. No outside body can operate it for a country, nor can any international code remove the need for national enforcement. However, more coordinated national action and use of international institutions as complements and supplements is desirable.

Data collection is expensive. Joint collection and prompt exchange of information among two to four countries with similar key goods and services could improve the data bank and/or reduce costs.

On the borderline between transfer-pricing and oligopoly-power cases (e.g. in cashew nuts three states export 90% of raw nuts and one imports 90% of them to process and export as kernels), exchange of data and analysis and coordination of bargaining far short of a cartel or formal commodity agreement could yield useful gains. Exchange of data on selling policy by national (public or private) commodity exporters could on occasion avert market collapses.[28]

For small countries and specialised products, joint companies are worth consideration. In terms of data collection, bargaining ability and scale of purchases/sales, they could provide gains. For example, if the Crown Agents were converted into a Commonwealth Corporation with enhanced technical/valuation services, they could be — and could be seen to be — a major joint focus of data analysis and bargaining capacity for thirty Third World states over a variety of goods and services. Proposals for a similar Latin American multinational (as opposed to transnational) enterprise are under study in SELA (Latin American Economic System).

International organisations can provide global and regional data. UNCTAD's initiatives toward a speedy reference price collection and publication system should be implemented. The World Bank's capacity for detailed product-by-product analysis of price trends and their probable future evolution should be promptly and generally accessible. UN Centre on Transnational Corporations' data on practices, procedures and control attempt experiences and their analyses of structures for particular goods and services can be valuable in building up systems, identifying priority areas for scrutiny, benefitting from the experience of others and providing basic contextual knowledge.

Such services cannot be more than secondary and supplementary. Global agencies must by their nature pay attention to the perceived self interests of all (or almost all) their members. To become identified as a committed partisan of one group of states is destructive of the institution's capacity to act as an honest broker or as a recognised source of broadly accepted data and analysis. Until most states perceive transfer pricing, as defined here, to be generally undesirable (not simply to oppose transfer pricing costly to them while supporting it when they are beneficiaries), the room for manoeuvre of international organisations is limited.

International organisations (in particular the UN and its extended family) collect and process data on a broad front for broad uses, not individual items for specific uses. They rarely achieve the speed in collection and evaluation of specific transactions needed for business operating purposes. They are more bureaucratic and less operationally-oriented than many government functional units, let alone business enterprises. Business management and business transactions are not an area in which they have much expertise. Relaxing some of these constraints is possible, as is the formation of small, specialised, transaction-oriented, quasi-autonomous units (e.g., the UNCTAD/GATT International Trade Centre). To expect international organisations to serve as case-by-case business advisors is rather like asking an elephant to behave like a hummingbird. Only in part is this a criticism of the UN family; there are things elephants can do and hummingbirds cannot. One should pick the appropriate creature for the task in hand.

SOME CONSTRAINTS

It may happen that monitoring reveals *transfer pricing gains*. Real issues arise over revealing data and putting them into cross-national coordination processes. The point is not flippant. One West African producer's bauxite was shipped in the 1960s to a second West African state for conversion to alumina at 40-50% below the 'norm' price. Power for smelting was probably 20% underpriced and the alumina exports underpriced by 15-25%. In this case, joint action by the two states — if practicable — would have made sense. But a state with low taxes, a sophisticated commercial and financial sector and limited exchange control, set in a region with most countries having the reverse characteristics (e.g., Singapore) may be a substantial net gainer on regional transfer pricing. What then?

A *'perfect normal price' does exist*. Beyond some point a quest for perfection costs more than it gains. For each type of product one can set limits (e.g., ± 2½%) of variations not needing scrutiny. For 'one off' major contracts, wider ranges are inevitable — one can detect 100% overpricing for a used merchant vessel, 20% for a moderately standard sugar mill; but at least 10% is a bargaining zone of indeterminacy not subject to transfer price control.

Therefore, actual savings cannot be estimated with any precision. One can add up cases of *ex post* price alterations. However, if the system works well then its deterrent effect will reduce such cases. If *ex ante* checking, direct intervention in negotiations and/or national commercial units breaking the foreign enterprise chain are used, their gains should be larger than those of *ex post* checks but are not subject to direct estimation. To claim the whole difference between a first offer and a negotiated price for transfer price monitoring/control offends against truth in advertising. In bargaining it is prudent and normal to make an initial offer one intends to improve. Comparison with pre-programme prices or those of comparable situations without monitoring/control is of qualitative value but becomes less informative as distance in time and situation increases.

A related constraint is *limiting the cost of control*. To spend $100,000 a year checking crude oil imports when a $10 subscription, a quarter of a $5,000 a year officer's time, and the quantity/quality tests that an independent refinery needs for its own purposes would do as well, is a gross waste — as the Central Bank in question now realises. It is critical to avoid delays: time is money in terms of interest and availability of goods, shipping arrangements, lost contracts. If *ex post* checking will allow subsequent correction or future loss limitation with modest mistakes, it is usually better than monitoring and delaying transactions in midstream. *Ex ante* checking of major transactions during negotiation and *a fortiori* before contract signing is prudent. Like delay, disruption has high costs. Voiding or blocking contracts is a last resort in cases of fraud, gross deception or massive, otherwise irrecoverable transfer pricing. If used as a routine control mechanism, suppliers will charge more and buyers pay less because the risk of non-performance is unusually high: a counter-productive result.

Control from outside of units whose interests conflict with the controller's cannot be perfect. Broad formula 'solutions' may be possible, e.g., link the price of raw cashew nuts to the world kernel price, and may yield 'acceptable' results. Fully effective detailed intervention requires knowing the business better than its managers. Long before that point, it reduces their operational efficiency drastically; e.g., *ex ante* approval of every leather sale by a foreign subsidiary to every associated or potentially associated shoe maker would reduce the business to chaos unless approvals were 'rubber stamped' and thus ineffectual as checks. Spot checks and broad monitoring can help but will leave a range of undetectable/uncontrollable transfers.

If conflicts are basic and amounts at stake large, e.g., Zaire copper marketing, the cure is not surveillance to the point of mutual claustrophobia but changing operating unit ownership management to reduce or eliminate conflict of interest. In the Zaire case, if a copper brokerage company unconnected with processors managed the marketing company, the incentive for underpricing would be sharply reduced. If a Zairian managerial and analytical cadre were built up, it could be eliminated.

Transfer pricing control operations are not very glamorous or dramatic. They take time to build up personnel and data before they show results. Results are rarely spectacular (albeit one IDS seminar participant used data and the negotiating approach to save $5 million on a three-year commodity contract on the basis of two weeks' study and one of negotiating). Once the system is working well, the intended results are 'negative' — to avoid recurrence of wrong prices. The bulk of the work itself is tedious — 99 parts perspiration to 1 of inspiration and 99 of preparation to 1 of negotiation — but must be done regularly and consistently if it is to pay off. Despite these 'public relations' or 'image' handicaps, transfer pricing monitoring and control needs a handful of top quality personnel and full cooperation of public sector bodies, i.e., priority backing at the political decision-taking level.

There is a tactical reason for merging overall direction with exchange control within the Central Bank. Central Banks are usually respected and influential, with operations geared to avoiding spectacular failures rather than achieving spectacular triumphs (at least, not ones readily visible to the man in the field or on the street). Most day-to-day work is routine, repetitive and organised. It also underlines the case for operational use of national productive enterprises; once they realise that they can save or make money by cooperating in transfer price control, their managers will normally see good reason to give it attention and support.

Transfer price monitoring and control will not, by itself, build a New International Economic Order nor dramatically alter basic economic power balances between TNCs and peripheral economy states or companies. However, in any such broader effort it would be a component. Knowledge is often not an adequate condition for power; it is virtually always a necessary one.

An operational approach along these lines could yield significant initial gains — say, an average of 4% on imports and 2% on exports in a situation characterised by frequent but not abnormally high transfer pricing. These could be doubled as the system developed experience and data. These estimates are fairly conservative.[29] They are for total imports and exports; 20% gains on some products or 50% on some transactions are possible. They do not include physical preshipment checking of imports. Nor do they assume removal of 'unequal' or 'unfair' prices resulting from structural inequalities in power illuminated, but only marginally mitigated by greater knowledge. For countries with special trade patterns or TNC involvements gains could be far higher.[30]

Who would benefit from the gains is a different issue — normally whoever (or whatever class or interest group) benefits from growth in resource availability. Transfer pricing control is rarely a means to reorienting domestic socio-political and political economic priorities. But it can reduce resource constraints on priority allocations.

NOTES

*   I wish to thank participants in the March 1978 IDS Conference on Control of Transfer Pricing and Related Practices in Developing Countries for comments and criticisms which have been of value in revising an earlier text, and in particular to acknowledge the valuable comments of R. Murray, K. Lamaswala, R. Makane, G. Helleiner and C. Vaitsos.

1   National is used in contrast to territorial. Knowledge in the hands of foreign firms or their affiliates is not nationally available.

2   A special problem is that transfer pricing whose ultimate impact is on external account can take place on internal transactions. On any sale from a domestically controlled to a foreign controlled unit transfer pricing is possible. This is most evident of sales by local produce growers to domestic subsidiaries of international merchanting groups but the point is broader.

    If a local unit of a foreign owned firm can obtain abnormally high prices (e.g. via needlessly high protection) or pay abnormally low ones (e.g. because the local producer does not know of alternative buyers), then transfer pricing exists. For example, if a national power company sells power to a foreign smelter below global going rates for such sales, this is a foreign exchange loss and one at least probably due to transfer pricing, e.g. power sales to VALCO in Ghana.

3   The unequal interest rates arose from lack of knowledge of alternative sources and tax laws applying to borrowers and lenders resulting in the borrower effectively paying 40% company tax on the interest twice.

4   There are mixed and borderline cases, In the power sale case inadequate knowledge of going rates, an urgent need to get a base load contract to underpin a dam and a lack of known alternative buyers interacted. Only the first element is squarely within the transfer pricing rubric proposed here Similarly a hides and skins company sold domestically to foreign merchants who — often without ever physically taking delivery — sold to manufacturers at prices higher by 50% or more. Part of the cause was lack of knowledge, part institutional limits on extending external credit. In this case the institutional restructuring to overcome the transfer price loss would appear to be a subsidiary implementation point under transfer pricing control.

5 For more detailed discussion, see R.H. Green, 'The Peripheral African Economy and the MNC' in C. Widstrand, *Multinational Firms in Africa*, Scandinavian Institute of African Affairs, Uppsala, 1975, and 'A Guide to Acquisition and Initial Operation' in J. Faundez and S. Picciotto, *Nationalisations of Multinationals*, Macmillan, London, 1978.

6 'Public Interest' is used here to mean avoiding 'serious loss of foreign exchange to the economy'.

7 Domestic private enterprises may collect and deploy knowledge effectively; indeed in specialised plant and equipment or production input cases their achieved performance is often better than that of more generalized public sector units.

8 This assumes the agent has been checked to be sure it is independent.

9 Spares prices are set on a basis which means that a complete set costs in the order of 2-3 times as much as a complete vehicle.

10 Even what exists or can be built up is usually scattered.

11 The maximum proportion of their total fees and charges plausibly allocable to transfer pricing/cost control.

12 There are no such creatures as 'global experts'. There are experts on some issues in some contexts who can form useful members of, or complements to, basically national teams.

13 This source appears to be grossly under-used by peripheral economy enterprises and governments.

14 In an extreme case, a commerce ministry official queried a steel sheet price because he failed to understand that his 'reference price' related to sheet of different width and thickness.

15 Steel sheet for galvanising illustrates the problem. In 1968-71, and since 1975, buying dumped odd lots has been a way to save money compared to a medium term contract with one of primary producers. In 1972-74, however, odd lots were almost unavailable, cost about twice list prices and the primary producers refused to take on customers who had previously used the odd lot market.

16 It has been used to check Andean Pact, especially Colombian, import prices.

17 This is a test of whether the amount alternative buyers would pay would yield more net of the additional costs of reaching them.

18 The initial gain was about 15% of the final per tonne price or $3.5 million (over 1% of total domestic exports).

19 Even here it may not be totally impossible. Recently one TNC/national petroleum joint venture located and used channels other than affiliates for residual heavy oil sales increasing proceeds 25%.

20 This is a case in which decision takers may be unwilling to give more than limited power to the control body because they fear broader repercussions. In that event, power to demand data paralleled by independent analysis leading to 'moral' suasion and reporting to decision takers can achieve something.

21 This combination facilitates limiting import licenses issued to foreign exchange likely to be available.

22 Ironically the only case of prices less than 25% out of line was a foreign plantation selling to a brokerage/marketing company owned by the same shareholders! The worst record was that of a state export corporation.

23 See C. Vaitsos' work on Colombia (chapter IV of *Intercountry Income*

Distribution and Transnational Enterprises, The Clarendon Press, Oxford, 1974.)

24 In one country for one year the prices received by four commodity boards varied from the UK terminal market prices by (on average) 10%, 15%, 30% and 40%. Costs between the Board and the market all appeared to be the 10%-15% range.

25 That is Tanzanian experience. The legislative framework is not perfect but is broadly workable, adapted to particular party and state goals, drafted with attention to objective constraints, and moderately comprehensive and internally consistent. Few pieces deal with transfer pricing alone but that may be a strength. The time frame of its development is 1967-75, the high-level legal personnel input required at most four (even including some of the basic negotiations pursuant to, rather than forming part of, the legislation).

26 For a similar position elaborated in more detail, see the article by P. Fitzpatrick in this volume.

27 These comments are based on experience in Tanzania and examples presented at seminars in Accra (Ghana), Tagaytay (Philippines), and New York by the International Center for Law in Development.

28 For example the 1970-71 sisal price collapse was triggered by divergent selling tactics and misestimation of other sellers' tactics between Tanzanian and Kenyan exporters. Total export proceeds losses were about $25 million.

29 What scattered data there are suggest an average of 7½-12½% transfer pricing on imports and somewhat more on exports. These are rough orders of magnitude — transfer pricing like smuggling statistics are hard to collect!

30 Two macro questions arise. If all or most peripheral economies monitored/controlled transfer prices would this result in lower average prices or would sellers/buyers simply lessen deviations from the average? If transfer pricing were controlled would new leakages (channels of surplus 'repatriation') be developed?

16.
MULTINATIONAL COMPANIES' (MNCs) TAX AVOIDANCE AND/OR EVASION SCHEMES AND AVAILABLE METHODS TO CURB ABUSE*

INTERNAL REVENUE SERVICE UNITED STATES

INTRODUCTION
How do MNCs Operate?

The MNC, through its vast size, complex organizational structure, global nature of operations and transnational profit motivation, presents innumerable and serious audit problems. These include, but are not limited to, complex accounting, economic and legal questions. Moreover, the MNC, unlike an entity strictly conducting business on a domestic or one-nation basis, possesses the business ability and structural capability to create a global market for its technology, products, etc., as well as plan flows of funds irrespective of national borders.

The MNC, like any other business operator regardless of size, is keenly aware that a key profit motivator is tax minimization. However, through centralized control of policy decisions and integration of corporate functions (finance, marketing, R & D, etc.,) the MNC pursues a global strategy to minimize its tax burden. Further, it can avail itself of the simultaneous use of complex tax laws, corporate structural and other organizational law, etc., to achieve its overall goal of profit maximization.

The MNC is able to effectively manage large corporate enterprises as one unit, rather than as a group of separate autonomous corporate entities. This can be greatly attributed to the technological advances of computers as well as the ease of issuing worldwide communications. Moreover, with centralized control, it may conduct business activities within many industrial sectors simultaneously. For instance, in many cases, the multinationals are conglomerates earning profits from many industries while, in other cases, they operate both vertically and horizontally within a given industry.

Expansion of the US business community in foreign investment and commerce, as well as the increased use of the US as a market for direct investment by foreign entities, has resulted in the development of various tax avoidance schemes, principally

245

through the vehicle of business transactions between related parties located in different countries.

Taxation of foreign income has provided legal incentives to invest abroad and encouraged the proliferation of unfair (not arm's-length) transactions and financial manipulations. The MNC has dramatically brought this problem to the surface because of its higher potential for tax minimization due to its relatively larger magnitudes of profits, technology, research and development, advertising and complex products.

The tax haven subsidiary of a MNC occupies a pivotal position in profit manipulation operations. It plays the role of an intra-company bank with intra-company lending facilities and is one of the group's sources of foreign external finance.

Role of Tax Administrator

Taxation is one of the most contentious subjects concerning multinationals. Even leaving aside any problems with tax evasion, it is undoubtedly true that domiciliation in various countries, each with its own method and rates, and with independently conducted audits — each covering only half of a group's intercompany transactions — provides openings for tax avoidance.

There is no quantitative information available on this problem. Heads of MNCs freely admit, however, that if tax avoidance is not their *raison d'être* or their main source of profit, nevertheless they do logically operate a tax strategy that best serves the interests of their firm.

Merely by being true to themselves, the MNCs thus come into conflict with the states, which consider that they suffer undue losses of tax revenue and see in this a challenge to their sovereignty, and with domestic corporations which see in it a serious distortion of competition and one of the chief reasons for the rapid expansion of the MNC.

While the scope and magnitude of some MNCs alone present a tax administration problem in terms of manpower allocation, their evergrowing complexity raises problems of maintaining the proper expertise to handle tax issues and audit problems outside the traditional accounting or auditing function. This is most notable in cases dealing with the establishment of arm's-length criteria under allocation of income and expense provisions of US law (IRC 482) and further, in the valuation of property or stock in foreign entities, valuation and determination of rights to intangible property as well as in the general understanding of complex industrial business practices.

US experience has demonstrated that, even with detailed guidelines, the safe-haven rules, and substantial disclosure requirements, an arm's-length profit margin or mark-up is still often an elusive phantom. Attempts by the Service to secure information involving international transactions indicate that sophisticated taxpayers are well aware of the audit problems and time involved for an agent to trace a transaction, find a comparable transaction, secure books and records, deal with the peculiarities of foreign law and document the substance of a transaction. Moreover, some taxpayers are taking advantage of these complexities to thwart effective investigations by use of passive resistance or not cooperating during the audit.

Further, MNCs present unique and complicated logistics problems not often encountered in the domestic area. Taxpayers' outside accounting and legal counsel may be in one geographical location, the parent and several domestic subsidiaries in another, with foreign subsidiaries in several foreign countries. The books and records are scattered throughout the world. The complexities of intercorporate and interdivisional transactions (domestic and foreign) complicate the situation further.

When a tax administrator is considering the tax aspects of his particular segment of this worldwide taxpayer, he must keep in mind that this taxpayer, like all taxpayers, is trying to minimize his tax liability to the extent permitted by law. As such, the tax administrator must be thoroughly familiar with his country's tax law as well as having a working knowledge of the laws of the country in which his taxpayer's parent is residing. A tax administrator must get to know his taxpayer in order to understand and combat the various schemes that the taxpayer and its affiliates or parent may perpetuate in order to minimize their tax liability through illegal means.

Above all, the tax administrator must keep in mind that he does not, and should not, regulate the business activities of taxpayers be they the butcher, the baker or the MNC. Simply stated, the Service's role is limited to tax administration only. We are the tax collector and not a regulatory body.

SCHEMES THAT MULTINATIONALS USE

The reasons for profit manipulation to avoid tax are many and varied:

(a) To avoid high corporate income tax rates;

(b) To sustain a high rate of self-financed direct investment for further expansion;

(c) To hide information from competitors;
(d) To finance future research and development projects;
(e) To compensate losses of one or more subsidiaries;
(f) To finance portfolio investments in other firms or sectors;
(g) To finance joint venture enterprises;
(h) To counteract the effect of exchange rate fluctuations;
(i) To provide for loss due to expropriation (nationalisation);

This paper is limited to a discussion which focuses attention on transfer pricing, false invoicing and use of tax havens to accomplish the desired profit manipulation.

With the aid of unfair (not at arm's-length) transfer pricing in the exchange of goods and services between parent and subsidiary, profit can be transferred to the home country or to a tax haven where another affiliate is based.

Latest revelations in the area of slush funds, business bribes abroad and political kickbacks have uncovered a prevalent use of false invoicing by MNCs.

The use of a tax haven is both expedient and flexible as a tool to minimize risks of detection and improve worldwide returns on direct investment. Use of tax haven holding companies enables MNCs to retain their overseas earnings outside their home countries for further expansion as most countries do not tax foreign income until it is repatriated to the parent company. Some countries have commercial concepts under which they do not tax foreign income at all.

Transfer Pricing
What is it?

In the free market, transfer pricing represents the price a willing buyer will pay to a willing seller. It is an ordinary and necessary commercial practice within the international business community. Generally speaking, however, IRS views the term to mean the direct transfer of profits by *abnormal* or *unfair* pricing practices. In other words, we would not disturb any pricing practices which are comparable to those between unrelated parties dealing at arm's-length.

Generally, most MNCs follow normal commercial practices in their inter-affiliate transactions. Arm's-length prices realistically reflect the market values of the goods or services transferred. However, we are concerned about the unfair (not at arm's-length) transfer pricing policies dictated by some parent companies within the multinational corporate structure.

Why is it used?

In some cases, inter-company pricing practices are based not on market realities but rather on ways to maximize consolidated aftertax profits and minimize taxes by taking into consideration the differences in tax laws in the various countries of the world. The company's objective is to minimize all taxes, not just US taxes. MNCs have found that transfer pricing is the most convenient and effective way to direct and control the international operations.

These taxpayers disregard conventional economics or commercial considerations, such as reasonable rates of returns on investments in the various business operations and market conditions, as principal factors in determining inter-company pricing and transfer practices.

Who uses it?

Generally speaking, anyone can. However, the most substantive and substantial reduction in overall taxes is by the MNC. To paraphrase a comment made in a recent book in the Harvard Multinational Enterprise Series: The most widespread use of transfer pricing is to locate profits in an appropriate affiliate in order to reduce the systems' total tax burden . . . However, it is difficult to draw unequivocal conclusions regarding variations and practices among firms. Our impression is that the influence of size is felt. In establishing inter-company prices, multinational companies tend to establish uniform policies that involve standard mark-up. The Assistant Treasurer of one firm noted, 'We have regular inter-company billing prices and they determine the price list for everybody. We have standard formula and everybody does it the same way.'

Nevertheless, when special reasons exist, some companies will bend their rule-of-thumb procedures to adjust their transfer prices. Echoing this note, a regional official of the same firm added, 'If I cannot get dividends out and my royalty rate is fixed, and I want to remit more money, then I do this on an uplift of my transfer prices.'

Many so-called esoteric tax avoidance techniques have been used to manipulate the market in certain products and services. The maximum after-tax profitability and the tax consequences of these techniques are best illustrated by case studies which have been derived from factual situations.

How is it used?

One method frequently used in industry is known as multi-processing. Different components of a product are produced by the affiliates of the parent company in different countries, and these components may be assembled in yet another country or countries. Sale of the final product may be entirely or partly within the US or may be in other countries throughout the world. From an audit standpoint, the determination of an appropriate arm's-length standard for such multiprocessing and the complex transactions involved is, at best, difficult.

Another method raises the issue of intangible rights and patents rights. The situation below illustrates one of the most effective tax avoidance techniques used by industry.

Manipulation often exists where the original research and development (R & D) cost sharing may originally be satisfactory or apparently satisfactory, but the sharing of market profits is disproportionately slanted toward the tax haven country. Since the benefits of this research can be realised only by sales or licenses, and the larger the market the larger the benefit, any affiliate that has the right to sell and license in a larger country with a higher income level and a larger population clearly has disproportionate access to the profits produced by the research and development.

We try to pay very close attention to the distribution of cost. We also pay close attention to the allocation of the property rights and the licensing rights to the results with respect to the available and potential markets. In addition, we pay very close attention, and this is difficult, to inter-company pricing in a field where it is necessary for our agents, not only to be good auditors, but also to be good technicians and know the technology in manufacturing and formulation in a highly refined and highly developed industry.

The assignment of property rights to inventions and formulae is frequently made in such a way that the tax haven affiliate is exclusively authorised to exploit — make, sell, use or license — the product to which attaches a substantial intangible value created by R & D. In an arm's-length transaction, the developer of the product would charge a substantial royalty for this right.

A combination of research and development arrangements with multiprocessing techniques in production and an intricate functional division of uneven risks may further compound the tax effectiveness of such income and profit shifting.

In one of our cases, a company with a foreign parent had a number of agreements, each regulating some aspect of R & D.

Some agreements dealt with basic research and some with applied research or technical aspects of the already invented products. The research program was so complicated that, to make a proper audit of such arrangements, it was not sufficient to know merely the techniques of auditing. It was also necessary to understand the industry in technical detail, the technology of production, the flow and mix of products, the value of intangibles, the characteristics of financial arrangements which supported the manufacturing and selling operations, and finally, the laws of a number of countries. Only after a careful analysis of all of these factors were we able to formulate an opinion as to whether the respective actions and operations of the MNCs had any substance over and above the consideration to minimize taxes.

A special distributing or sales company in a tax haven country may utilize non-arm's-length transfer pricing to minimize income attributable to the US affiliate or to affiliates in other countries with taxes comparable to those of the US such as France, Brazil or Canada. This method is prevalent throughout many industries. Under the classic and simplistic example, a domestic parent will sell to a related sales organization located in a tax haven country and the sales organization will resell the product to foreign subsidiaries for further manufacturing, processing or marketing, thereby lodging income, and usually excessive income, in the tax haven country. The audit problem is to determine the arm's-length price of the transaction between the domestic parent and the tax haven sales organization and also the price between the sales organization and outlets in other countries.

False or otherwise incorrect invoicing (form vs. substance)
Why do some Multinationals use this device?
There is considerable disparity between the tax accounting standards of the various nations of the world. One nation may consider an expense or item of income fully accountable in computing taxable income. Whereas, for one reason or another, that same item of income or expense is not recognized by another country in which the international company is conducting business. For example, one nation may require the reporting of royalties and technical assistance fees as income for tax purposes. On the other hand, the company owing the royalty payment or payment for technical assistance may well be doing business in a nation that does not recognize the payment of these expenses for tax purposes when paid to a foreign entity.

In these instances, the international company is placed in a dilemma. One taxing authority will insist that taxes be paid on income that another taxing authority refuses to recognize the payment as a deductible expense or allow remittance to be made. In these instances, the international company will resort to devising schemes (label it something else that is recognized by the other country) or not provide the services or allow the use of patents. Schemes add to the cost of doing business. However, discouraging the rendering of services or use of patents works toward the detriment of technological advancement of the receiving company and country.

When schemes are developed with regard to these particular problem areas, they are generally disguised as transfer of profits, concealed as transactions that are recognized by the paying country's tax authorities, or simulated exports to obtain the desired income to cover the royalties and technical assistance fees otherwise not permitted by law.

As you may have noted, the schemes discussed above are basically accounting schemes that result in income being correctly reported in the nation providing the technical assistance or the patent. While there is technical avoidance in the paying country, the resulting net income is correct in the eyes of the receiving nation as their tax accounting standards were met. There is, however, a serious evasion problem both for the paying and receiving nations when a taxpayer resorts to an arrangement that is not normal in sound business relations.

What is false invoicing?

A preliminary step towards attacking this evasion devise is to attempt to define the phenomenon. In this connection, we support the definition reached by the OECD Panel at its meeting in Paris in November 1976. The Panel concluded that:

> 'from the fiscal point of view, false invoicing could be defined as a transaction intended to evade tax by putting taxable objects outside the reach of the national tax authorities by means of an invoice that does not accord with economic facts.'

In many cases, false invoicing involves, in principle, the invoicing of a sum which is either higher or lower than the sum actually owed. This act may be considered fraudulent. Where goods or services are correctly priced but the indicated goods or services are different or may not exist at all, it is always a matter of fraud. Other cases may also arise, for instance, those in which the invoiced price is correct, but the invoicing company prints a false name on the invoice to avoid having its true name recorded in the purchaser's books, and thereby enabling it to receive the payment without entering it in its books.

Examples uncovered

An investigation of a large corporation revealed that a slush fund was both initiated and largely devised by the corporation president who was concerned because the corporation did not have funds available for which no public accounting was required. This scheme, which was in operation over a number of years, involved the contracting of foreign consulting services at an inflated rate with the understanding that the excess over normal fees would be returned to the corporate officer in the US who had complete control over these funds. No accounting was maintained for the amounts received or the purpose for the expenditures.

Another corporation removed assets from normal inventory control and distributed them to its various local offices. The decontrolled assets were subsequently sold by the local offices and proceeds remitted to the home office in cash. The purpose of the diversion of these assets was to generate funds to be used at the discretion of certain corporate officials.

One MNC devised a complex scheme of kickbacks from the construction of a foreign facility and from contracts to supply raw materials. False invoices were used in the diversion of funds. The contracts written specifically provided for the payments to be made outside the US and would not be made from any person or corporation subject to US law. All payments were directed through foreign conduits, and at least two foreign bank accounts before being placed into various Swiss accounts. On occasional European trips, the US corporate officers would pick up cash from these accounts to be used at their discretion.

General observations

The diversity of techniques used in these schemes is practically unlimited. Illegal payments have been reflected as legal services, loans, and corporate officer's bonuses. False invoices and supporting data have been created for these expenditures. Collusion by corporate officer has aided in the disguise of these payments.

These matters are of concern to all of us. They are matters dealt with rather clearly by our existing statute and regulations. The problem is principally one of enforcement, and more particularly, one of detection. In this respect, our task is certainly made more difficult by the complexity inherent in transnational corporate activity, as our authority to regulate and track corporate financial activities is diminished by the boundaries of our national sovereignty.

Tax havens

The methods used by some MNCs to shift income to the tax havens are varied and diversified. We are aware of many areas of concern: transfer pricing; transfers of research and development benefits; movement of capital; transactions involving technical 'know-how'; the transfer of parts and accessories; negotiation of loans and setting of interest rates; and the transfer of securities. We also recognize that there are other avenues to explore which may disclose schemes to avoid tax in entirely new areas.

The fact is — and this must be stressed — that every country, large or small, is a tax haven to some degree. The US for example, does not impose any income tax on the interest paid to foreign nationals on their US bank deposits, thereby encouraging foreign nationals to leave their money on deposit. Should this exemption be eliminated, however, billions of dollars would leave the US. In short, it is not the use of tax havens that cause government officials to wince; it is their abuse by people who are trying to evade taxes in their home country.

Attempts to cope with tax avoidance or evasion schemes with regard to MNCs have been the bane of tax administrators in many countries for many years. The accumulation of earnings and profits in tax haven countries have affected not only tax revenue but also the balance of payments and can have a deleterious effect on the economic health of many countries. Experience has clearly demonstrated that legislation and unilateral tax compliance measures are wholly inadequate to maintain proper tax administration as to MNCs. The corporation conglomerates have astutely used tax avoidance schemes with amazing deception and flexibility in the tax haven area. These schemes, based largely on legal fiction which does not reflect economic realities, severely abuse the intent and spirit of our tax structures.

What is a tax haven?

The term 'tax haven' is used to describe a country or locality which charges no tax at all on income or profits, or charges a rate which is relatively low in comparison with the rates commonly charged in the major industrialized countries, or which has some peculiarity in its tax laws which affords favorable tax treatment to particular persons or transactions.

The orientation of this paper is from a US viewpoint. US tax administrators are particularly concerned with tax havens who encourage secrecy and provide protection for transactions which are not at arm's length. It should be kept in mind, however, that any country or territory can be a tax haven to the person who pays little or no tax to that place.

There are different types of tax havens and they can be classified, at the risk of appearing subjective, into different categories. The following categories can, as a practical matter, overlap. However, they are basically intended to indicate the different types of tax havens that exist and examples of each type best described by the applicable category. The classification is by no means an exhaustive list and description of tax havens, as this is beyond the scope of this paper.

First, there are tax havens which have virtually no taxes or provide complete tax exemption; such as, The Bahamas, Bermuda, the Cayman Islands and New Hebrides. Second, there are those which impose taxes, but do so at very low rates: such as Liechtenstein, Switzerland, the British Virgin Islands and Gibraltar. Third, there are havens which tax income from domestic sources but exempt income from foreign sources. Included in this category are Hong Kong, Liberia and Panama. Fourth, there are tax havens which allow special tax incentives and privileges for certain types of companies such as holding companies. Included in this category would be Luxembourg and the Netherlands Antilles. Fifth and finally, there are places which allow exemptions and privileges for certain types of activities. The Free Trade Airport Zone at Shannon, Ireland, is an example of this.

There are many factors considered by taxpayers in selecting an appropriate haven. These include, among others, communication facilities; political stability; freedom of currency movement; tax treaty network; liberal commercial, corporate and trust laws; presence of bank and corporate secrecy; availability of professional and financial services; and the nature and level of taxation. One basic similarity among tax havens, however, appears to be low or no tax on at least one important category of income. Further, low taxation plays an important part in the determination of whether or not MNCs should invest in a certain tax haven.

The expanding activity of MNCs has resulted in the development of a variety of techniques to minimize their total income taxes. This minimization is not limited to US income taxes but applies to the MNCs worldwide tax liability. A US parent would have just as much incentive to shift US income to a tax haven country, as it would to shift income of a Canadian subsidiary to a sister corporation in a tax haven country. These companies generally report earnings on a worldwide basis and their objective is to enhance their worldwide net earnings and minimize taxes paid to all countries. We are concerned with non-arm's-length transactions used to accomplish this.

1. Foreign Trusts

The person wishing to start an investment portfolio of some substance with an eye to accumulating the income produced is likely to be concerned with the advantages of a tax haven. In one of many variations, it is possible for a US person to create a trust resident in a tax haven whose income is not subject to US taxing jurisdiction. The trust would invest its funds in assets producing passive income. If the tax haven has, for example, favorable tax treaty arrangements, investment income from outside the haven flows to the trust at reduced or exempt rates. Similar tax consequences may occur if the trust finds passive investment opportunities either in the tax haven where it has established residency or some other tax haven. An example of this is the foreign trust which invests in shares of a mutual fund based in one of the tax havens. The foreign situs trust situated in a tax haven is frequently used to avoid tax on its passive investments.

As US persons have been able to establish foreign trusts in which funds could be accumulated tax free, the Tax Reform Act of 1976 provides new rules to tax the income of a foreign trust to the US grantor if the funds are accumulated for a US beneficiary, or for his benefit. Other rules provide for an interest charge on the amount of any tax paid by a US beneficiary where the trust income is not taxable to the grantor; revise the provisions for taxing capital gains to US beneficiaries; and increase the rate of the excise tax on transfers to foreign entities.

2. Holding Companies

A holding company is used here to describe a company which acts as a conduit for funds as opposed to goods. A holding company may be used, for example, to pass intercorporate dividends, finance other companies within the corporate family, or license patents or other intangible rights.

Certain island in the Caribbean offer holding companies

attractive tax benefits. For example, Antigua, Barbados and Jamaica have special 'International Business Companies' which are desirable for many holding company operations. The 'International Business Company' of the investment company variety pays a 2½% insular income tax on investment income after deducting management expenses and dividends paid to nonresident shareholders are also subject to a 2½% tax in the form of withholding. One other significant feature of an 'International Business Company' is that it may be entitled to income tax treaty benefits. The US-UK treaty, for example, applies to the previously mentioned insular areas that allow 'International Business Companies'. To illustrate how an investment type 'International Business Company' might be utilized, consider the following situation: If a corporation from a non-treaty country has a wholly owned subsidiary in the US, dividends paid to the parent by the US subsidiary would be subject to a 30% withholding tax. By using one of the insular 'International Business Companies' to hold the shares of the American subsidiary, the US withholding tax on the dividends would be equal to 5% . . . the rate provided for under the UK treaty. As previously mentioned, the holding company would pay only a slight insular income tax on the dividends income.

Holding company tax benefits are also to be found outside the Caribbean. For example, a Netherlands holding company is free from tax on income resulting from its direct participation in both Dutch and foreign subsidiaries. Examples of the types of income receiving this beneficial treatment are dividends received from a subsidiary and gains from the sale of the subsidiary's shares. Dutch holding companies are particularly attractive in some cases because of the lack of withholding imposed by the Netherlands at source on certain types of income. To be more specific, there is no Dutch withholding tax on interest and withholding tax on dividends going to a foreign parent is often reduced to zero under income tax treaties with other countries. Consequently, Dutch holding companies are particularly lucrative as a conduit for funds.

3. Intercorporate Transactions

Making intercorporate loans across National boundaries may depend on the use of holding companies or the availability of a treaty provision. If the Canadian corporation borrows funds for such purpose, it must relend them to its UK subsidiary at a rate to compensate for withholding on the interest under the UK/ Canadian treaty. But if an affiliate US corporation borrows funds and relends them to the UK company, the US-UK treaty permits interest to be paid from one country to the other free of tax. Consequently, in the case of the US affiliate, the interest chargeable to the UK corporation is likely to be nearer the borrowing rate than if the Canadian corporation makes the loan (save some other manipulation to minimize the overall tax burden of the corporate family). To achieve similar results, if for some reason routing the loan through the US affiliate is not feasible, a Swiss holding company is a likely alternative in making the loan to the UK subsidiary.

4. Corporate Residency

Because of the variation in corporate residence rules in some instances, a corporation may be entitled to the most favourable tax benefits offered under more than one treaty with a particular country. We understand, for example, corporations which have neither their place of management nor their seat in Germany are subject to German corporate income taxes only with respect to certain income derived from German sources. Aside from the German concept, countries use other criteria for defining place of management such as the place where the board of directors meet (United Kingdom), the location of the center of the administrative management (New Zealand) or even the territorial source of a corporation's prevailing income (Pakistan).

Legally required connective factors, such as the location of the management or the place of incorporation, can be easily manipulated or avoided. Thus, companies place economically and financially important operations outside a state's jurisdiction by means of a foreign incorporation regardless of 'home' country connections. The present corporate residency rules appear to place too much weight on the location of the corporate seat, or on the mechanical and formal act of legal creation. These residency criteria give competitive favor to the corporation able to take advantage of these rules. Such rules invite tax avoidance and may result in complicated counter-legislation to mitigate the adverse effects on a country's revenue and balance of payments.

5. Captive Insurance Companies

Another strategy used by MNCs is the use of a captive insurance company. Many large US manufacturing companies form captive offshore insurance companies in tax haven countries for the purposes of insuring their and their affiliates' properties and risks. In most cases the wholly-owned insurance subsidiaries are insuring only the risks of their parents and affiliates. Promoters of the use of captive insurance companies describe an off-shore company as a means of exporting dollars for investment abroad, a vehicle for obtaining a tax deduction as opposed to non-deductible informal self-insurance (self-insurance is not deductible on the US tax return), and as a means of generating foreign source income for the purpose of using excess foreign tax credits. Although we are still studying the matter, our initial approach to this problem is to deny the premium deduction as being self-insurance.

6. Income shifting

The following illustrates a classic tax haven arrangement. The principals behind a particular US corporation engaged in selling automobiles overseas also control a foreign subsidiary and a Liechtenstein 'Anstalt'. Each of the entities participate in the transactions giving rise to the income. However, a disproportionate part of the profits are shifted to the 'Anstalt'. The 'Anstalt' is not subject to tax in the country where the sales take place, presumably because its contacts with that country are minimal. Subpart F of the Internal Revenue Code, designed to lessen the value of the tax haven *modus operandi*, was found to be inapplicable as the purchases and sales that make up the transactions giving rise to the income are from and to unrelated parties. Further, the services are performed within the country where the subsidiary was created. The most effective weapon the Service has in this type of case is to reallocate income.

7. Transfer pricing

This method (direct shifting of income to tax haven countries through under or over pricing of commodities in inter-company transfers) is a well known tax avoidance technique. Transfer pricing is a common issue due to its implications along broad industrial lines and variance in use by selling, trading, distributing and manufacturing organizations. We have taken an aggressive stand against this issue by strong enforcement of IRC 482.

8. Research and Other Arrangements

US audits of certain MNCs clearly established that cost-sharing and other research arrangements are becoming an important tax haven technique. However, it is not so much in the area of the cost distribution between a tax haven and other affiliate that the income is shifted. More significantly, the income and profit is shifted by a disproportionate regional distribution of the sales and other exploitation rights to research results ensuing from joint research and development (R & D) efforts.

For example, while the research costs may be nominally divided evenly between an affiliate in a member country and one in a tax haven country, the assignment of property rights to inventions made under a cost-sharing arrangement will be divided in such a way that, invariably, the tax haven affiliate is exclusively authorized to exploit (sell, use, license) worldwide the product to which a substantial intangible value, created by R & D is attached.

Moreover, deducting current R & D expenses and other write-offs for R & D in one member country may result in an apparent loss situation which decreases a tax liability not only in this country but possibly also affects a tax position of the respective company in another member country. Operations of a chemical and drug company in the US where it carries on R & D and shows perennial losses well projected into the future, with obvious implications for the parent's profits in the UK is one example. This company, insofar as we know, transfers the knowledge and results of R & D to the parent which in turn gives licensing rights to a Swiss affiliate. The case was brought to our attention by the UK. Similar techniques resulting in losses in the US are being discovered. A combination of R & D arrangements with multi-sourcing techniques in production and intra-network division of functions of uneven risks may further compound the effectiveness of the income and profit shifting.

Tax shelters compared
As mentioned earlier, tax haven techniques are such business selling, accounting, financing, management and other practices and arrangements which shift the income flows and the capital stock (income producing assets) to no tax or low tax-rated countries.

From the point of this discussion only such tax haven techniques (and respective countries) are of interest, insofar as they were not part of legislative intent to create the respective tax havens. For instance, neutralizing the impact of foreign taxation on investment; or favoring particular regional developments, and thus, directing the flow of investment to Less Developed Countries (LCDs), or special entities (Western Hemisphere Corporation).

Tax shelters, as far as the present discussion is concerned, are such lawful techniques which permit a reduced tax liability — usually in the high tax-rate countries — chiefly by laws which allow deductions for noncash outlays; such as, write-offs, depreciation, depletion, etc. Deductions for certain outlays, usually considered capital expenses, as current expenses can also work, over a certain period, as a tax-shelter technique in shifting profit to the later years.

The purpose and effect of a tax shelter practice is to produce or increase cash flows which otherwise would have been, at least partially, used for paying taxes. This tax-negative impact is further compounded, if a stream of such tax flow can be diversified by the utilization of some money (debt) management techniques to a tax haven country.

PROGRAMS USED TO CURB ABUSE

The United States, aware of the fact that many conventional audit methods and techniques are not effective in the area of international audits, has initiated various programs and procedures in an effort to encourage maximum tax compliance by MNCs. The major programs, discussed below, include the International Enforcement, Coordinated Examination, Industry-wide, and On-site Examination Program.

International Enforcement Program

Overall responsibility for coordination of this program is vested in the Assistant Commissioner (Compliance) with broad functional responsibilities delegated as follows:

(1) *National Office Audit Division* — has responsibility over domestic corporations doing business in foreign countries.

(2) *Office of International Operations (OIO)* — has responsibility over foreign corporations doing business in the USA and US citizens residing in foreign countries.

The program's objective is to obtain voluntary compliance in the international area through a vigorous but reasonable audit program. Basically, our discussion will concentrate on those international issues which comprise activities and other transactions that involve foreign affiliates of a domestic parent.

The National Office Audit Division provides broad program direction, exercises functional supervision over regional activity, and coordinates examinations involving taxpayers in industry-type cases having international features. Experience has taught us that central program guidance ensures nationwide uniformity in the application of tax laws as well as nationwide coverage of significant international tax abuses. A senior member of the staff of each ARC (Audit) coordinates the program within each of our seven regional offices. The program is managed in each district by a District Program Manager (DPM). International examiners, supervisors, conferees and reviewers are stationed in twelve

'Key Districts'; however, they service the various district needs throughout the entire region.

This program covers a complex and sensitive area in which we are still gaining experience. Therefore, examiners are instructed to exercise care and good judgment when recommending adjustments between domestic taxpayers and their foreign affiliates. *De minimus* adjustments are discouraged. Rather agents look to situations involving significant deviations from arm's-length dealings, or significant shifting of income to a foreign affiliate.

Coordinated Examination Program

The Coordinated Examination Program closely monitors the activities of our 1,200 largest taxpayers. Included in this program are all taxpayers (except financial institutions and utilities) whose group assets exceed $250 million. Financial institutions and utilities are also included in the program if their gross assets exceed $1 billion. As may be seen, due to the asset criteria, almost all US multinationals of consequence and in some cases US subsidiaries of MNCs, are included in this program.

The overall objective of this program is to effectively plan and manage (with central monitoring) the tax examinations of large cases to produce a maximization of US tax compliance efforts. We recognize the audit problems created by size, complexity, diversification of or geographical dispersion of operations and assets owned or effectively controlled (both within and without US borders) by the principal taxpayer (parent company). The accomplishment of this objective requires that the key taxpayer (usually the parent company of the multinational group) and all effectively controlled entities will be considered as one unit for the purpose of planning and executing the audit.

The key to implementing and carrying on a large case audit is the concept of the team audit. Team audits are executed according to a written plan by a team of highly trained auditors and other specialists managed and directed by a case manager, who is directly responsible for, and the focal point for control and decision making with respect to the overall audit plan. Usually from two to nine revenue agents will be assigned to the audit of a large MNC. Included in the team may be various specialists. In most audits of multinationals, an engineering specialist and an international examiner will be assigned. As needed, a specialist in computer audit techniques, a pension trust examiner and other audit specialists will be assigned. The audit team may also include, at times, an economist who will assist and advise agents particularly concerning the economic realities encountered in audits of international transactions between related parties. The international examiner is trained to deal specifically with international issues, most notably, controlled foreign corporation issues and allocations of income and/or expenses between related taxpayers.

The entire audit team (case manager, revenue agents and all specialists) takes part in planning the depth and scope of the audit. Also, the various members of the audit team, when necessary, will consult with experts from other US governmental agencies or arrange private consultation with industry experts.

The team audit concept is an effective tool for dealing with MNCs. In addition to providing a diversified allocation of manpower along a specific line of expertise, it promotes and encourages communication and exchange of technique between examiners, and provides the best possible uniform treatment of issues.

Industry-wide Examination Program

We have found that taxpayers within a given industry tend to treat items (business and/or operating functions and practices, special income or expense categories, etc.) peculiar to that industry basically the same, perhaps with slight variations due to differences in accounting. As a result, we have instituted an audit concept referred to as an 'Industry-wide Examination'.

One of the primary purposes of Industry-wide Examinations is to identify significant tax issues predominant within an industry. In most instances, transfer pricing and the use of tax havens are targeted as issues. The use of this type of examination not only enables us to make consistent audit adjustments, but also allows for the study of industry patterns and pricing techniques.

An Industry-wide Examination is a simultaneous audit of several principal US taxpayers, usually six (6) to ten (10), within a given industry. Invariably, due to US corporate structure, certain taxpayers within the industry-wide study will be MNCs. This tends to enhance our study since it gives us the opportunity to look at worldwide business operations and tax practices within the targeted industry.

Our examination experience has indicated that we can rely, to a great extent, on results developed in one audit area to determine whether or not we should concentrate on, or bypass, that area with other taxpayers who operate within the selected industry but were not part of the initial Industry-wide Examination. Some of the procedures followed in organizing and implementing an Industry-wide Examination are as follows:

— Selection of major taxpayers within the targeted industry;
— Assignment of a nationwide audit coordinator who is responsible for organizing, planning, and handling of meetings;
— Selection of specific audit issues to be investigated;
— Planning the coordination and exchange of audit information, techniques, procedures, etc., among all personnel taking part in the industry study;
— At the conclusion of the audit, prepare audit techniques and guidelines to be utilized in future audits of all taxpayers who operate within the specific industry studied.

We believe the application of an intense and coordinated audit effort through an industry-wide approach provides a greater degree of uniformity and consistency in raising and resolving tax issues and will reduce the audit time expended in future audits.

On-site Examination Program

As mentioned earlier, the Office of International Operations has the primary responsibility for the Service's Compliance effort outside the US. As a result of IRS' concern over the illegal activities of MNCs and the related potential for unlawful reduction of taxable income, we have allocated additional resources and established more effective procedures for conducting the examinations of foreign entities related to domestic MNCs. District offices are now seeking the assistance and support of the Office of International Operations whenever the facts surrounding foreign transactions should be more fully explored.

Our current and planned on-site examination program involves a cross section of American industry. Intensive IRS activities abroad are not limited to controlled foreign corporations. They also include branch and partnership operations. In some instances, we plan to expand our Industry-wide Examination Program into foreign countries. Using this approach, the Service will simultaneously examine all the activities of major US corporations engaged in specific line of business in particular countries.

Foreign on-site audits are not new to the administration of the US Federal income tax law. However, we are increasing our administrative efforts in this area to meet the growth of the MNCs in our present business world. We believe this is the right way to go if the IRS is to achieve its mission of ensuring proper tax compliance.

AUDIT TOOLS TO CURB ABUSE
Through legislation
Subpart F
The United States legislative efforts to deal with international tax avoidance or evasion schemes gained prominence with the Revenue Act of 1962. This Act introduced Subpart F, which represented a major step in attacking the use of tax havens for accumulating foreign earnings. The concept used in Subpart F was the imposition of tax on the US shareholder with respect to the earnings of controlled foreign corporation regardless of whether the foreign earnings were repatriated. This concept was based on the alleged right of the home country to tax income produced by the capital investment of its nationals. The concepts of Subpart F have been adopted by a few other countries, such as Canada and Germany, and are being discussed by the international organizations as a possible solution to problems which they have encountered.

Section 367
A further tool available to the US government regarding tax affairs of MNCs is Code Section 367. This section denies recognition of the tax free reorganization of a foreign entity unless an advance ruling from IRS is obtained. Section 367 is intended to prevent the tax free transfer of appreciated assets to foreign tax havens and, of significant importance, provides the US with substantial information about proposed transactions.

Allocation of Income and Expenses (Section 482)
Section 482 of the Internal Revenue Code gives the Commission of Internal Revenue authority to allocate income and deductions between or among organizations, trades, or businesses owned or controlled by the same interests in order to prevent the avoidance of tax or clearly reflect income.

To accomplish this, allocations and adjustments are based on standards which would be applied by unrelated parties dealing at arm's-length. For example, the Commissioner may make allocations to reflect adequate reimbursement for services rendered by one member of a group of corporations to another member of the group, where the services are for the benefit of the latter member. He also has the authority to adjust the prices charged for goods sold by one member to another, where the prices charged are not a fair reflection of the proper price, or to require a proper charge where money or property of one member is made available to another. In other words, in the case of transactions between controlled taxpayers, income for tax purposes is to be determined by placing the parties on a tax parity (state of equality) with uncontrolled parties.

Administration of Section 482 is accomplished by regulations which describe the application of the arm's-length standard first, in a general way, and then, in detail covering five specific transactions:

1. Loans or Advances
2. Performance of Services
3. Use of Tangible Property
4. Transfer or Use of Intangibles
5. Sales of Tangible Property (Transfer Pricing)

In each of these five areas, the general rule is first stated — that is, that the proper arm's-length consideration will be determined with reference to all relevant facts and circumstances. Next, in some instances, a safe haven or *prima facie* rule is provided. This rule provides a specific rate or charge that will be accepted arm's-length, unless the taxpayer (and not the Government) desires to establish a more appropriate rate.

In view of the aforementioned arm's-length standards, we have issued general guidelines to our examining personnel for developing Section 482 cases. This is preferred rather than applying specific or concrete allocation methods. This permits the examiner to apply the law to a particular factual pattern and determine the best evidence resources which would be necessary or helpful in sustaining any Section 482 allocation. This is not to say that we will not apply the same allocation method in different cases if the factual pattern and circumstances are similar. For example, if in one case we allocate Research and Development expenses between related parties in accordance with each party's proportionate share of worldwide sales, we are not precluded from making the same allocation in another particular case if the facts and circumstances are similar. This allocation method attempts to match each party's cost with the benefits they derive. However, an attempt must also be made to measure each party's risks. Further, in some instances, a safe haven rule is provided where the taxpayer is not regularly engaged in similar dealings with unrelated parties. For example, we have instituted a safe haven rule for inter-company loans where the creditor does not regularly engage in the 'business' of making loans and advances of the same general type to unrelated parties.

We also feel, particularly with our application of an arm's-length standard, that the large variety of factual patterns which arise in Section 482 cases will not allow for the development of specific allocation methods for every type of situation. Further, this procedure would result in a document too complex and difficult to be useful.

The nature and complexity of the problems in the application of Section 482 do not lend themselves to stereotyping. Therefore, we have also found it not feasible to establish or specify minimum evidentiary standards. Each Section 482 problem should be resolved basically upon its particular facts and circumstances. We feel, to some extent, that the kind of information required to arrive at accurate and defensible allocations is the same or very similar for most Section 482 issues. This statement holds true whether the issue involves pricing, services, royalties, or any other Section 482 transaction.

Therefore, in every Section 482 issue, it is essential that our examiners know the following:

1. *The details of the questioned transactions as they actually occurred.* For example, if there are inter-company sales, what products are involved; in what form are the goods sold (i.e., bulk, small packages, unbranded, etc.); in what quantities; at what price; and what credit terms are available? If resold, at what prices and to whom? If not resold, what use did the buyer make of them, etc.?

2. *The functions performed to accomplish the transaction.* This (step one) is what we refer to as a 'functional analysis'. We try to determine what economically significant functions were performed in accomplishing the questioned transactions. A functional analysis goes behind the books and records to discover the realities of the transactions and beyond the form of the transactions to determine economic and business reasons.

3. *Which organization performed each function.* Step two of our functional analysis normally begins with the organization which initiates a particular transaction and carries through until the transaction has generated income from outside the related or controlled group. This means that, for each step of a transaction, a determination must be made concerning the worth or economic value which should be attached to the specific function. This determination can only be achieved through inspection of the pertinent books

and records and, in most cases, from actually questioning appropriate officials (not just accounting or tax officials) of the organization.

4. *The method or basis upon which the inter-company charge (price, fee, commission, royalty, etc.) was determined by the taxpayer.* It is important to obtain whatever information is available as to how the taxpayer and its affiliates arrived at the price or charge they used. That is, it is necessary not only to determine what price, royalty, or commission was charged, but how and why it was decided to use that figure rather than some other figure. Was the price in a controlled sale the same as the price in some uncontrolled sale? Was it computed as an arbitrary mark-up on cost, or was it computed in some other fashion? These are important questions.

We find the managers in accounting departments may not have been involved in the pricing decisions and may not know the details, considerations and computations used in an inter-company charge. In this case, the agent should find out who made the decision, and obtain information as to how the inter-company transaction was invoiced. Thus, it may be necessary to talk to or secure information from, operating officials and executives in the company who made the decisions.

5. *The determination of arm's-length comparables upon which the examiner is basing his recommended method of allocation.* In the search for arm's-length comparables, it is always advisable to exhaust the possibilities on obtaining acceptable comparables from within the controlled group's own operations before proceeding to alternative sources. In most cases, we frequently discover identical transactions which are substantially similar. When this occurs, it may be possible to isolate significant differences, if any, measure them and, after an adjustment for any differences, determine a good comparable.

However, when an arm's-length comparable is not available within the controlled group, we have resorted to the use of third-party data (information obtained from various government sources, industrial organizations, investment services and the public business sector) to determine an arm's-length standard. Regardless of where comparables are obtained, it is important to develop sufficient information which will demonstrate that, in fact, they are comparable.

As may be seen from the above discussion, the enforcement of Section 482 by application of an arm's-length standard does not lend itself to specific or concrete methods. Rather, Section 482 requires an analysis based on the merits of the particular facts and circumstances of each case.

For this reason, the development of any Section 482 issue is time-consuming, complex, and requires imagination and ingenuity in resolution. Further, a Section 482 allocation must withstand the test of reasonableness to be sustained throughout the legal process. Arbitrary allocation will result in lost court cases, set bad court precedent, waste our most precious asset (manpower) and perpetuate non-compliance in the area of international business transaction between related parties.

In order to avoid the problems mentioned above, our examiners exercise complete flexibility both as to Section 482 allocations and techniques used in the audit. Only those situations where there have been significant deviations from arm's-length dealings or significant shifting of income should be examined in detail. Finally, in all cases, our examiners enforce Section 482 within a spirit of reasonableness. We hope, of course, that taxpayers will exhibit this same spirit of reasonableness in their dealings with related parties.

Information-gathering ability

We are severely hampered by the lack of information about MNCs. Because of the relatively recent awareness of the impact that tax havens have on various countries' tax laws, there is very little historical data with regard to these companies. Most of the data which has been gathered has not been publicised for obvious reasons. There is a critical need for such historical data. Through the team audit approach in our examinations of MNCs, and by special studies, central coordination, etc., much useful information and statistical data is being accumulated.

The ability to conduct any quality audit or investigation, or successfully measure tax compliance, whether it be an individual or the largest MNC, is dependent upon the tax administrator's access to the books, records and other pertinent information.

We are keenly aware that investigations which require tax officials to cross national boundaries, whether physically or through correspondence, often present unusual difficulties in obtaining information. This is particularly true in the examination of transactions between related parties, and most notably, in cases dealing with the allocation of income and/or expense between related parties.

In the discussion which follows, we have outlined some of the procedures we utilize, under the dictates of US laws, to obtain the necessary information to properly evaluate tax compliance and measure the self-assessment system. The discussion will be limited to methods employed to obtain information concerning foreign affiliates of US taxpayers. In all instances, we strive to establish a spirit of cooperation with US taxpayers and pursue all avenues open to have the taxpayer voluntarily provide the information necessary to complete a timely quality audit.

1. U.S. Taxpayer's Copies of Foreign Affiliates Records

The US can require a domestic corporate taxpayer to produce and disclose copies of balance sheets, profit and loss statements, and books and records of its foreign affiliates which are physically present in the files of the domestic corporation. The information requested must, in all cases, be relevant and material to a proper investigation. In these cases, the officers and directors of the US parent corporation are well within the reach of US law.

2. U.S. Taxpayer's Correspondence with Foreign Affiliates

The US can require a domestic corporation to produce and disclose such written communications and correspondence which may be relevant and material to an investigation. However, here the term correspondence is nonspecific and may include many corporate documents unrelated to tax liability under investigation. Therefore, information requests for correspondence should be pertinent to certain subjects and transactions under investigation and should be described with reasonable particularity.

3. Records from Foreign Members of a U.S. Controlled Group

As previously noted, the first action taken to obtain foreign information is to request it directly from the US domestic taxpayer. Generally, parent corporations are able to get information from foreign subsidiaries they control. Also, US subsidiaries usually can obtain data from their foreign parent companies. However, there can be exceptions with respect to particular records where the law of the foreign country may prohibit records being removed from the country. Other difficulties may arise concerning the production of records in the possession and custody of a foreign corporation located outside the USA. Accordingly, if the US taxpayer corporation refuses or is unable to obtain books and records in possession of a foreign affiliate which is important to the US government's case, the problem will be referred to our Office of International Operations for advice and assistance.

As a general guideline to examiners, we recommend that all sources of information which are available, or can be made available, in the US should be thoroughly explored before requesting information from foreign countries through the Office of International Operations. We recognize that there is a limit to the reach of US law when we audit the accounts of a US affiliate of a foreign parent. In these cases, we have some difficulty in obtaining data in the hands of the foreign parent. However, we are aided by our Revenue Service Representatives (RSRs) operating abroad.

The Office of International Operations is responsible for enforcing US tax laws in all areas of the world outside the USA. It maintains tax liaison with tax representatives of foreign countries. Information available in foreign countries varies from almost full accessibility to very little, depending upon the degree of tax cooperation enjoyed between the respective nations. This cooperation has been established, fostered and maintained by our Revenue Service Representatives (RSRs) situated at fourteen (14) strategic locations overseas. The RSRs are under the direct supervision of the Director of International Operations.

Special Audit Techniques
One major responsibility under the International Enforcement Program is to provide our international field examiners with current basic and detailed audit techniques. This is accomplished via the distributing of our Audit Techniques Handbook.

Basic techniques are those which are generally applicable in all field examinations of income tax returns. They are mainly planning and procedural activities that will ensure a uniform approach to the audit. Detailed techniques apply whenever a more intense and thorough review is necessary in a specific area or account (e.g., in determining the validity and accuracy of receipts and disbursements, balance sheet items, etc.). These detailed techniques were not devised to be all-inclusive or restrictive. The degree of their use is entirely optional. Examiners usually modify or amplify the application of these techniques, whenever warranted, to cover the specific audit situation encountered in the examination.

Although International Specialists receive five (5) weeks of intense, formal training before they are assigned to an International Audit Group, there is a continual need to keep them up to date concerning nationwide uniform practices, special studies completed, impact from legislative changes, etc. To some extent, the Audit Techniques Handbook serves as a useful vehicle for this purpose because of the complexity of and interrelationships of the tax law applicable to international activities.

A typical example of the information provided by the Audit Techniques Handbook is the comprehensive discussion on the development of Section 482 issues. Another area discussed is the use of summons and other related problems in obtaining information.

Citing a recent example: we are about to distribute to our field offices a list of thirty-four (34) pointers to international tax avoidance (see the Appendix). We believe they may find it helpful in their initial screening process for the selection of highly suspect returns. The list can also be used by all examiners for pre-audit analysis and audit planning purposes.

APPENDIX A

Pointers to International Tax Avoidance
The guidelines are divided into the following three general categories:
  A. General Matters.
  B. The Balance Sheet.
  C. Profit and Loss Items.

General Matters
1. *Member(s) of corporate group located in tax haven(s).* A tax haven can be described as any country whose laws provide an escape from taxes on an economic gain which would otherwise be taxable in another country. For example, a country may have a low or no tax on income or a type of income. It may also allow a deduction that is not allowable in the other country. There is a great incentive to divert profits and other income to parent or subsidiary corporations organized in tax havens.
2. *Dual use of tax havens.* A multinational group may use a tax haven to advantage both in the purchase and sale of goods. By adroitly invoicing goods through a tax haven affiliate, the greater portion of the profit, unrelated to any functions performed by the tax haven affiliate, can be erroneously recorded in the affiliate. Likewise, reversing the technique, a United States corporation can be overcharged for goods purchased from a tax haven affiliate, thereby creating an unallowable tax deduction for the United States corporation.

3. *Consolidated figures for world group better than domestic corporation results.* This type of situation can be an indication that the profits of the United States corporation are being diverted to a tax haven.

4. *Group Organization.* In a corporate group structure, ascertain if each corporation has a valid function. An 'unexplained' corporation may be a vehicle for tax avoidance. An analysis of the taxpayer's copies of Securities and Exchange Commission Forms 8K and 10K and the Form 959 print-out, maintained by the Regional Manager-International, can be used as a starting point to determine all foreign entities owned by a United States taxpayer.

5. *Associated by common control rather than group membership.* There is need in practice to watch for transactions between companies which are under common control but which do not simply belong to the same group.

6. *Domestic branches of foreign corporations.* It should be ascertained whether or not the foreign corporation is engaged in a trade or business in the United States and subject to United States taxation.

7. *Permanent loss-makers.* This can indicate the possibility of less than arm's-length transactions and relationships with suppliers and/or customers.

8. *Domestic International Sales Corporation.* DISC transactions should be scrutinized to determine if the election, qualifications and pricing arrangements are proper.

The Balance Sheet
9. *Repatriation of foreign profits as loans.* Loans from foreign affiliates may represent the repatriation of foreign profits and an attempt to avoid payments of dividends to an affiliated United States corporation.

10. *Excessive balances with affiliates.* Excessive credit or debit balances with foreign affiliates may indicate non arm's-length transactions between the parties which have not, and perhaps will not, in fact be paid.

11. *Write-offs of inter-company debt.* This can be an attempt to reduce accumulated inter-company balances that may have resulted from less than arm's-length transactions.

12. *Investment and receivables held through or by foreign subsidiaries.* Banks may lend funds to tax haven subsidiaries for investments, but allege that they are only lending as part of ordinary banking business at commercial rate. Loans or

investments may be made in United States property, subject to dividend consideration.

13. *Absence of expected assets or liabilities in a company's accounts.* Such omissions may indicate the assignment, transfer or sale of such intangible assets as patents, know-how, trade secrets, etc., to a tax haven affiliate.

Profit and Loss Items

14. *Research and development.*

(a) *High technology industries.* These industries are intensively engaged in research and development. They are particularly prone to tax avoidance schemes because of their high gross profit margins. The US in this respect, provides tax sheltering opportunities as I.R.C. Sec. 174 allows a current deduction for research and development expenditures.

(b) *Hidden research and development expenditures.* Certain expenses are sometimes booked in specific accounts; however, larger amounts may be passed through cost of sales accounts. The total expense (including payments to other group members) should be established.

(c) *Pooled research and development expense.* When a group pools its research and development expenses, all the companies involved should be dealt with on the same basis and reciprocal benefits should be closely watched. Both capital and current operating expenses should be taken into account and the total pool expenditures should be scrutinized.

(d) *Pooling of research and development expense not entirely in one company.* One company in a group may centralize the expenditure (that is, reimburse the other members for their expenditure) but another corporation in a tax haven may assess the group for the user. The excess of assessments over expenditures may then be diverted to the tax haven.

(e) *Research and development expenditure but no indication of royalties received.* The reason for the absence of royalty income should be ascertained.

15. *Royalties*

(a) *Royalty and licensing rates.* Rates paid to foreign affiliates may be excessive or the rates charged to such affiliates may be too low in comparison with arm's-length rates charged by third parties.

(b) *Unlikely recipients of royalties.* Royalties paid to recipients who are unlikely to be conducting the research and development, such as Liechtenstein or Swiss holding companies, may indicate tax-avoidance schemes.

(c) *Round sum royalties*. Payments which are not directly related to the number or value of particular goods produced are suspect (e.g., round sum payments or percentages of total sales).

(d) *Royalties payable on sales of goods purchased from affiliates*. The total royalty and purchase price should equal an arm's-length price. If the total exceeds the arm's-length price, either the royalty or purchase price or both are excessive.

16. *Patents and trademarks*

(a) *Monopolistic position*. Corporations which have valuable patents which are not licensed directly to third parties may exploit their monopoly position by transferring the patents to tax haven subsidiaries to serve as licensors.

(b) *Payments in respect of expired patents*. Any payment in respect of patents which have expired needs further investigation.

(c) *Reciprocal benefits*. Where a corporation pays royalties to a foreign affiliate for use of a patent, consider whether the company is adequately compensated for know-how etc., deriving from its own research and development.

(d) *Payments to affiliates for use of trademarks*. These should be examined with a view to determining if the charge meets arm's-length criteria.

17. *Home Office Expenses*

(a) *Failure to charge foreign affiliates for service*. Make sure that companies within a group (particularly the parent) are charging foreign affiliates adequately for services rendered to them such as home office administrative support, research and development, etc.

(b) *Payments to foreign parent*. Payments for home office administrative support, research and development, etc., may be excessive and may contain hidden profits which are not assessed in the country of receipt.

18. *Interest income as expense*. The rate of interest received and paid in dealing with foreign affiliates should be checked to ascertain if the interest is being properly accounted for.

19. *Sales of partly finished goods*. Such sales to foreign affiliates provide considerable scope for manipulation especially if there are a few or no comparable third-party sales.

20. *Third-party commission or discount to foreign affiliates*. An inflated import price from an unrelated party may be com-

pensated by payment of a commission or discount by the unrelated party to a foreign affiliate of the domestic corporation.

21. *Discounts to foreign affiliates.* The sales price to a foreign affiliate may be arm's-length. However, excessive discount by the seller may then be allowed in the same sale.

22. *Market value less than cost.* Writing down of inventory purchased from affiliates may indicate overcharging in the first place.

23. *Unexpected purchases or sales.* Transactions with a foreign affiliate in a foreign country different from its home country may indicate that the non-home country is being used for tax avoidance purposes.

24. *Invoice to one party; shipment to another.* Separation of a transaction in this way may indicate a tax avoidance scheme.

25. *Adequate compensation of offices.* If officers of a United States corporation also serve as officers of foreign affiliates, check if the offices' compensation is being properly allocated as an expense of the affiliated foreign corporations relative to the executive services the officers perform for each corporation.

26. *Rental accounts.* Details of the use of premises occupied by foreign affiliates may indicate the extent and nature of their activities.

27. *Internal chartering arrangements in shipping groups.* Non arm's-length rates may be charged between companies in a controlled group, particularly to or by affiliates in tax havens. Long term charters may be concluded to take advantage of unusual rises or falls in the general level of the freight rates.

28. *Changes in the pattern of accounts.* Any major changes such as decrease in gross or net profits, volume of business, debit and/or credit balance inter-company accounts as they relate to dealings with foreign affiliates, should be analyzed to ascertain the reason for the changes.

29. *Travel expense.* If a domestic entity deducts expense of travel to its foreign affiliate, such expense, along with similar expenses, could be allocated to the foreign corporation under Section 482, depending upon the facts of the instant case. Also, in which case, such travel expenditures would be considered allocable to foreign sourced income for the purposes of computation of the foreign tax credit limitation of the domestic affiliate.

30. *Domestic parent companies with affiliates within possessions of the United States.* Some possession corporations are exempt from taxation. In these circumstances, transactions between parent and subsidiary should be watched closely.

31. *Net operating losses of affiliates.* During a period of world-wide economic recession, sales affiliates of foreign corporations should be closely watched for large net operating losses carried back to profit years, and the recapture of all previously paid tax. Foreign corporations with excessive losses, or in bankruptcy status, may make excessive charges to their affiliates.

32. *Presence of ruling letter.* If any transactions involved a reorganization between a domestic and foreign entity, a ruling letter should be present.

33. *Liquidation or sale of a foreign affiliate.* This may reveal areas where foreign income was accumulated or shifting occurred. Also, the possible conversion of ordinary income into capital gain may be present.

34. *Payments to foreign entities by domestic corporations.* Where a payment of income has been made to a foreign entity from sources within the United States such as wages, rents, dividends, interests or other fixed or determinable annual or periodic income not effectively connected with the conduct of a trade or business in the United States, it should be determined whether a liability for withholding tax exists and whether Forms 1042 were filed.

NOTE

*   This article is the text of a lecture given at the XVII Conferencia Tecnica (Technical Conference) held in Montevideo, Uruguay in March 1977. We are grateful to the US Internal Revenue Service for permission to publish it in this collection.

17.
A BLUEPRINT FOR A TRANSFER PRICING COMMANDO UNIT
PANAYOTIS ROUMELIOTIS

LIMITATIONS OF EXISTING MECHANISMS OF CONTROL
Many countries have attempted to control transfer pricing by legal instruments. They range from formal controls on the establishment of foreign companies and conditions attaching to the importing of foreign technology, to the daily examination of accounts, the prescribing of maximum and minimum prices for imports and exports, and the creation of trading companies to control the export of the country's basic natural resources. In some countries there are strict regulations, involving severe penalties, designed to prevent and discourage transfer pricing. In practice, however, most state bodies are incapable of dealing effectively with the problem.

On the one hand we have a cumbersome uncoordinated and out-moded public machinery based on the traditional codes of business practice, with a competence mainly restricted to the national level. On the other hand, there are the highly flexible centralised multinational corporations which operate at the international level and whose development relies on modern business methods and the principle of confidentiality. The activities of the multinational corporations, including transfer pricing, can be controlled only if the state bodies responsible gain a flexibility of action and radically change their attitudes towards the whole question of the codes of business practice.

For example, many governments have departments which exercise control over the prices of imports and exports. Their authority derives mainly from laws relating to currency exchange. This control tends to be preventative and designed to pre-empt transfer pricing. The authorities rely for their information on specialist journals, on their own comparisons of prices of similar imports and exports, and on economic advisers of their country's foreign embassies for information on international prices.

In practice, however, these services are powerless because

278

they cannot obtain the requisite data on international prices to form a comparative basis for the control of transfer pricing. The mechanisms for the determination of many international prices are invisible. International trade is, by and large, controlled by multinational enterprises, whose pricing practices and methods of operation remain hidden from governments. This is quite apart from the question of the capacity of the commercial advisers maintained abroad by various countries.

Even if these services succeeded in obtaining comparable international prices, this may be of little avail, for much legislation is so couched as to put the burden of proof of over- or underpricing on the government services themselves.

Consequently, under present law, the information obtained by the services from their connections abroad does not constitute proof of over- or underpricing. In order to establish an infringement of the law on transfer pricing, the government is compelled to demonstrate that the multinational's declared prices are false. This presupposes that there exist forged import and export invoices, which it is difficult to establish.

Further, even if the courts take up a particular case of transfer pricing, it is open to the company accused to dispute the government's data. Companies use many arguments: the lapse of time between the conclusion of an import or export transaction and the acquisition of the data, the particular specifications of the goods in question, special trading agreements between the parties concluding the transaction, monopoly conditions, etc. In the majority of cases where the courts have taken up transfer pricing cases, the verdicts have gone against the government.

As a result, the services often react by fixing unrealistic limits on prices of imports and exports. This can paralyse a country's foreign exchange or encourage over- or under-pricing even further.

There is the additional problem of the lack of coordination and cooperation between the various bodies interested in controlling transfer pricing, each of which approaches the question from its own standpoint. To take a specific example: in many countries the bodies responsible for foreign exchange are not permitted to seek information about particular companies either from the tax authorities, or from the banks, since this would infringe the confidentiality of the tax return or the bank account.

This information is essential, however, for transfer price control. The currency control authorities, moreover, have no legal basis for examining company accounts, nor are the tax authorities permitted to seek essential information from the banks about the financial position of companies.

Serious efforts are being made to eliminate these loop-holes. In some countries, France is one example, the burden of proof rests with the party concerned and not with the government body in assessing taxable income or company profits, where it is suspected that profits are being concealed by the device of transfer pricing. It is the party concerned which is required to show that the assessment made by the government body is unreasonable.

Other countries have dealt with the cumbersome nature of government transfer pricing control in currency exchange by transferring responsibility to the commercial banks. These banks, in Italy for instance, are answerable to the administrative authorities and at law if they fail to exercise proper control over the flow of foreign exchange.

However, neither laying the burden of proof on the tax payer nor modernising the system by which transfer pricing is controlled by placing the responsibilities on the commercial banks, helps to solve the problems of the data that form the basis for comparison.

Finally, in certain less-developed countries (such as Kenya), control of transfer pricing is undertaken by a private company which issues certificates on imports. The government control services require, prior to the final approval for import, the relevant certificate of the private enterprise approving the price. The supposed advantage of this organisation is its possession of information on international prices and qualities which states can gather only with difficulty.

Apart from the principle that a State should be in a position to control its own economic policy enforcement, there is a danger of corruption when control of transfer pricing is given over to private enterprise.

Experience has shown that these monitoring enterprises do not want to help the State to acquire the relevant experience in controlling transfer prices, nor appealing to the confidential nature of the research, to provide it with details about the research methodology, their sources and difficulties. They merely say that the import prices are or are not 'justifiable', with nothing else to support their conclusion. But, as we have seen above, it is difficult to demonstrate manipulative transfer pricing, and more evidence is required to convince enterprises and courts of the irregularity of an import price. It should be noted, too, that such enterprises have no control in the sector of exports.

FUNCTION AND ORGANISATION OF THE COMMANDO UNIT

I have indicated that there are serious weaknesses in the control of transfer pricing as currently exercised by the State. I have also maintained that private enterprises should not, nor is it possible for them to, decisively control transfer pricing. I shall now try to show that it is possible for this control to be founded on a new organisational base within the government itself, which I will call a Transfer Pricing Commando Unit.

Formation of the Commando Unit

The precondition for this new organisation is the recruitment of eight or ten experts including engineers, accountants, economists and lawyers who should get to know the technical details of the main products imported and exported, the manner of their production and marketing, the structure of the international market, the main enterprises which produce or market them, the different restrictive business practices as well as the legal *status quo* for foreign enterprises in developing countries.

Where such people are not already available in the government, they would have to be recruited from the private sector. If they cannot be found, foreign specialists who have already dealt with the problem of transfer pricing and who are known to international organisations (UNCTAD, United Nations Centre on Transnational Corporations, etc.) should instruct new personnel.

Work Programme and Methods of Operation

The Commando Unit ought, first, to select those products whose prices are to be controlled. As a rule, they should be products of high value which count significantly in the trading accounts. They should also choose products whose production and marketing is controlled by large multinational companies. The specialisation of the experts in the Commando Unit will depend on the choice of products, and they should aim to gain maximum foreign exchange and income from taxes, thus justifying the operation costs of the Commando Unit.

One fundamental problem for the team is access on an international level to information that would enable it to rapidly assemble the relevant data on international prices and market conditions.

To this end, the team must have completely reliable associates working abroad, who either themselves have access to the required information or can gain access to the international circles trading in the products. There are many foreign representatives, themselves middlemen, who act as inter- mediaries and who can therefore enter these circles relatively easily. Commercial advisers attached to embassies cannot do this because of the restrictions placed upon them by their office.

The possibility of finding such middlemen from the various countries presents no practical obstacles. When it has been decided which product or enterprises will be controlled by a particular country then the specialists in these products must be sought either through international organisations (UNIDO, FAO, UNCTC, UNCTAD, etc.), or through other countries which already exercise such control, or even through the country's embassies abroad.

One thing to ensure is that the Commando Unit is not dependent on one sole middleman. It should be able to verify the information of one middleman against that of another, as well as against that which the Commando Unit obtains from official trading organisations of foreign countries or international organisations. In many countries, for example, there are producers or consumers organisations for specific products such as aluminium, bauxite, copper, fish, etc., which either publish the prices of these products, the market conditions, the fluctuations of supply and demand, the trading in a specific product, the main supplies and buyers, transport costs, etc., or can communicate these details.

With the required information, the team can proceed to monitor the fluctuation of all the factors mentioned above and thus be in a position to know at any given moment the forces determining the international prices of the basic products in which it is interested. Its members based abroad should telex information every day on the international prices of basic products or enterprises, which should be stored on a computer, along with all other relevant information.

To reach this stage, the transfer pricing control team would have first to clarify certain problems surrounding the iden- tification of the products in question. For an effective comparison of prices the basis for comparison must be the same: that is, the specifications of the product imported or exported to or from a country must be the same as those of the product with which it is being compared.

It should be observed here that, as far as possible, information on international prices should derive from, and be accompanied by, specific offers to buy or sell the products. This would put the validity of the prices at the disposal of the team beyond dispute.

The Commando Unit will assume the following duties:

1. Reading, selecting and recording data:
   —from documents such as contracts, applications of export and imports customs clearances, payments requests, etc.;
   —from the specialised press, covering product-markets, conditions and events related to producers and consumers;
   —from experts on the identification of the products and their varieties, normal trade terms and conditions of the products, such as commissions, credit, insurance, transport, surveillance, laboratory analysis, tests, etc.
2. Checking the above and tracing material errors and apparent irregularities in relation to:
   —trade;
   —negotiation;
   —company performance.
3. Determining reference prices computation in relation to all the above.
4. Over/underinvoicing calculations.
5. Elaboration of surveys.
6. Drafting reports for the government.

Functions of the Commando Unit

The central idea of the proposal set out above is that the responsibility for controlling transfer pricing, at least for basic products, should be assigned to a special team, and that the kind of control exercised should be preventative. This would automatically prevent tax evasion and loss of foreign exchange. A number of legislative changes would be required to ensure the effective working of the team. It would undoubtedly need information concerning the practices of a variety of companies in the financial sphere, and also details of the administration of the enterprises. It would therefore be useful if it could draw on the relevant information at the disposal of other state bodies and that of the banks.

The best approach to the control of transfer pricing is its prevention. Often, however, this kind of preventative control cannot be implemented immediately. The team would not have rapid enough access to the data needed to establish a particular price, and to avoid interrupting foreign trade, it would have to act in a restrictive manner. This, too, would require legislative changes. Specifically, in all three areas of currency control, customs and taxation, it would be necessary to establish the principle that the burden of proof should rest with the interested party. In other words, the interested party should be called upon to demonstrate that the prices quoted by the transfer pricing control team are unreasonable, rather than vice-versa.

If the enterprises are unable to prove that the prices of their imports or exports are normal, then they should be liable to monetary penalties. For the Commando Unit to be in the position to gather full information, exercise the above control, and impose prices, a new law should be passed by the Parliament, or the Government should implement a new policy administratively.

As the Commando team gains experience in the control of the prices of a limited number of products, it should extend its field of action. The number of products or services whose prices it monitors should be increased, and the team should be in a position to make suggestions for the prevention of transfer pricing. In particular, the team should be able to produce cost-benefit analyses for specific enterprises, particularly multi-national companies, and to make suggestions to the Government on the criteria for giving approval to the establishment and functioning of multinational corporations. The team should also examine alternative sources of technology including possible local development and offers of technological aid, giving due weight to the broader aims of socio-economic development.

The latter proposals are, of course, long term. In the short run the creation of a Commando team would yield, as the Colombian experience has shown, immediate benefits in the areas of foreign exchange and taxation.

(c) Control in Practice

18.
THE CONTROL OF TRANSFER PRICING IN GREECE: A PROGRESS REPORT*
TOM GANIATSOS

Although its *per capita* GNP of $3,000 is moderately high, Greece has several features in common with many of the developing countries which are attempting to transform their economies through the import of technology. It is technologically backward compared with other developed countries and a substantial part of the population is still engaged in agriculture. Its foreign-trade sector is large in relation to GNP and it has a sizeable chronic trade deficit held in check by delicately managed monetary and foreign-exchange controls. It is a market economy whose successive governments have given priority to private enterprise in the country's economic developments. Having neither extensive natural resources nor a large domestic market to offer, they have felt obliged to maintain a hospitable climate for foreign investors, and to offer generous incentives to attract foreign capital and technology.

The conservative economic philosophy suggested by the above two characteristics of national economic policy was not inconsistent with the action initiated by the Government, under the impulse of the Governor of the Bank of Greece (the central bank), to curb the extremes of transfer pricing in 1975, at a time when the country found itself faced with an impending balance-of-payments crisis.

EXISTING CONTROLS
At this time Greece already had an extensive structure of controls to check import and export prices. Every customs house, for example, had a valuation service charged with assessing the validity of import prices. They kept files which allowed them to compare the declared valuations by different importers of a given good and of the same importer at different times. They also used prices quoted in international trade journals and data provided by overseas commercial attachés as a basis of comparison. They had full power to adjust prices — but as a Customs authority, their

interest was in high valuations (to maximise tariff revenue), rather than controlling overinvoicing.

The Ministry of Finance was likewise empowered to adjust import-export valuations in assessing a firm's taxable income, but it was not organised to do this on a regular and systematic basis with other monitoring departments of the Government, and indeed was restricted from divulging to other government services tax data given to it confidentially.

Thirdly, an elaborate control apparatus operated under the authority of the Ministry of Commerce. All commercially traded goods passing through customs in Greece had to secure the prior approval of the Chamber of Commerce and Industry, whose main task was to check prices, to prevent unlawful flights of foreign exchange. The practice, which still operates today, is as follows. Each importer submits to one of the thirty-six Chamber offices a form detailing the particulars of the importer, the exporter, any intermediary, the goods traded, its tariff classification, quantities, prices, commissions, and so forth, together with other documents such as the *pro forma* invoice and commonly a copy of the seller's catalogue. The documents are then assigned to Chamber employees specialising in the commodity groups in question (there are ten such groups) for review and approval. For imports whose invoice value is under $20,000 a routine check and approval is given after a comparison of price with that of a previously approved invoice for the same good. If the price is 10% above the previous approval, or the invoice value exceeds $20,000 a more detailed control is made, taking into account official international quoted prices for the product published in trade journals and periodicals[1] or contained in the catalogues supplied to the importer by the exporter. If it is not possible to compare with price lists, prior invoices or published prices, the international price data is requested from the commercial attaché of the Greek Embassy in the country of origin of the good. In general, the firm approached for the price data will turn out to be the same as the one doing the exporting. The employee who does the check then makes a brief recommendation on the invoice which he is obliged to forward to the Invoice Control Committee of the Athens Chamber of Commerce for examination and final approval.

For exporters, the clearance by the Chamber of Commerce once the application/declaration and invoices are submitted is much more routine than for imports.

Transfer pricing monitoring machinery could, therefore, be

said to exist, but such a system has a number of weaknesses;[2]

(a) For certain internationally traded products there are no published price figures. Even where available, the prices given in trade journals and used by the Chamber of Commerce, being averages or simply quoted basic prices applicable only to certain product specifications, are only a rough approximation of prevailing international prices at which transactions actually take place.

(b) Prices contained in sellers' catalogues are of dubious value for comparative purposes in cases where the sellers and importers are affiliated, since it is hardly likely in these circumstances that the sale invoice will state a price that deviates materially from the catalogue price, though both may be overvalued in comparison with arm's-length prices between independent entities. Seldom has the Chamber of Commerce actually requested information from commercial attachés overseas. However, this data may also originate from the exporting firm which probably quotes the same price to the attaché as that charged to its importing affiliates in Greece.

(c) Relying on the price given in the previously approved invoice as a reference price overlooks the fact that all prices are constantly changing. However, if the old invoice was wrongly approved the error will be compounded in subsequent approvals, leading to systematic overpricing of imports (or underpricing of exports).

(d) In some invoices approved by the Chamber of Commerce there is no indication of what reference price, if any, was used for comparison.

(e) The Athens Chamber of Commerce has never been staffed adequately to examine thoroughly the enormous volume of invoices it must handle daily. Its staff of approximately 300 persons handles invoices equal in value to half of the country's foreign trade. Importing and exporting firms exert a constant pressure to have their invoices approved without delay, so that shipments can be loaded and the factory wheels kept moving. As a result, only the most superficial investigation of the invoice can be made by the employee, who moreover lacks the specialised technical background required for analysing the goods traded in particular industries. In general, the work has consisted mainly of registering, recording, and keeping the flow of paper moving and to some extent responding to the requests for international price information from Greek firms.

(f) Lack of a sufficiently fine breakdown and classification of products by the Chamber has resulted in the use as reference prices of price averages previously approved for an entire product category. As a result of this aggregation error, some applications have been wrongly rejected or their approval delayed.

(g) The examination procedure of the Chamber has not given adequate attention to the commissions (added to the prices) paid to trade representatives acting as intermediaries between the seller and buyer or to the size of financial charges (sometimes representing 25% of the value of the products) where the settlement of payment is effected by credit.

Beyond the inadequacies of the approval procedures of the Chamber of Commerce there is more profound weakness in the overall governmental machinery in dealing with foreign transactions in Greece, namely an absence of an integrated pursuit of national policy objectives with respect to balance of payments, foreign investment and technology transfer and taxation, where these overlap with one another. Thus, as already noted, there is no connection between price valuations on imports approved by the Chamber of Commerce (of the Ministry of Commerce) and those of the Customs Service (of the Ministry of Finance). One side effect is that importing firms are encouraged to overprice in the invoice they submit to the Chamber of Commerce.

Similarly there is no systematic link between control over false price declarations on internal trade and the enforcement of tax legislation; nor indeed between the establishment of upper limits on profit, royalty and interest outflows (which was the responsibility of the Foreign Currency Committee of the Bank of Greece) and the surveillance over import and export prices which could be manipulated by technology suppliers in order to get round those limits.

THE ESTABLISHMENT OF EPETEE

It was in the light of this experience that the three Ministers of Co-ordination, Finance and of Commerce established a specialist committee for the Surveillance and Control of Prices of Imported and Exported Goods (Epitropi Parakoloytheseos kai Eleghou Timon Eisaghomenon kai Exaghomenon Eithon, or EPETEE). The committee consisted of a chairman and seven high-level administrators drawn from the three ministries, and met on average once every three weeks. It was more than an interdepartmental committee, however, for it established a technical unit — composed of three professionals and six university students with scientific, engineering and economic backgrounds — to develop a more thorough and systematic system to monitor transfer prices.

The Technical Unit itself was quite independent of any of the three government ministries concerned (although it was formally housed in the Ministry of Co-ordination). It was funded by the autonomous Bank of Greece, its staff were not classed as civil servants and it reported directly to EPETEE.

MAIN POLICY CONSIDERATIONS

EPETEE began to function in April 1975, very soon after its creation, under the chairmanship of a retired director from the Customs Service. There were three matters of strategy that it had to decide upon at that time. One was the choice of products or product groups to be examined. The second was whether the investigations were to be carried out *ex ante* — that is, at the time that the application/declaration and *pro forma* invoice were submitted for clearance to the Chamber of Commerce (but before the actual import or export had been completed) or *ex post*, that is, some time after the transaction was concluded and payment made. The third was whether the remedial action that EPETEE would propose to the Ministers would be of a judicial or administrative nature.

The main criterion for the selection of sectors to be studied was to be their relative importance in the balance of payments. This criterion was dictated by the need to establish as soon as possible that the surveillance of transfer prices was a useful activity whose administrative cost would be outweighed by the amount of foreign exchange saved.[3] The other main criterion was availability of usable data. The studies not only had to be carried out as quickly as possible but also yield findings, the validity of which would stand up to attacks from the firms in question and from any government officials that might be critical of EPETEE. Hence, choice was confined to the sub-set of goods that could be easily studied, that is, in (a) branches having a reasonably stable composition of marketed goods; (b) branches for which there is little or no product differentiation; and (c) branches for which there exists some semblance of an international market. The latter condition excluded goods lacking a market price because they form part of productive processes that are proprietary secrets and are only exchanged between affiliated firms.

Views in EPETEE on the relative merits of *ex ante* and *ex post* investigations were divided. On one side, the Bank of Greece member took the position that *ex post* studies presented the Government with a *fait accompli*, the foreign exchange already having left the country; whereas *ex ante* studies gave the Government a bargaining hand in negotiating price reductions on cargo waiting to be loaded. On the other hand, the Ministry of Commerce participant was concerned that *ex ante* or preventative investigations would hold up the approval process in the Chamber of Commerce and Industry and hamper the free flow of trade. It was decided to do mainly the *ex post* and only a few *ex ante* investigations, especially at the beginning until the Technical Unit had built up its experience in processing information and producing soundly-based price comparisons.

The preceding discussion is relevant to the question of whether EPETEE was to recommend *judicial* as opposed to *administrative* action to the ministers in cases where transfer pricing abuses were identified. The ostensible advantages of recommending judicial action are that it would permit the state to recover any losses it may have sustained on account of the wrongdoing, and also to establish an example to deter other firms from doing the same thing. However, these advantages are outweighed by the serious disadvantage of having to prove intent to defraud or some other kind of criminal act. In order to even hope to accomplish this fact, the state would have to expend considerable time and resources to amass the necessary evidence, and it would never have as much information at its disposal as the accused firm. Moreover, in an institutional environment that is supposed to be benign towards private enterprise — as is the case in Greece — it would not be possible to tolerate the adverse political repercussions that would result from reactions in the business community. On the other hand, administrative measures such as holding up shipments would be inexpensive to implement and would put burden of proof on the firm to justify the disparity between its price and that of the market. They would also be discreet and more capable of bringing an improvement in behaviour without undermining the confidence of the business community. The intention was to avoid having to resort to action any more extreme than confronting a violator with the evidence. The main effect that the Government hoped to achieve as a result of the Technical Unit's findings was psychological: to obtain improved behaviour by instilling in firms the knowledge that the Government was aware of, or had the means of discovering, what was going on.

The methodology of the Technical Unit

The Technical Unit began to operate soon after the establishment of EPETEE in April 1975. Its staff was young, bright and motivated. It was given an office equipped with a telephone having direct dialing to other countries (a scarce and jealously-guarded asset in the government bureaucracy). In addition, it was given access to telex facilities, making it possible to obtain daily price quotations from major international commodity exchanges. Because of the pioneering nature of the attempt to control transfer pricing it was necessary to proceed slowly in an experimental fashion, taking a few products at a time. Gradually, as more experience was acquired through trial and error, it would become possible to increase the number of products covered and introduce a systematic control system. The basic source of information and focus of attention of the analysis were the invoices that had passed through the Chamber of Commerce and Industry for clearance. Using the criteria described above, the Technical Unit examined over the ensuing year the import invoices of a sample of 75 products (84 cases) falling within the categories of chemicals (including pharmaceuticals), fabricated metals, and minerals. The sample consisted of any one of the following: (a) all invoices for imports of a certain product, or (b) all invoices with a value in excess of $100,000, or (c) invoices arbitrarily selected from those sent to the Technical Unit by the Chamber of Commerce. The specific products included in the samples accounted for approximately 10% of the total value of chemicals imports and 20% of fabricated metals and minerals. Invoices were examined for shipments made during an interval of six or twelve months or even longer (if, as in the case of some products, the frequency of shipments was low). The Technical Unit also examined a sample of exports for evidence of under-pricing. As with imports, the sampling procedure was not random but, conforming to the criteria previously described, centred on three leading exports from the metallurgical and mining sectors. Together, these products accounted for 6% of the value of the country's total exports during 1976.

To calculate the percentage of over-pricing of imports or under-pricing of exports, the Technical Unit used the formula:

$$\frac{P_a - P_r}{P_r} \times 100$$

where P_a is the observed price paid by the importing firm in Greece or received by the exporting firm in Greece, as shown on the invoice; and P_r is the reference of arm's-length price with which P_a is compared. In broad outline, the procedure followed was first, to record on large worksheets the price or prices P_a and all other data relevant to the analysis extracted from approved invoices (pertaining to previously-concluded transactions) obtained from the Athens Chamber of Commerce and Industry; secondly, to record the reference prices P_r obtained from published and other outside sources; thirdly, convert the two sets of prices P_a and P_r to a comparable f.o.b. basis by allowing for freight and other charges; and fourthly, to calculate the extent of under- or overpricing and estimated loss of foreign exchange to the country according to the above formula.

The actual procedure was somewhat more complex than this and bore a closer resemblance to detective work than to statistical analysis. For each case the analyst would establish the exact identity of the product and ascertain the dates of submission and approval of invoices, the date of contract between buyer and seller the importer, the exporter, the producer (if different), the trade representative or broker (if there was one) and his commission, the unit price, quantity, total value, terms of payment (including financial charges), delivery dates, method of transport, form of packaging, freight and insurance charges, foreign-exchange parity rates and any other data bearing on price. The primary source of much of this information analysed in each case was the approved invoices and other documentation appended to them, provided by the Chamber of Commerce and Industry.

For reference prices, the Technical Unit recorded either (a) prices paid by other importing (or received by other exporting) firms in Greece on or about the same dates; (b) prices paid or received by the same firm but at other times; (c) published prices contained in catalogues, trade journals and periodicals; (d) unpublished international prices based on actual transactions obtained from expert sources; and (e) prices (inclusive of a reasonable rate of return) calculated from analysis of production costs. When the Unit could obtain them, it recorded all of the first

three types of price figures. It made an initial estimate of the
extent of transfer pricing. In the majority of instances it then
confirmed these estimates with the information provided by
expert sources. Only in a very few instances did it have the
information to calculate reference prices on the basis of cost data
for the product in question.

The most demanding part of the process of detecting the extent
of overpricing of imports or underpricing of exports was the task
of specifying precisely the identity of the product. Despite the
high degree of homogeneity of the goods forming the sample of
imports and exports being investigated, considerable variation
was still possible from the base prices of particular products on
account of: packaging; form of shipment; concentration; grade;
quality; nature and quantity of impurities present; special
chemical, physical or heat treatment; finish and other properties.
Here knowledge of the tariff classification or n-digit SITC
number used in tabulating statistics for balance-of-payments
purposes was rarely if ever sufficient to permit identification of
the product. Consequently, in addition to their general scientific
or engineering backgrounds, the analysts also had to acquire a
familiarity with the nature of the production technology and
market characteristics of the various products.

To facilitate its work in determining reference prices, the
Technical Unit took out subscriptions to a number of periodicals
which regularly publish data on prices and market conditions,
such as the *Financial Times, Metal Bulletin*, and *European
Chemical News*. As it gained experience in the first months the
Unit was also able, for certain products, to fall back on the
confidential bi-weekly digest of published world prices circulated
by the Invoice Control Committee of the Athens Chamber of
Commerce for the use of its own examiners and for the various
local Chambers.[4]

Apart from its direct exploitation of published sources, the
Technical Unit did not hesitate at an early stage to seek help from
outside persons and organisations in carrying out its research. It
contacted Greek commercial attachés by telephone and telex for
information on prices and markets in overseas capitals. This
source proved to be of limited usefulness, in part because of a lack
of the necessary background and experience amongst all but a
minority of attachés. Consequently an effort was made to
establish information channels from private commercial sources.
Two alternatives were encountered: the delivery of 'packaged'
price inspection services and the delivery of 'unpackaged' price

data. The price inspection service offered by one company with many years experience in this domain was turned down, chiefly because it was confined to inspection before shipment of goods (whereas EPETEE had wished to investigate already completed shipments), it did not cover export prices, and it would have entailed a politically unacceptable transfer of price surveillance responsibilities from the state to a foreign private enterprise. A decision was made in favour of unpackaged arrangements. After investigating several firms, EPETEE decided to engage the Economist Intelligence Unit (London) and Chase World Information (New York) for the supply on a regular basis of price data on a list of designated products. For data on shipping rates other than what could be obtained from maritime reviews, the Technical Unit contacted shipping offices and the UNCTAD secretariat (which supplied shipping conference rate figures). Information on the prevailing financial charges for transactions involving deferred payment were communicated by the Bank of Greece. A senior official of the Bank and member of EPETEE with many years experience in dealing with balance-of-payments matters provided guidance on a part-time basis to the Technical Unit on the intricacies and mechanics of international trade transactions. Where relevant, information on the terms of approval of import of foreign capital and of licensing agreements covered by Law 2687 were obtained from the Ministry of Coordination and the Ministry of Industry. Industry specialists (engineers and scientists) from Greek universities provided expert opinions on particular products on an *ad hoc* basis and in some instances carried out laboratory analysis in order to help identify correctly and to specify these products.

The investigations were carried out product by product. As they progressed it became apparent that the price data supplied by the Economist Intelligence Unit and by Chase were identical to data obtained by the Technical Unit from listings in price catalogues and published periodicals and trade journals. This was encouraging because it showed that the ability to make use of published sources had been acquired. However, for many products the base prices obtained directly from these sources (or indirectly via EIU and Chase), while they gave an indication of the approximate range of world prices, bore no relation to the actual prices paid for products with the qualities and specifications that were actually bought and sold in Greece by importing and exporting firms, respectively. Consequently, after several months, contact was established with a small number of expert consultants in the USA and Europe who agreed to supply unpublished price information based on actual offers in foreign markets for the specific qualities and varieties of products imported in or exported from Greece that were being investigated by the Technical Unit.

Empirical findings

This section, based on an article by Roumeliotis, summarises the results of the investigations for the two groups of products that were studied.[5]

The rate of overpricing of imports ranged between 5 and 88% (weighted average of 19.4%) for the metals, metal products and minerals sample and between 12.5 and 229% (weighted average of 34.5%) for the chemicals sample. The resulting foreign-exchange loss for the first group of products was $8.4 million, of which 95% was accounted for by foreign-owned companies;[6] the corresponding loss for the second group of products came to $1.8 million, of which virtually all was accounted for by foreign-owned companies. If one were to assume for imports of the whole sector in 1975 the same incidence and percentage of overpricing as in the sample, the total foreign-exchange loss for metals, metal products and minerals would amount to $42.4 million; whereas the corresponding figure for chemicals would be $17.8 million. It was also estimated that the first of these two figures represented nearly two and a half times the size of declared profits by the firms in question.

Although the analysis of underpricing of exports centred on only three products, the coverage for each of them was more complete than in the case of imports. The findings were as follows. For the first of the three products, the sample covered 74% of its total exports and the estimated average underpricing was 8.3% for a loss of $4 million in foreign exchange in 1976. For the second product, the coverage was 78% and the estimated average underpricing 8.8%, giving an estimated loss of foreign exchange equal to $3.9 million. For the third product, the coverage was 42% and the underpricing 16.9%, giving an estimated foreign-exchange loss of $0.5 million. One of the three products studies was produced by a 90% foreign-owned company; one by a joint venture and one by a company which was locally-owned but had external financial links, evidenced by its importation of foreign capital under Law 2687.[7] It was also estimated that the foreign exchange outflows attributable to underpricing represented 35%, 26% and 13%, respectively, of the declared profits of the firms in question in the preceding year.

Problems and Prospects

The work of EPETEE and its Technical Unit in the first two and a half years of their existence provides strong support for the view that developing country governments have the means at their disposal to begin to tackle the problem of transfer pricing. A systematic statistical assessment of the results of the investigations has yet to be made by EPETEE. Nevertheless, it has been strongly emphasised that each case in which individual firms have been confronted with solid evidence of wrongdoing has led to a cessation of the transfer pricing abuses that had been previously observed, without the need for recourse to further remedial action. Moreover, subsequent periodic spot checks of the studied product groups made by the Technical Unit and the Bank of Greece show a distinct tendency for both import and export prices to converge very closely to corresponding world prices. A comparison of the cost of operation of EPETEE — about $110,000 per year[8] — with the foreign-exchange cost of the transfer pricing practices that have been brought to a halt as a result of its operation shows that it has already paid for itself several times over.

However, as EPETEE itself is aware, some problems remain to be solved. With respect to methodology, it has already been pointed out that the Technical Unit did not devote its efforts to all imports and exports but only to a sample of products imported or exported over a year's period, whose importance in the balance of payments was quite large relative to the number of transactions, and whose simplicity, homogeneity or degree of standardisation rendered them comparatively easy to identify. It was thus possible for a somewhat untrained staff using trial-and-error methods to come up with striking revelations. But as coverage expands, the number of products possessing these characteristics will become fewer and fewer. In addition, it must be borne in mind that the investigations were *ex post* and covered invoices which had all been approved by the Chamber of Commerce and Industry. Now that knowledge of the change in regulatory climate brought on by the activity of EPETEE has spread, firms can be expected to use more subtle means to disguise their transfer pricing. For these reasons it will become progressively more difficult for future investigations of individual cases to produce findings as dramatic as those in the past. To justify its continued existence, therefore, the Technical Unit will have to cover a greater number and variety of products with a perfected methodology and on a continuous basis, rather than take samples for short time periods as before. However, for some important categories of highly heterogeneous products such as imported capital equipment, much of which is only traded between related firms, the Unit does not have the vast resources that would be necessary to determine what would be a reference price and it has already had to turn down requests for guidance in evaluating invoices from the Chamber of Commerce.

There exist alternative or supplementary analytical techniques of which the Technical Unit has not made much use. One is to examine suspected firms' income statements to try (in the case of exports) to calculate whether they are selling their outputs at prices sufficient to cover costs and yield normal rates of return on capital invested in Greece. Similarly, low profits or losses repeated year after year could be a sign of overpricing of imported inputs, particularly if the firm's operations are expanding simultaneously. Unfortunately, the ability to undertake this kind of analysis has been hampered by inadequate access to the information required. EPETEE has lacked the authority to subpoena accounting data from private firms; while fiscal authorities are barred by law from releasing tax-return data to other government services. Another technique, which can supplement the more conventional analysis and which is now being introduced by the Technical Unit in its investigation of pricing of exports of certain highly homogenous products, entails running statistical regressions between Greek f.o.b. export prices and unit values appearing in balance-of-payments statistics in various export markets to see if any systematic patterns are observable that would suggest the existence of transfer pricing. The method could also be applied to imports. However, errors of aggregation and myriad other factors that create discrepancies in the trade statistics of importing and exporting countries[9] disqualify regression methods as a means of proving, as opposed to inferring, that overpricing of imports or underpricing of exports is actually taking place.

A degree of refinement is possible in the way that samples of world market prices are used for comparison purposes. The tendency of the Technical Unit to simply choose an arithmetic average or the mid-point between two extremes as the reference price may permit some cases of malpractice to escape detection as, for instance, where a firm reduces its rate of overpricing or underpricing per transaction and instead spreads it over a greater number of transactions but for a prolonged period of time in order to achieve the same result. Selection of the average as reference price is a questionable practice in that it fails to distinguish whether some of the prices in the international sample are themselves biased upwards or downwards as a result of manipulation. Although it may be difficult in practice to determine with theoretical rigour and precision[10] the 'correct' reference price, it is preferable to make some allowances for such biases rather than to settle invariably on the average or adopt some other arbitrary decision rule.

As already mentioned, EPETEE's efforts have evidently been fairly successful in curbing undesirable transfer pricing practices for the products which it investigated. This success is subject, however, to certain qualifications. First, it is not at all certain that the firms that had been caught engaging in these practices in the past are not now transferring income illegally out of the country by other means; that is, by switching their transfer pricing to other outputs or inputs whose complexity or heterogeneity makes their investigation difficult or to payments for technology or other services which are at present less subject to administrative control. If, in fact, transfer pricing abuses in all their possible manifestations have ceased for these firms, the fact should be reflected in some way in the flow of their accounts — either in higher payments to domestic factors of production or in increased taxable income, or both. But without access to the firms' books or to the tax returns that they file with the revenues service, there is no way to ascertain whether this actually has occurred.

Secondly, because it has lacked power to prosecute, EPETEE has not been able to recover damages to the Greek state stemming from the past losses of foreign exchange and of tax revenues as a result of its investigations. There has been no evidence of an inclination to take the necessary action at higher levels of government, where the costs of such measures in terms of unpredictable political repercussions weigh more heavily than the immediate benefits to the economy. In part, this inaction has been favoured by the secrecy of EPETEE's meetings and of its findings, however justified such secrecy may be on other grounds. The one instance in which legal proceedings were initiated against a company was the outcome of a 'leak' to the press.

Thirdly, it is evident that the pressure on firms to refrain from malpractices in the pricing of their imports and exports is not very strong, except on products for which such malpractices have already been exposed. The only adverse consequence that a firm engaging in such behaviour has to reckon with is the possibility of getting caught. The temporary embarrassment that this causes to a firm that wishes to maintain cordial relations with government authorities with whom it must deal in order to operate smoothly is not to be minimised. However, this risk is likely to be more than offset by the transfer of income out of the country that it is able to achieve before getting caught.

Finally, despite the existence of EPETEE since 1975, there continues to be an absence of co-ordination in Greece between the control of transfer pricing and other interrelated areas of government policy such as transfer of technology, foreign investment and taxation. In practical terms this means that the finding of EPETEE that firm alpha was overvaluing imported intermediates in year t does not, as it should, enter into the consideration of the rate of royalty payments on foreign know-how that will be approved for that firm by the Ministry of Industry in year $t+1$, or the terms and conditions accorded by the Ministry of Co-ordination for an importation of foreign capital under Law 2687, or the deductions that it will be permitted to make in calculating its net income by the Ministry of Finance. In so far as a transfer of technology is involved, the country is thus deprived of the opportunity of sharing as fully as it might in the benefits likely to arise from that transfer.

In June 1979 Parliament voted a law which attempts to address at least some of these problems.[11] It established a new body, called the Price Research Council (Symvoulion Erevnis Timon), in place of and similar to EPETEE. The Council which functions under the auspices of the Currency Committee, has close connections with the Bank of Greece, which covers all the operational expenses and supplies the Technical Unit with the required specialised staff. This fact invests the Council with the prestige and material support of a politically independent institution that has a continuing vested interest in minimising foreign exchange outflows. Close connection also exists with the Minister of Commerce, who is made ultimately responsible for implementation of the law, thus ensuring that potential political repercussions of such recommendations can continue to be taken into account at Cabinet level if necessary. The authority previously assigned to EPETEE is considerably expanded and now includes the power to examine long-term issues concerning the pricing of imports and exports as well as of invisible items — patents, trademarks and know-how; to provide general guidance and current information to the Chamber of Commerce and to the Ministries which are concerned with these matters, including tax authorities, and to subpoena the information necessary for its investigations from private firms — including their books — and from other government services (thus overruling previous laws prohibiting the release of such information). The new law, following previous legislation, makes misbehaving parties subject to criminal proceedings with the possibility of up to two years imprisonment and fines up to an amount equal to the value of trade involved. More important is the fact that independently and irrespective of the outcome of any judicial action, the law empowers the Minister of Commerce or the Council or customs officials acting on his behalf, to levy similar fines by administrative decisions. Serious violators may also be excluded from engaging in foreign trade for up to one year or from participating in the competitive bidding for the award of government contracts for up to five years.

The enactment of the new law increases the credibility of the Government's intention to control transfer pricing. The task of analysing prices, particularly those of the more complex products, would be facilitated by having access to company data and to information from tax authorities and other services. Moreover, the power to impose administrative sanctions not only increases the pressures on companies to refrain from malpractices but also facilitates the process of investigation. Through an increase of co-operation between government services on the exchange of information the law would also mark a first step towards a unified approach to the formulation of transfer of technology policies.

Since the law was passed, steps have been taken to organise the Technical Unit on a more permanent footing with various sections devoted to the study of a number of commodity groups. A freight monitoring section and a section dealing with technology payments (royalties) are also provided for. Data processing procedures are being systematised and computerisation is being introduced so as to reduce the amount of time required to train new staff and permit a greater volume of invoices to be handled.

It will also free personnel to spend more time analysing prices and the markets in which they are determined and carrying out special studies, including research on the factors influencing transfer pricing behaviour in Greece. Up till now the Technical Unit has concentrated entirely on detection, whereas the causal factors affecting transfer pricing — government policies and overall managerial objectives — have not been systematically explored. It is interesting to note that, apart from the control on profit remissions mentioned in this study, the government policy environment *per se* is not particularly conducive to moving company surpluses out of Greece: corporate tax rates are as low or lower than in most parent-company countries, the level of tariff protection on final goods is moderate and was already declining as the country's entry into the European Common Market was approaching, and the black market rate on foreign exchange is well under 10%. This may explain why the average level of overpricing of imports in Greece has been lower than in other less developed countries where research has been carried out.

As to the new law, it is difficult to speculate on how vigorously the Government will implement its provisions. What emerges from the recent Greek experience is that further progress in controlling transfer pricing abuses appears to be less a question of technique than one of political will.

In conclusion, it should be noted that the present study has described how one country in isolation has tried to come to grips with transfer pricing abuses. Similar detailed studies have yet to be carried out on the kinds of measures that have been enacted in other countries — both developing and developed — in accordance with their own national policy objectives and institutional constraints. Such studies would show common problems which all governments face and would help point the way to greater international co-operation as a means of increasing the effectiveness of national measures.

NOTES

*   This paper draws heavily from the UNCTAD study *The control of Transfer Pricing in Greece: a Progress Report*, (TD/B/C.6/32). However, the views expressed are strictly the personal responsibility of the author and should in no way be attributed to the UNCTAD secretariat of which he is a staff member.

1   A bi-weekly bulletin, giving a resumé of published international prices, is published and circulated for internal use by the Athens Chamber of Commerce and Industry.

2   P. Roumeliotis, G. Harokopos, C. Golemis, J. Kalogeros, E. Petsalas, *Melete tes arnitikes epidraseos ton hyperkostologheseon ton eisaghoghon sto eisozyghio pleromon tes Hellados kai diethnes empeiris*, Athens, July 1976, mimeograph.

3   It should be noted that the Committee's approach focusing on products rather than firms meant that it did not restrict itself to intra-firm trade, but to all trade whose prices deviated from international norms for arm's-length transactions between independent firms. In this paper I have used the term 'transfer pricing' to cover deviations in this broader sense.

4   *Deltion Timon tes para to E.B.E.A. Kentrikes Epitropes Eleghou Timologhion*, containing price data on 15 commodity groups plus foreign exchange parities between the major currencies and the drachma and the dollar, respectively.

5   Panayotis Roumeliotis, 'La politique des prix d'importation et d'exportation des entreprises multinationales en Grèce', *Revue Tiers Monde*, vol. XVIII, No.70, April-June 1977.

6   A foreign-owned company was defined as one in which foreign equity holding came to 30% or more. According to this definition, of the 23 enterprises engaged in overpricing, 15 were foreign and 10 were local.

7   See chapter I, section D, for a description of this law.

8   This figure assumes that the Technical Unit is operating at full strength, which it has not done so far. Of the total, approximately $70,000 goes to cover the salaries of a director plus ten other professionals and a typist, rent and office expenses, subscriptions to periodicals, computer time, and the small honoraria of the eight members of EPETEE. The balance is accounted for by the use of overseas consultants.

9   See Oskar Morgenstern, *On the Accuracy of Economic Observations*, Princeton University Press, Princeton, New Jersey, 1963.

10 See UNCTAD, *Report on the Sussex Seminar on Intra-Firm Transactions and their Impact on Trade and Development*, Institute of Development Studies, Brighton, 7-11 November 1977, UNCTAD/OSG/174 (UNCTAD Seminar Programme Report Series No.2, May 1978).

11 *Efimeris tis Kyvernisios*, 144/30-6-1979 t. A', Ethnikon Typografeion, Athinai, 1979.

19.
INCOMEX AND TRANSFER PRICING CONTROL IN COLOMBIA
OSCAR HERNANDES SIERRA

In Colombia the control of import and export prices is exercised by the division of international price control of INCOMEX, a government agency. The division was created by Decree no.691 of April 1967. The principle function of the division is to control the invoicing of all transfers in the external trade of Colombia. The control covers the case of both overpricing and underpricing of imports and exports.

MECHANISMS OF PRICE CONTROL
The price division of INCOMEX has three sections:
(i) storage of information: for this, information on the import and export of goods is filed for reference purposes from periodicals, books and technical papers, including data sent by trading offices and lists of established suppliers in the Colombian import trade. The objective of this section is to classify available information in a systematic way.
(ii) analysis and concepts: the technical section contains professional personnel such as mechanical engineers, pharmaceutical chemists, economists, and specialists in international trade. This section also contains the people who process information as it comes in, and therefore it requires people who are able to work in more than one language. The section publishes price lists which give 'maximum import prices' for products with a low tariff level, and 'minimum import prices' in the case when tariff levels are high. It also publishes information on 'normal prices' which are principally derived from the observation of international trade prices.
(iii) the selection and subsequent execution of investigation: this section contains economists, lawyers and other technical personnel. It examines customs declarations of imports and exports, and compares them with information previously analysed and filed.
The prices division, which has a total staff of thirty, is able to

exercise some control of licensing for imports and exports, and its aim is to limit the outflow of foreign exchange to the exterior. Annual operational costs of the division are estimated at approximately US $200,000 per year as of 1978. The saving in outflow of capital is estimated at approximately US$80 million per annum. In addition, the operation of this division helps to constrain the possibilities of tax evasion. Unfortunately it has not been possible to estimate the extent of saving in this form.

DESCRIPTION OF THE PROBLEM
Abnormal operations have been detected as follows:

Imports
1. Overinvoicing. This is usually found to be associated with multinational corporations. It is identified in the following cases with the greatest frequency:
   (a) In commodities with low import tariffs and especially for those which enter free of tariffs. The principle objective is that of confounding exchange control by illegal repatriating of capital to head offices. This phenomenon was detected initially in 1967, although it has been demonstrated that it existed for many years before and probably from when multinational corporations first began to arrive in Colombia. At the present time, there is a law suit going on in US courts in which five pharmaceutical companies are involved, charged with selling raw materials to Colombia at substantially overvalued prices between 1955 and 1965. The amount involved in the lawsuit is $50 million. Around 1970, considerable overinvoicing was discovered in relation to certain major international drug companies (Pfizer, Abbott, Baxter, Squibb, Eli Lilli, Ciba-Geigy, Roche, Hoechst, Glaxo, etc.) The companies involved were subjected to sanctions when the invoicing was discovered. Subsequently, overvaluation has been detected in other sectors of economic life such as industrial chemicals, rubber and electrical goods. Gradually control over these sectors is being undertaken.
   (b) In sectors where there is internal price control implying maximum legal consumer prices, there has been substantial overinvoicing. This takes the form of increasing the apparent costs of production in order to try and obtain an increase in official prices.
2. Underinvoicing of imports. This has been found in all

economic sectors and is defined as follows:

(a) In relation to products with high tariffs or with a high sales tax. It is estimated that some companies both overinvoice some products and underinvoice others. With these mechanisms, they try essentially to undermine the tax system of the state. Sometimes there is not a greater outflow from the country but rather the transfer pricing is used by head offices to assist subsidiaries to avoid taxes.

(b) In some cases the National Planning Department has refused capital investment applications by multinational companies because proposed investments have not met legal requirements. In this case underinvoicing occurs on raw materials and capital goods in order to capitalise the differences between real values and those invoiced.

Exports

1. Overinvoicing. This is practised by certain multinationals which produce or assemble manufactured products. The objective is to obtain a greater value from the government subsidy scheme which the state provides to the tune of 12% of the value added on certain exported goods.

2. Underinvoicing. This is undertaken by companies who wish to avoid the stipulated quantity of foreign exchange which they have to deposit with the banking authorities. In this way, they are able to directly transfer profits to head office. There are also illegal transfers in relation to technical assistance contracts, gifts, royalties and so on, but none of these are at present controlled in Colombia.

In all the foregoing problems, what has most worried the Colombian authorities is not whether purchases or sales are undertaken at high or low prices or not, but rather the case in which multinational companies fix special prices for Colombia alone. It is on these cases that INCOMEX concentrates its work.

Ways in which the Authorities can exercise a legal means of control

In Decree no. 444 of March 1967, INCOMEX was given considerable powers to exercise control over price levels even for those items classified as duty-free imports. In the same decree, certain powers were given to the Superintendent of Exchange Control and to the National Customs Authority. In the case of overinvoicing of imports, it is necessary to first prove that such overinvoicing has occurred. If a license to remit exchange to the exterior has not yet been issued, INCOMEX is able to correct prices. If permission has already been granted by the office of exchange control, it is still possible to apply sanctions which may go up to 200% of the exchange infringement. In the case of underinvoicing of imports, INCOMEX is able to prevent foreign exchange outflows where permission has not yet been granted. Where permission has been granted, the customs authorities may apply sanctions under the law relating to smuggling, and the office of exchange control can apply sanctions for illegal exchange flows between real and invoiced values. The office of exchange control also applies sanctions when there is no invoicing of exports.

INCOMEX has the responsibility, in the law, to inform the customs authorities and the office of exchange control of international price levels and of evidence of wrongful valuations.

Results

The results of the ten years in which the price division has functioned may be considered as satisfactory; but it is estimated that there are still many transactions which require examination. The efficient discharge of price-control mechanisms will only be achieved when developing countries are able to interchange detailed information between each other. In this, international organisations like UNCTAD can obviously be helpful, and in addition, if the governments of developing countries were to take measures to control the problem, further advances could be made.

20.
SUMMARY STUDY OF INTERNATIONAL CASES INVOLVING SECTION 482 OF THE INTERNAL REVENUE CODE*
UNITED STATES TREASURY DEPARTMENT

COMPILATION OF DATA

1. A total of 871 international cases were identified in which examining agents considered making one or more section 482 adjustments. Where a taxpayer's returns were audited for more than one year, or where an entity related to the US taxpayer also filed a US tax return, in general all returns were treated as one case.

2. The 871 cases in which section 482 adjustments were considered were first analysed to determine in which cases one or more section 482 adjustments were made, and in which cases no adjustments were made (Table 1). All section 482 adjustments that the examining agents considered making in the 871 cases were then characterised as 'potential' adjustments and were broken down into categories showing the various types of adjustments that were considered in the cases, and to what extent the various types of potential adjustments considered were actually make by the agents[1] (Table 2). The study then made a detailed breakdown of those adjustments that were actually made in the cases by the examining agents (Tables 4, 5, 6, 8, 9 and 10). Data were then compiled showing the effect in the cases of participation by an International Examiner (Table 7). Finally, data were compiled where possible showing the size of the taxpayer in each case, without regard to the types of adjustments that were considered in the cases (Table 3).

3. Where a transaction involving a US taxpayer and many foreign subsidiaries was concerned, in general all potential adjustments were treated as one potential adjustment. For example, where the agent considered allocating among many foreign subsidiaries a particular expense claimed by the US taxpayer, all potential adjustments were treated as one potential adjustment for purposes of the study. Similarly, where the agent considered making adjustments affecting a number of separate but similar transactions between the US taxpayer and many foreign subsidiaries (such as a pricing adjustment where the US taxpayer

had sold identical or similar products to a number of different foreign subsidiaries), all potential adjustments were treated as one adjustment.

4. Where the study file did not contain sufficient information to determine the exact reason that an adjustment was made or not made, no effort was made to secure clarifying information due to the cost and time that would have been required (it is noted that only the international issues treated in each examination report were examined in the study). Such adjustments are reported under the heading 'Not Clear' in Tables 9 and 10, and 'Unknown' in Tables 1, 2, 4, 5, 6 and 7. Similarly, where information concerning the size of the US taxpayer was not readily available, the taxpayer was included under the heading 'No Category' in Table 3.

STUDY AND DATA COMPILATION HIGHLIGHTS

Adjustments were actually made in slightly more than half of the 871 cases in which one or more adjustments involving section 482 were considered by the examining agent (458 cases out of 871; see Table 1). Similarly, out of a total of 1,706 potential adjustments that were considered in the 871 cases, slightly more than half (886 adjustments) were actually made (Table 2). The aggregate dollar amount of all the 886 adjustments made totalled more than $662 million (Table 4).

1. *Frequency of Adjustments Made* (Tables 1 and 2)

Among the 1,706 potential adjustments that were considered, a larger number of pricing adjustments were *considered* than any other type of potential adjustment (591 out of 1,706 considered). On the other hand, pricing adjustments on a percentage basis were actually *made* less frequently (29.5% of potential pricing adjustments were actually made) than any other type of adjustment for which the statistics were meaningful.[2] The types of adjustments that were made most frequently on a percentage basis among all potential adjustments were those involving the allocation of net income[3] (89.0% of all adjustments considered were actually made) and allocation of expense items (83.8%), followed by interest adjustments (66.5%). Out of the total 886 adjustments made, more interest adjustments were made (258 interest adjustments) than any other type of adjustment.

The figures showing the number of cases in which adjustments were made and not made (Table 1) were broken down further to show the 'principal' adjustment that was made in each case where one or more adjustment was made, and the 'principal' adjustment that was considered but not made in each case where no adjustment was made.[4] Those figures parallel fairly closely the figures given in Table 2 for all potential adjustments that were considered (discussed above). For example, a pricing adjustment was the principal adjustment made or not made in almost half of the cases (390 out of 871 cases), while on a percentage basis pricing adjustments were actually made less frequently (33.3%) than any other type of principal adjustment for which the statistics were meaningful. Similarly, the principal adjustments that were actually made most frequently on a percentage basis were those involving the allocation of net income (86.1%) and allocation of expense items (86.4%), and interest adjustments (76.7%). The percentage of the 871 cases in which one or more adjustments were made (52.6%) was also fairly close to the percentage of all potential adjustments considered that were actually made (51.9%).

2. *Dollar Amounts of Adjustments Made*

(a) *Aggregate Dollar Amounts* (Table 4)

Of the total $662,101,000 of adjustments made in all cases, pricing adjustments totalled $312,526,000, or almost half of the total dollar amount of all adjustments made (Table 4). The total dollar amount of services adjustments — $126,996,000 — was the second largest dollar amount by category, and the total dollar amount of interest adjustments — $75,936,000 — was the third largest.

The total dollar amount of adjustments made in each category was broken down further in Table 4 into 11 different dollar ranges showing the frequency that adjustments of particular sizes were made in each category. In every category except those in which the total dollar amounts were insubstantial (rental adjustments and gain allocations), the overwhelming proportion (well over 90%) of the total dollar amount of adjustments in each category represented single adjustments of at least $100,000 in size. The aggregate amount of all adjustments that were less than $100,000 in size for all categories totalled less than $16,000,000 out of the total sum of $662,101,000 for all adjustments made.

(b) *Average Dollar Amounts per Adjustment* (Table 5)

The total dollar amount of adjustments made in each category was also broken down further in Table 5 to show the average dollar amount for each category of adjustments made, and the average dollar amount *per year* for each category of adjustments made. The average amount per adjustment made for all types of adjustments was $747,000. Since the average number of years audited in each case was slightly more than two years, the average amount per year for all adjustments made was $330,000.

Pricing adjustments accounted for the largest average dollar amounts — $1,796,000 per adjustment made, and $679,000 per year for each adjustment made. These amounts were more than twice the average dollar amounts for any other category. The next largest average dollar amounts per adjustment made were for services adjustments and allocations of net income ($847,000 average for each category). Although interest adjustments accounted for the largest number of single adjustments made out of all potential adjustments that were considered (Table 2), the average dollar amount for all interest adjustments made — $294,000 — was lower than the average dollar amount in all other categories for which the statistics were meaningful.

3. *Percentage of Adjustments Agreed to* (Table 6)

A separate analysis was made showing the extent to which the total 886 adjustments made were agreed to or not agreed to by the US taxpayer in each case (Table 6). For purposes of this study, an adjustment was treated as 'agreed' if it was recorded as agreed in the revenue agent's report of examination. Of the 886 adjustments made, 51% were agreed to by the taxpayer and an additional 8% were partially agreed to. Cases involving interest adjustments were agreed to most frequently (59% agreed, and 6% agreed in part), followed by adjustments involving the allocation of expense items (57% agreed, and 11% agreed in part). Of the cases involving pricing adjustments, 41% were agreed, 11% were partially agreed, and 48% were not agreed.

4. *Participation of International Examiner* (Table 7)

The 458 principal adjustments made (see Table 1) were further analysed in Table 7 with reference to whether an International Examiner participated in the case or not (where an International Examiner participated in the case only nominally, he was considered not to have participated in the case at all).[5] International Examiners made principal adjustments in roughly three-fifths of the cases in which they participated (364 adjustments out of 607 cases in which they participated), while principal adjustments were made in slightly more than one-third of the cases in which an International Examiner did not participate (94 out of 264 cases in which an International Examiner did not participate). An International Examiner participated in more than two-thirds of the cases in which the principal adjustment that was *considered* was a pricing adjustment (272 out of 390 cases), and an International Examiner participated in almost all of the cases in which the principal adjustment that was *made* was a pricing adjustment (122 adjustments out of 130 made). However, in more than half of the cases in which an International Examiner considered a potential pricing adjustment, he did not make the adjustment (150 pricing adjustments not made out of 272 pricing cases participated in).

5. *Analysis of Most Frequent Adjustments* (Tables 8, 9 and 10)

Data concerning three of the four most frequent types of adjustments — pricing adjustments, services adjustments, and adjustments involving intangibles — were analysed in detail to determine the reason that the agent did or did not make a particular adjustment. Because both the safe haven for interest charges contained in the regulations and the rules to be applied in making interest adjustments are extremely precise [Treasury Regulation §1.482-2(a)(2)], no detailed analysis was made of potential interest adjustments, even though more interest adjustments were made than any other type of adjustment (see Table 2).

(a) *Pricing Adjustments* (Table 8)

The present pricing regulations [Treasury Regulation §1.482-2(e)] provide for three methods in determining an arm's-length price for the sale of tangible property between related entities. In order of priority they are the comparable uncontrolled price method, the resale price method, and the cost-plus method. Under the regulations other unspecified methods can be used to determine an arm's-length price if none of the specified methods may reasonably be applied, or if some other method is clearly more appropriate.

Of the 174 pricing adjustments made in the study, 20.7% were based on the comparable uncontrolled price method, 10.9% were based on the resale price method, 27.6% were based on the cost-plus method, and 40.8% were based on an improvised fourth method. Where a pricing adjustment was not made, however, the comparable uncontrolled price method was applied in 56.1% of the cases (234 cases out of 417 in which a pricing adjustment was considered but not made), usually on the basis of evidence of sales to third parties offered by the taxpayer. A fourth method was applied in 27.6% of the cases in which a pricing adjustment was not made (115 out of 417 cases).

(b) *Services Adjustments* (Table 9)

Where one entity renders services for the benefit of a related entity, the regulations provide that an arm's-length charge for the services may ordinarily be determined on the basis of the costs incurred by the entity rendering the services [Treasury Regulation §1.482-2(b)(3)-(6)]. If the services are an 'integral part' of the business activity of either entity, however, an arm's-length charge must be based on the amount that an unrelated third party would have paid.

Of the 288 potential services adjustments that were considered, 150 (52.1% of the total) were actually made (Table 2). Approximately 60% of the services adjustments were made either on the basis of the taxpayer's costs or on the basis of third-party transactions (Table 9). Approximately 40% of the services adjustments were made by application of a hybrid method.

(c) *Adjustments Involving Transfer of Intangibles* (Table 10)

Where intangible property (such as patents or know-how) is transferred or made available by one entity to a related entity, the regulations provide that an arm's-length consideration must be received [Treasury Regulation §1.482-2(d)(1)]. Where the property has been developed jointly by the related parties pursuant to a *bona fide* cost-sharing arrangement, however, each entity will be permitted to use the property free of charge to the extent that it shared in the costs of development. Where an arm's-length consideration must be determined, the standard to be applied is the consideration that would have been received from an unrelated third party for the intangible property under the same circumstances. Where similar transactions with third parties cannot be found, the regulations set forth 12 factors that may be examined in determining an arm's-length consideration.

Of the 188 potential adjustments involving intangibles that were considered, 100 (53.2% of the total) were actually made (Table 2). Of the 100 adjustments made, no consideration had been received in 73 instances (Table 10). In 6 instances where no consideration had been received, the parties had shared the research and development costs under a cost-sharing arrangement which the agent determined had not properly reflected the costs and risks of the parties to the arrangement. Accordingly, in those cases the agent reallocated the development costs in order to properly reflect such costs and risks, as required by §1.482-2(d)(4) of the regulations, instead of imputing an arm's-length consideration from one entity to another.[6] The remaining 93 adjustments were made by imputing an arm's-length consideration to the entity that had transferred or made available the intangible property to the related entity. The consideration received by the taxpayer from unrelated third parties was used as the basis for 54 of these adjustments, while the various other methods prescribed in the regulations were applied in making 24 of these adjustments.

Of the 88 potential adjustments involving the transfer of intangibles that were considered but not made, the existence of a cost-sharing arrangement among the related entities was the basis for not making an adjustment for only 9.1% of the adjustments not made. The consideration received by the taxpayer from unrelated third parties was relied upon as the basis for not making an adjustment in 23.9% of these cases, while the various methods prescribed in the regulations were relied upon as the basis for not making an adjustment in 35.2% of these cases.

6. *Size of Taxpayers Examined* (Table 3)

An examination of the size of the primary taxpayer was made for each of the 458 cases in which one or more adjustments were made, and for each of the 413 cases in which no adjustment was made (Table 3). Among the 378 primary taxpayers that experienced adjustments and for which this information was readily available (in other words, 458 taxpayers that experienced adjustments minus the 80 taxpayers listed by asset size in 'No Category'), more than half the adjustments made affected primary taxpayers with more than $50 million in assets (199 taxpayers out of 370). In general, the frequency with which taxpayers experienced adjustments increased with the size of the taxpayers. Among taxpayers with assets of less than $50 million that were audited in connection with a section 482 problem, 50% or less actually experienced adjustments. The percentage of taxpayers that experienced adjustments increased sharply with respect to taxpayers having assets of more than $50 million, increasing to 76.6% for taxpayers having assets of more than $250 million.

NOTES

*   This study was first published in January 1973. We are grateful to the US Treasury Department for permission to reprint it in this collection.

1   An adjustment was treated as having been 'made' for purposes of this study if it was written up in the revenue agent's report of examination, even though technically an adjustment is not made in an agent's report but only *recommended*. An adjustment that is recommended in the report filed by an agent is made at that point only if it is agreed to by the taxpayer. An adjustment that is recommended by an agent and *not* agreed to by the taxpayer at that point is not actually made until a later stage in the case.

2   Adjustments involving the rental of personal property were made less frequently on a percentage basis (27.3%). However, rental adjustments were considered in only 11 out of the 1,706 potential adjustments that were considered (Table 2), and the aggregate dollar amount of all rental adjustments totalled only $555,000 (Table 4).

3   An agent was treated as having made an allocation of net income where he allocated particular items of gross income from one entity to another, together with any deductions attributable to such items.

4   In each case where more than one adjustment was made, the adjustment in the largest dollar amount was treated as the 'principal' adjustment made in the case. Similarly, in each case where no adjustments were made, the potential adjustment which the agent believed would have been the largest if it had been made was treated as the principal adjustment considered in the case. In each case where only one adjustment was made, that adjustment by definition was treated as the principal adjustment made in the case, even though larger potential adjustments were considered but not made in the same case. For example, if an interest adjustment of $100,000 was made in a case and a pricing adjustment of approximately $1 million was considered but not made in the same case, the interest adjustment would be the principal adjustment made in the case.

5   In general, an International Examiner is asked by his regional program manager to participate in a case where a large potential adjustment with international aspects is being considered, and where the regional manager does not feel that the district agent has the expertise to examine the issue properly.

6   In one instance where inadequate or excessive consideration had been received by the developer, and where no cost-sharing arrangement had been entered into among the parties, the adjustment was made by allocating development costs among the parties, rather than by imputing an

arm's-length consideration to the developer. This case is recorded under the heading 'Cost Sharing' in Table 10 in order to reflect the manner in which the adjustment was made.

APPENDIX

Table 1

Analysis by Case of Principal Adjustments[1] Made and Not Made

	Total Cases	Adjustments Made[2]	No Adjustments Made	% Made
Pricing	390	130	260	33.3
Intangibles	70	46	24	65.7
Interest	163	125	38	76.7
Services	133	64	69	48.1
Rental	7	2	5	28.6
Allocation of Net Income	36	31	5	86.1
Allocation of Expense	66	57	9	86.4
Allocation of Gain	5	2	3	40.0
Unknown	1	1	—	100
	871	458	413	52.6%

1 See p.309-10 for definition of 'Principal Adjustments'.
2 See p.324n1 for definition of 'Adjustments Made'.

Table 2

Analysis of All Potential Adjustments[1]

	Total Potential Adjustments	Adjustments Made	Adjustments Not Made	% Made
Pricing	591	174	417	29.5
Intangibles	188	100	88	53.2
Interest	388	258	130	66.5
Services	288	150	138	52.1
Rental	11	3	8	27.3
Allocation of Net Income	55	48	7	89.0
Allocation of Expense	179	150	29	83.8
Allocation of Gain	5	2	3	40.0
Unknown	1	1	—	—
	1,706	866	820	51.9%

1   See p.308 for definition of 'Potential Adjustments'.

Table 3

Number of Cases Analyzed by Asset Size of Primary US Taxpayer

Asset Size of Primary U.S. Taxpayer (in thousands)	Adjustments made	No Adjustments made	% made
Under 50	1	2	33.3
50-100	1	4	20.0
100-250	4	4	50.0
250-500	3	10	23.1
500-1,000	13	21	38.2
1,000-5,000	47	74	38.8
5,000-10,000	31	38	44.9
10,000-50,000	79	89	47.0
50,000-100,000	40	22	64.5
100,000-250,000	38	20	65.5
Over 250,000	121	37	76.6
No Category	80	92	46.5
	458	413	52.6%

Table 4

Total Amounts of Adjustments (in Thousands)

Dollar Range of Adjustments	Pricing	Intangibles	Interest	Service	Rental	Allocation of Net Income	Allocation of Expense	Allocation of Gain	Total
$ 0 — $ 5,000	$ 2	$ 9	$ 117	$ 27		$ 3	$ 57		$ 215
5,000 — 10,000	16	43	343	83			66		551
10,000 — 25,000	188	198	837	313	$ 14	116	619		2,285
25,000 — 50,000	453	512	1,335	802		105	1,040		4,247
50,000 — 100,000	691	1,869	1,967	1,883	91	334	1,576	$ 95	8,506
100,000 — 500,000	12,101	6,790	9,013	9,696	450	3,575	4,165		45,790
500,000 — 1,000,000	18,194	5,683	5,548	8,353		3,929	4,973	558	47,238
1,000,000 — 3,000,000	61,048	10,852	12,332	20,888		21,032	8,177		134,329
3,000,000 — 6,000,000	46,540		4,000	6,931			9,065		66,536
6,000,000 — 9,999,000	55,252		8,536	21,436			6,492		91,716
9,999,000 — Above	118,041	26,468	31,908	56,584		11,561	16,080		260,642
Totals in (Thousands)	312,526	52,424	75,936	126,996	555	40,655	52,310	653	662,055
Type of Adjustments Unknown									46
Grand Total— All Adjustments									$662,101

Table 5

Average Dollar Amount, Per Year and Per Adjustment
For Adjustments Made in Each Category

Category	Number of Adjustments Made	Total Number of Years	(In Thousands) Total Amounts	(In Thousands) Average Amount Per Adjustment Made	(In Thousands) Average Amount Per Year
1. Pricing	174	460	$312,526	$1,796	$679
2. Intangibles	100	227	52,424	524	231
3. Interest	258	480	75,936	294	158
4. Services	150	368	126,996	847	345
5. Rental	3	11	555	185	50
6. Allocation of net income	48	117	40,655	847	348
7. Allocation of expense	150	339	52,310	349	154
8. Allocation of gain	2	3	653	327	218
Unknown	1	2	46		
TOTALS	886	2,007	662,101	747	330

Table 6

Adjustments Made
Agreed, Agreed in Part, Not Agreed

	Total Number	Agreed		Agreed		Not	
		#	%	#	%	#	%
Pricing	174	71	41	20	11	83	48
Intangibles	100	52	52	8	8	40	40
Interest	258	153	59	15	6	90	34
Services	150	65	43	10	7	75	51
Rent	3	1	33	—	—	2	66
Allocation of Net Income	48	21	44	—	—	27	56
Allocation of Expense	150	85	57	17	11	48	33
Allocation of Gain	2	1	50	1	50	—	—
Unknown	1	—	—	—	—	—	—
TOTALS	886	449	51%	71	8%	365	41%

Table 7

Participation of International Examiner
(Principal Adjustments)

	Participation		Non-Participation		Totals	
	Adjustment made	Adjustment not made	Adjustment made	Adjustment not made	Total Adjustments made	Total Adjustments not made
Pricing	122	150	8	110	130	260
Intangibles	39	17	7	7	46	24
Interest	83	22	42	16	125	38
Services	51	43	13	26	64	69
Rental	1	2	1	3	2	5
Allocation of Net Income	27	2	4	3	31	5
Allocation of Expenses	39	5	18	4	57	9
Allocation of Gain	2	2		1	2	3
Category Unknown			1		1	
TOTAL CASES	364	243	94	170	458	413

Table 8

Methods Used for Pricing Adjustments

Adjustments Made Method Used	Totals	Percent of Pricing Adjustments Made
1. Uncontrolled Sales	36	20.7
2. Resale Price	19	10.9
3. Cost Plus	48	27.6
4. Proportionate Profit	12	6.9
5. Ratio of Return on Investment	1	.6
6. Other formula	27	15.5
7. Others	31	17.8
	174	100.0%

Adjustments Not Made Method Used		Percent of Pricing Adjustments Not Made
1. Uncontrolled Sales	234	56.1
2. Resale Price	11	2.6
3. Cost Plus	57	13.7
4. Proportionate Profit	3	.7
5. Rate of Return on Investment	2	.5
6. Other formula	32	7.7
7. Others	78	18.7
	417	100.0%

Table 9

Adjustments for Services Performed

	Total	Taxpayer's Cost	Taxpayer's Transactions with other Parties	Transactions between other Parties	With Unrelated and between Unrelated	Not Clear	Other
			Adjustments Made				
No Charge	77	21	19	4	—	17	16
Inadequate Charge	73	14	21	9	1	16	12
	150	35	40	13	1	33	28
	(100%)	(23.3%)	(26.7%)	(8.7%)	(0.7%)	(22.0%)	(18.7%)
			Adjustments Not Made				
	138	19	34	18	—	34	33
	(100%)	(13.8%)	(24.6%)	(13.0%)		(24.6%)	(23.9%)

Table 10

Adjustments Involving Transfer or Use of Intangibles

	Total	Cost Sharing	Taxpayer's Transactions With Other Parties	Transactions Between Other Parties	Other Method	Not Clear
Adjustments Made						
No Consideration Received by Taxpayer	73	6	47	1	11	8
Inadequate or Excessive Consideration Received	27	1	7	—	13	6
	100 (100%)	7 (7.0%)	54 (54.0%)	1 (1.0%)	24 (24.0%)	14 (14.0%)
Adjustments Not Made						
	88 (100%)	8 (9.1%)	21 (23.9%)	6 (6.8%)	31 (35.2%)	22 (25.0%)

BIBLIOGRAPHY

Arpen, J.S. (1972), *International Intracorporate Pricing*, Praeger.

Bhagwati, J.N. (ed.) (1974), *Illegal Transactions in International Trade*, North-Holland.

Brooke, M.Z. and Remmers, H.L. (1970), *The Strategy of Multinational Enterprise: Organisation and Finance*, Longman.

Carlson, G.N. and Hufbauer, G.C. (1976), *Tax Barriers to Technology Transfers*, Office of Tax Analysis, U.S. Treasury Paper No.16, November.

Chown, J.F. (1974), *Taxation and Multinational Enterprise*, Longman

Collins, M.H. (1977), *Suggested Guidelines – Payments for goods, technology, services*, Paper to United Nations Expert Group in Tax Treaties between Developed and Developing Countries, 6 October, ST/SG/AC.8/L.26.

Duerr, M.G. (1972), *Tax Allocations and International Business: Corporate Experience with Section 482 of the Internal Revenue Code*, The Conference Board, New York.

Ellis, F. and Joekes, S. (1977) *Intra-firm Transactions and their Impact on Trade and Development*, a report of the UNCTAD/ IDS Conference, IDS, November Girvan, N. (1976) *Corporate Imperialism: Conflict and Expropriation*, Sharpe.

Green, R.H. (1977), 'International and Intersectoral Statistical Development of Peripheral Economies as a means to exercise of sovereignty in relation to MNC's', Paper to Study Group 23, on Statistical Policy in Developing Countries, IDS, University of Sussex.

Greene, J. and Duerr, M.G. (1968), *Intercompany Transactions in the Multinational Firms*, The Conference Board, New York.

Helleiner, G.K. (1977), 'Transnational Enterprises and the New Political Economy of US Trade Policy', in *Oxford Economic Papers*, Vol. 29, no. 1, March.

—— (1981), *Intra-Firm Trade and the Developing Countries*, Macmillan.

Holland, S.K. (1975), *The Socialist Challenge*, Quartet.

Hopkins, E. (1978), 'Illegal Foreign Exchange Transactions: the Zambian Experience', IDS Discussion Paper, 125.

Kopits, G.F. (1976a), 'Taxation and Multinational Firm Behaviour: a Critical Survey', IMF Staff Papers, 23.

—— (1976b), 'Intra-Firm Royalties Crossing Frontiers and Transfer Pricing Behaviour, *Economic Journal*, 86.

Lall, S. (1973), 'Transfer Pricing by Multinational Manufacturing Firms', in *Oxford Bulletin of Economics and Statistics*, no. 3, August.

—— (1979), 'Transfer Pricing and Less Developed Countries: some Problems of Investigation', in *World Development*, January.

Lall, S. and Bibile, S. (1977), 'The Political Economy of Controlling Transnationals: the Pharmaceutical Industry in Sri Lanka 1972-76', in *World Development*, July.

Lall, S. and Streeten, P.P. (1977), *Foreign Investment, Transnationals and Developing Countries*, Macmillan.

Plasschaert, S. (1979), *Transfer Pricing and Multinational Corporations*, Saxon House and the European Centre for Study and Information on Multinational Corporations (ECSIM).

Roumeliotis, P. (1977), 'La politique des prix d'importation et d'exportation des entreprises multinationales en Grèce', in *Revue du Tiers-Monde*, XVIII, no. 70, April-June.

Roumeliotis, P. (1978), *Entreprises Multinationales et Prix de Transfert*, Athens.

United Nations, Dept. of Economic and Social Affairs (1974), *The Impact of Multinational Corporations on Development and on International Relations*, Technical Papers — Taxation, New York.

United Nations Conference on Trade and Development (1977), *Dominant Positions of Market Power of Transnational Corporations: Use of the Transfer Pricing Mechanism*, ST/MD/6.

United Nations Conference on Trade and Development (1978), *The Role of Transnational Corporations in the Marketing and Distribution of Exports and Imports of Developing Countries*, TD/B/C.2/1.97/February.

United Nations Commission on Transnational Corporations (1978), *Transnational Corporations in World Development: A Reexamination*, E/C.10/38, 20 March.

United Nations, Senate Committee on Finance (1973), *Impli-*

cations of Multinational Firms for World Trade and Investment and for US Trade and Labour, Washington.

Vaitsos, C.V. (1974), *Intercountry Income Distribution and Transnational Enterprise*, Clarendon Press, Oxford.

—— (1978), *Transnational Enterprises and Latin American Integration*, UNCTAD, Geneva.

—— (1980), 'Corporate Integration in World Production and Trade', in D. Seers, C. Vaitsos, M-L Kiljunen (eds.), *Integration and Unequal Development: the Experience of the EEC*, Macmillan.

Van den Bulcke, D. (1971), *Les entreprises étrangères dans l'industrie Belge*, Ghent.

Verlage, H.C. (1975), *Transfer Pricing for Multinational Enterprise*, Rotterdam University Press.

Ward, M. (1978), 'Accounting for the Missing Millions: the Case of Tax Havens (with special reference to Bermuda)', *Review of Income and Wealth 24* (2), June.

INDEX

(Transfer pricing has been abbreviated to t.p.)

329